RIGOROUS CURRICULUM DESIGN

How to Create Curricular Units of Study that

Align Standards, Instruction, and Assessment

RIGOROUS CURRICULUM DESIGN

How to Create
Curricular Units
of Study that
Align Standards,
Instruction, and
Assessment

Larry Ainsworth

LEAD+
LEARN
PRESS

ENGLEWOOD, COLORADO

The Leadership and Learning Center
5680 Greenwood Plaza Boulevard, Suite 550
Greenwood Village, Colorado 80111
Phone 1.866.399.6019 | Fax 303.504.9417
www.leadandlearn.com

Published by Lead+Learn Press.

Library of Congress Cataloging-in-Publication Data

Ainsworth, Larry.
    Rigorous curriculum design : how to create curricular units of study that align
standards, instruction, and assessment / Larry Ainsworth.
        p. cm.
    Includes bibliographical references and index.
    ISBN 978-1-935588-05-4 (alk. paper)
    1. Curriculum planning--United States. 2. Education--Standards--United States. I. Title.
    LB2806.15.A375 2010
    375'.001--dc22

                                                                                2010032955

ISBN 978-1-935588-05-4

Printed in the United States of America

        05 06 07 08   19 18 17 16 15 14

4500507590   B C D E F G

It is with gratitude and respect that I dedicate
this book to the leaders, curriculum supervisors,
curriculum designers, and educators of West Haven,
Connecticut. What they have accomplished together
in such a relatively short amount of time is nothing
short of remarkable. I want to especially thank
Superintendent Neil Cavallaro for his unflagging
support and Assistant Superintendent Anne
Druzolowski for her visionary leadership, tenacity,
and genuine caring for all. It continues to be both
an honor and a privilege to work with such
dedicated professionals and truly wonderful people.
You have all contributed greatly to make this
process both real and doable, and your work will
have a far-reaching impact on education, both
within and beyond the West Haven community.

Contents

List of Figures

Acknowledgments

So many of my professional colleagues, clients, and friends assisted me greatly with the preparation of *Rigorous Curriculum Design*, and I would like to sincerely thank each of them for their individual contributions.

Connecticut Schools

Bristol Public Schools: Superintendent Philip A. Streifer, Deputy Superintendent Susan Kalt Moreau, and a very special thank-you to Denise Carabetta, Director of Teaching and Learning, for contributing Chapter 19. Denise and Sue, it has been my singular honor and privilege to know you all these years and to see how you have kept the work you began with Mike Wasta alive and ever growing in Bristol. You are an inspiration to us all.

East Hartford Public Schools: Scott Nozik, Marcia Huddy, Kristie Bourdoulous, Michelle E. Daigle, Bonnie Fineman, Karen Radding, Tod Kenney, and their respective design team colleagues for sharing their initial drafts of their unit planning organizers, and Debbie A. Kaprove, Assistant Superintendent, for your supportive leadership and permission to publish these documents.

Hartford System of Schools: Superintendent Steven Adamowski, Chief Academic Officer Penny MacCormack, Jennifer Allen, Sandra Inga, Sharon Heyman, Marianne Lalama, Beryl Bailey, James Thompson, Leon McKinley, Thomas Faniel, Desi Nesmith, Brenda Greene, Darren Schwartz, and the principals and educators of the Powerful Practices Cohorts 1 and 2. My sincere appreciation for all you do for Hartford students.

Middletown Public Schools: Kristen Freeman, Bob Fontaine, Tracey Koff, Karey Stingo, Eric Marszalek, Trevor Charles, and Lisa Geary. Special thanks to Superintendent Michael Frechette and Assistant Superintendent Barbara Senges for your passionate commitment to education and your permission to include the Middletown daily lesson plan templates in this publication.

New London Public Schools: Tommy Thompson. For years, your hands-on leadership to both implement and sustain best practices in your schools has demonstrated what an instructional leader should be.

West Haven Public Schools: Superintendent Neil Cavallaro and the outstanding curriculum supervisors and assistants who have proven the worth and practicality of the Rigorous Curriculum Design model: Ann Valanzuolo, English language arts; Amy Jo (A.J.) Palermo, mathematics; Raffaela Fronc, science, and Mark Consorte, social studies; Jonathan Capone, health/physical education/athletics; Judith Drenzek, early childhood; Dana Martinez, world language/English Language Learners (ELL); Francine Coppola, fine arts/adult education; Cassandra Marcella, secondary fine arts; Garrett Grant, career and technology education; Marilyn Lynch, senior library/media specialist. Special thanks to Kathryn Shea for her scoring guide student testimonial and especially to *all* of the dedicated educators that have worked so diligently to redesign West Haven's curricula. Raffaela, Ann, A.J., and Mark, we couldn't have done this without you. My heartfelt thank-you to Assistant Superintendent Anne Druzolowski for contributing Chapter 18 and for your inspiring motivation to improve the life of every student. You epitomize all that is best in education.

Herbert Lehman High School English Department, Bronx, New York

My sincere appreciation and respect for Assistant Principal Karen Andronico and her dedicated English Department colleagues: Lambrini Mavromatis, Aubrey Cunningham, Judy Rath, Jason Mulero, Anibal Bruno, Jeannette Chico, Sarah Richard, Stephanie Schochet, Carl Manalo, Britt Strickland, Kevin Kearns, and Claire Thomason. Keep up the outstanding work you are doing for all of the students you so selflessly serve. Working with each of you has been one of the high points of my professional career.

The Leadership and Learning Center

Grateful appreciation to Pam Zetterlund Clark for her hours of research and other contributions to this project; and to all my Center colleagues, particularly those who played a key role in this publication: Peggy Lush, Kristin Anderson, Katie Schellhorn, Mike Wasta, John Van Pelt, Stephen Ventura, Jay Trujillo, Loan Mascorro, Cathy Lassiter, Connie Kamm, Angela Peery, and Juan Cordova. And to my mentor and friend, Douglas Reeves, with my continuing gratitude, respect, and appreciation for all you have done for education, for The Center, and for me.

A singular acknowledgment of thanks and appreciation to Robert Kuklis, whose incisive feedback and suggestions for improving this publication proved invaluable;

to Mary Jane O'Connell for her detailed suggestions to assist administrators in the implementation of curriculum design; to Linda Gregg for her generous help in providing specific information regarding Response to Intervention strategies and specially designed instruction; to Bonnie Bishop for her assistance with English Language Learner strategies; to Tony Flach for his thought-provoking feedback on the chapters; and to the other reviewers who invested their time, thought, and energy to provide meaningful feedback and perspectives: Rachel Syrja, Barb Pitchford, Debbie Lee, and Kris Nielson. I am grateful for your validation and encouragement.

A very special thank-you to Katie Schellhorn for "shepherding" this publication from its inception to publication, and to the wonderfully conscientious Alan Bernhard and his editorial staff at Boulder Bookworks.

And on a Personal Note

To my beloved wife, Candy, who is always there to support me in countless ways, both seen and unseen.

About the Author

Larry Ainsworth is the Executive Director of Professional Development at The Leadership and Learning Center in Englewood, Colorado. He travels nationally and internationally to assist school systems in implementing best practices related to standards, assessment, and accountability across all grades and content areas. He is the author or co-author of ten published books, including *Rigorous Curriculum Design*, *"Unwrapping" the Standards*, *Power Standards*, *Common Formative Assessments*, *Student Generated Rubrics*, and *Five Easy Steps to a Balanced Math Program*, including three 2006 editions, one each for the primary, upper elementary, and secondary grade spans. His chapter "Common Formative Assessments: The Centerpiece of an Integrated Standards-Based Assessment System" appears in the 2007 assessment anthology *Ahead of the Curve: The Power of Assessment to Transform Teaching and Learning*, edited by Douglas B. Reeves. Larry regularly works on site in school systems to assist leaders and educators in understanding and implementing standards-based practices: prioritizing and "unwrapping" the standards, developing common formative assessments, designing authentic performance tasks, and creating rigorous curricular units of study in all content areas, pre-kindergarten through grade 12.

Larry has delivered keynote addresses and breakout sessions across North America and in Latin America, most notably for the U.S. Department of Education, Argentina's ESSARP (English Speaking Scholastic Association of the River Plate) institute in Buenos Aires, the New York Department of Education, Connecticut Department of Education, North Carolina Department of Education, Ohio Department of Education, Michigan Department of Education, Harvard University Graduate School of Education's Principals' Center, Solution Tree of Canada, Solution Tree in the U.S., 21st Century Learning Group, California Staff Development Council, Louisiana Staff Development Council, Indiana Staff Development Council, Archdiocese of Los Angeles, Diocese of Fort Worth, the Southern Regional Education Board, Ohio's Battelle for Kids conference, Virginia Title I and STARS (Supporting Teachers and Achieving Results for Students) conferences, the California Math Council, the California International Studies Project, the Alabama CLAS (Council for Leadership in Alabama Schools) Summer Institute, the Delaware Professional Development Conference, the National Council of Teachers of Mathematics, and the national ASCD (formerly the Association for Supervision and Curriculum Development).

With 24 years of experience as an upper elementary and middle school classroom teacher in demographically diverse schools, Larry brings a varied background and wide range of professional experiences to each of his presentations. He has held numerous leadership roles within school districts, including mentor teacher and K–12 math committee co-chair, and has served as a mathematics assessment consultant in several San Diego County school districts.

Larry holds a Master of Science degree in educational administration.

Preface

Over the years, busy educators and leaders have often expressed their appreciation that my books are short, focused, and easy to read. With regard to length, *Rigorous Curriculum Design* had to be different. Whereas my previous works have each focused on a *single* professional practice (*Priority Standards*, "*Unwrapping*" *the Standards*, *Common Formative Assessments*), the broad subject of curriculum must unavoidably take into account *multiple* professional practices. That, coupled with the fact that the first word in the title is "rigorous," meant that I just had to accept the fact that to present the education community with a comprehensive model of curriculum design meant writing a longer book.

The framework of *Rigorous Curriculum Design* is straightforward, sequential, and explicit. Comprehensive and highly detailed, it presents a step-by-step process that educators/curriculum designers can successfully follow—*over time*—to create wonderful curricular units of study in any grade, course, and content area.

The majority of my work in education continues to take place on site in school systems across North America, presenting powerful standards-based practices to our educators and leaders and helping them implement these practices in their own classrooms and instructional programs. The following two notes of appreciation from the same educator, sent to me after my first and second presentations of the *Rigorous Curriculum Design* seminar several months apart, greatly reaffirmed for me the value of the model:

> "I just wanted to touch base with you about the state of our curriculum development for secondary English. In a nutshell, it's going great! The five of us are completely 'sold' on your method. We are enjoying every moment of our work (if you can call it 'work'). Our first eight documents are comprehensive, clear and all very strongly based on the standards. Curriculum makes so much sense now!"
>
> BONNIE FINEMAN
> *East Hartford High School Curriculum Design Team, January, 2010*

> "I can't wait for you to see our final product. Right now, we've completed four units for each grade level (ninth and tenth); these units are quite rich. Our group worked tirelessly to follow the recommended framework and to make the curriculum accessible to the teachers. More importantly, I believe it is going to be extremely

valuable to our students. As I said before, it all makes sense now! I hope that the implementation goes as well as the actual creation of it."

BONNIE FINEMAN
East Hartford High School Curriculum Design Team, June, 2010

My sincere hope is that this book and its related seminars will serve educators for years to come as they continue their all-important work of educating our students for the future.

—LARRY AINSWORTH
Encinitas, California
July 31, 2010

Introduction

The subject of curriculum is a vast one—as huge in scope as the topics of standards, instruction, and assessment. Because there are numerous interpretations of exactly what the term *curriculum* means, as well as a multitude of ideas and opinions about what curriculum should include, a topic this broad needs narrowing and defining.

When educators and leaders consider all that a solid curriculum can and should take into account in order to engage and prepare students for the future—breadth and depth of content knowledge, procedural skills and conceptual understanding, meaningful learning activities that take into account students' interests, strengths, and developmental levels, constructivist thinking, college and career readiness, human values, character development, student-generated learning tasks, parent involvement, and so on—it's no wonder that the mere idea of creating a comprehensive curriculum to address all of these worthy aims can be daunting.

Educators must juxtapose this lofty ideal with the reality of education's focus in school systems today—a relentless concentration on preparing students to score proficiently on high-stakes tests based on a partial sampling of certain academic concepts and skills.

How can our educators and leaders strike the desired balance of designing their curricula to accomplish both the ideal and the reality—preparing students to successfully pursue whatever life pathways they choose in this 21st century *and* preparing students to succeed on state, provincial, and national tests without sacrificing rich and worthwhile learning?

Thoroughly addressing all of these considerations in exhaustive detail would result in an encyclopedic volume that many working professionals simply would not have the time to read and study, let alone be able to systematically apply. Instead, the process presented in these pages is a comprehensive, yet doable, approach to curriculum design that endeavors to achieve this desired balance, one that educators and leaders in any school system can successfully use to create rigorous curricular units of study for every grade and content area. Think of this design model as a road map—a practical pathway to a clear destination with opportunities to stop along the way for further information and course correction, as needed.

The Need for a Curriculum Design Road Map

The need for a cohesive and comprehensive curriculum that intentionally connects standards, instruction, and assessment has never been greater than it is today. For educators to meet the challenging learning needs of students—comprehend all the standards, prepare for a variety of formative and summative assessments, and demonstrate proficiency on high-stakes state or provincial tests—they must have a clear road map to follow throughout the school year.

Such a road map must offer busy educators an overall organizational plan to meet these needs, a plan that:

- clearly specifies standards-derived student learning outcomes;

- includes the different categories of instructional strategies: research-based, differentiation (additional supports for all students plus strategies for enrichment), intervention, and those most appropriate for English Language Learners and special education students;

- offers engaging learning experiences that incorporate 21st-century learning skills, such as authentic performance tasks, *in addition to* the more traditional types of textbook- or program-based learning activities;

- provides an aligned set of assessments to gauge student progress before, during, and after each instructional unit of study; and

- includes enough detail in the unit design to facilitate the writing of weekly plans and the designing of daily lessons.

This comprehensive road map needs to present *new* teachers with a detailed structure and pace to follow and *experienced* teachers with a flexible framework within which to apply their expertise. Essentially, it must offer *all* teachers a collaborative model for creatively planning and delivering an accessible and user-friendly curriculum that collectively addresses these multiple requirements.

Commercially Produced or Internally Created

Designing or redesigning rigorous curricula is a major undertaking. In preparing to undertake this work, school systems have options to consider. They may investigate commercially produced "turnkey" curricular programs that promise to save school systems from having to invest in the enormous expenditure of time, effort, and resources required to create their own. Expensive to buy, such component-heavy programs require both initial and ongoing professional development for educators so they are able to thoroughly understand the program and to use it effectively. No commercially produced program or textbook *by itself* should ever be regarded as "the curriculum." However, a carefully selected commercial program or text can certainly be effective when used as *part* of a school system's curricular redesign efforts.

For school systems that lack the necessary resources to purchase such a costly program and/or believe that the educators and leaders within their own system should be active participants in the custom design of their own rigorous curricula, this book is meant to provide a straightforward, do-it-yourself guide for doing so. Regardless of the choice that school systems make—commercially produced, internally created, or a blend of both—it is important to cultivate "in-house" ownership of the curricula throughout the process.

A Road Map Ready to Follow

Rigorous Curriculum Design presents a carefully sequenced, hands-on model that curriculum designers and educators in every school system can follow to create a progression of units of study that keep standards, instruction, and assessment tightly focused and connected.

Applicable to every grade, course, and content area, you will learn:

- what a rigorous curriculum *is* and how to create, sequence, and pace such a curriculum;
- why seeing the "big picture" connections *first* is essential to beginning curriculum design;
- how to build the foundation for designing a rigorous Pre-K–12 curriculum;
- how to design a grade- or course-specific curricular unit of study, from start to finish;
- how to use formative assessments and data analysis to guide instruction before, during, and after each unit; and
- how leaders can organize, implement, and sustain this model throughout the school and/or school system.

Overview of Book

This book is divided into four parts. Here is a brief overview of each part:

Part 1, Seeing the Big Picture Connections *First*, defines curriculum in terms of rigor, provides the background of this model, connects curriculum design to the "big picture" of standards, assessments, instruction, and data practices, previews the step-by-step design sequence, and introduces end-of-chapter reader asssignments.

Part 2, Building the Foundation for Designing Curricular Units, explains the five steps that must first be taken to lay the foundation upon which to build the curricular units of study, and provides explicit guidelines for applying each step.

Part 3, Designing the Curricular Unit of Study—From Start to Finish, gives the "nuts and bolts" directions for designing a rigorous curricular unit of study, from beginning to end, and concludes with an overview of how to implement the unit in the classroom or instructional program. Formatively assessing students along the way, educators analyze resulting student data to diagnose student learning needs and then adjust ongoing instruction accordingly.

Part 4, Organizing, Monitoring, and Sustaining Implementation Efforts, addresses the role of administrators in beginning and continuing the work of implementation. These final three chapters provide first-person narratives and advice to administrators from administrators who have personally led the implementation and sustainability efforts of curriculum redesign and related practices within their own school systems.

I have endeavored to pull together all of the elements necessary for designing a rigorous curriculum, to position these elements in a sequential order, and to provide a step-by-step approach for constructing each one. My hope is that this road map will not only "show you the way" to design your own curriculum, but also allow you the flexibility of customizing it to fit your own purpose and needs.

As with the realization of any lofty vision, it will take a great deal of time, thought, energy, and collaboration to create and revise a *single* curriculum, let alone multiple curricula. The best advice I can offer is to regard whatever you produce as a continual "work in progress," to be accomplished over one, two, or three years, or even longer. As my friend and colleague Robert Kuklis points out, curriculum designers "shape and modify the process as they move through it. It is important that they know this is not a rigid, prescriptive procedure, but rather an opportunity for learning, adapting, and improving. This preserves fidelity to the process, encourages flexibility, and promotes local ownership."

Whenever people's spirits need lifting because the work seems so demanding, remind everyone that it is a *process*, not a one-time event. You are creating something truly significant—a comprehensive body of work that is going to serve your educators, students, and parents for years to come!

PART ONE

Seeing the Big Picture Connections *First*

CHAPTER 1
What *Is*
Rigorous Curriculum Design?

Before defining curriculum design in terms of *rigor,* let's first start with a fundamental definition of the general term, *curriculum.* There are varying definitions, all useful for providing an important foundational understanding of the term. Among them are the following:

According to the New Oxford American Dictionary, the origin of the word *curriculum* is from the Latin *curricle,* meaning "course, racing chariot," and *currere,* "to run." Loosely interpreted, a curriculum is a course to be run.

Peter Oliva (2005) defines *curriculum* as:

> A number of plans, in written form and of varying scope, that delineate the desired learning experiences. The curriculum, therefore, may be a unit, a course, a sequence of courses, the school's entire program of studies ... (p. 7).

W. James Popham offers two related explanations of *curriculum:*

> By curriculum, I mean the *outcomes* that educators hope to achieve with their students. The three most common kinds of outcomes sought are students' acquisition of *cognitive skills, bodies of knowledge,* and their *affect* (such as particular attitudes, interests, or values) (2003b, pp. 16–17).
>
> In this time-honored definition, a curriculum represents educational *ends.* Educators hope, of course, that such ends will be attained as a consequence of instructional activities which serve as the *means* of promoting the curricular ends (2004, p. 30).

Douglas B. Reeves (2001) writes:

> An effective standards-based curriculum is planned "with the end in mind." The selection of a standards-based curriculum implies focus, discernment, and the clear exclusion of many things that are now in textbooks, lesson plans, and curricula (p. 13).

Apart from these clear and compatible definitions of the word, many broad synonyms for curriculum, often used interchangeably, include: standards, lesson plans, textbooks, scope and sequence, learning activities, and prescribed courses of study provided by the state, province, district, school division, or professional content area organizations. The result is a rather nebulous understanding of the term whenever educators use it in dialogues and discussions.

For purposes of this book, I am defining curriculum as *the high-quality delivery system for ensuring that all students achieve the desired end—the attainment of their designated grade- or course-specific standards.* My vision for designing such a curriculum is founded upon the intentional alignment between standards, instruction, and assessment.

The Current Need to Update and Redesign Curricula

School systems have been working hard over the past several years to get the *means* for achieving this desired end firmly in place and accepted within their professional culture. These "means" include, but are not limited to, the effective use of standards, differentiated instructional practices, formative assessments, and corresponding data analysis.

Today, educators and leaders are well aware of the need to update and redesign their existing curricula—particularly in the U.S., where forty-three states and the District of Columbia have adopted the rigorous Common Core State Standards in English language arts and mathematics. Equally rigorous curricula aligned to these new standards must be created to help educators prepare their students for the national assessments that will be first administered in 2014–15. In addition, stronger links are needed between curricula and the many professional best practices being implemented. Not only have curricula not kept pace with the updated versions of state or provincial standards and assessments, often the established curricula are reflective of only the more traditional components:

- A general listing of content and performance standards (student learning outcomes or objectives) for each content area
- A yearlong scope and sequence of what to teach and in what order
- A pacing calendar of when to teach it and how long to take in doing so
- A list of related learning activities
- A suggestion of assessments to use
- A list of required or recommended materials and resources

All of these traditional components are, of course, necessary to retain, but they need to be further clarified. In addition, other important components should be added. We must broaden our view of what we want our curricula to be and do.

Curricular architects must acknowledge that the function of a rigorous curriculum is to *raise the level of teaching* so that students are prepared for the 21st century with skills that "drive knowledge economies: innovation, creativity, teamwork, problem solving, flexibility, adaptability, and a commitment to continuous learning" (Hargreaves and Shirley, 2009).

Think about the following *blend* of both traditional and new components for an updated and redesigned comprehensive curriculum:

- *Specific* learning outcomes students are to achieve from pre-kindergarten through grade 12 in all content areas

- *Vertical representation* of those learning outcomes (grade-to-grade, course-to-course) in curricular frameworks

- Units of study—*topical* (literary devices, character traits, narrative writing); *skills-based* (making text-to-text connections, simplifying fractions); *thematic* (patterns, ecology, composition and creativity, personal rights)

- Emphasis on standards-based skills *and* content knowledge

- Academic vocabulary specific to each discipline and pertinent to each unit of study

- Explicit linkages to state or provincial assessments and to college and career readiness

- 21st-century learning skills

- Higher-level thinking skills

- Interdisciplinary connections

- Authentic, student-centered performance tasks that engage learners in applying concepts and skills to the real world

- Ongoing assessments to gauge student understanding

- Sequencing of "learning progressions" (Popham, 2008), the conceptual and skill-based building blocks of instruction

- Research-based effective teaching strategies

- Differentiation, intervention, special education, and English Language Learner strategies to meet the needs of *all* students

- A common lexicon of terminology (curriculum glossary) to promote consistency of understanding

- Embedded use of resources and multimedia technology
- A parent communication and involvement component
- A curriculum philosophy that is compatible with or a part of the school system's mission statement

Another factor—this one external—that is driving the need to update and redesign curricula is the curriculum audit. In some school systems where low student performance on standardized tests has identified the system as being in need of improvement, a curriculum audit administered by an outside agency examines a particular content area curriculum to evaluate its strengths and point out its omissions. Although an external audit may initially seem disciplinary, it can, upon further consideration, be looked upon as a helpful diagnostic. The findings and recommendations of the audit report can provide a specific focal point for beginning needed revision efforts.

Rigor for the 21st Century

There are many definitions of the noun *rigor*, most of them related to some form of physical or mental rigidity or severity. Merriam-Webster's Online Dictionary definition of *logical* rigor—"strict precision or exactness"—seems at least relevant to the educational context. The Oxford Pocket Dictionary of Current English defines the related adjective *rigorous* as "extremely thorough." Yet neither of these definitions satisfactorily conveys the intent behind the word. To me, rigor refers not only to a level of difficulty and the ways in which students apply their knowledge through higher-order thinking skills; it also implies *the reaching for a higher level of quality in both effort and outcome.*

In many U.S. communities, the public perceives a decline and loss of rigor in their schools. School systems with a majority of underachieving students are facing very real external accountability pressures to perform well on state assessments. The response to these pressures in some, though certainly not all, school districts has been to *lower* expectations of what their students should learn and be able to do. This "lowering of the bar" has resulted in a loss of instruction and learning rigor for *all* students in those systems. Conversely, in other school systems with a majority of *high*-performing students, the comfortable status quo—as related to rigor—may need a healthy "bump up" in terms of redefining what rigor ought to mean and look like in both instruction and student work.

School systems preparing for a partial or complete overhaul of their existing curricula to emphasize increased rigor may find support in these insightful words of

Arthur L. Costa and Bena Kallik (2010): "We must ask ourselves, are we educating students for a life of tests or for the tests of life?" (p. 225).

In his article "Rigor Redefined," Tony Wagner (2008) names seven 21st-century "survival" skills students today need to "master [in order] to thrive in the new world of work: (1) critical thinking and problem solving; (2) collaboration and leadership; (3) agility and adaptability; (4) initiative and entrepreneurialism; (5) effective oral and written communication; (6) accessing and analyzing information; and (7) curiosity and imagination" (pp. 21–22).

Wagner extols an exemplary algebra II teacher he observed who carefully structured a lesson so that his students learned the academic content while *simultaneously using all seven of these skills.* In contrast, Wagner laments what he has seen in hundreds of U.S. classroom observations: the reduction of curriculum down to only one component—test preparation. He concludes, "It's time to hold ourselves and all of our students to a new and higher standard of rigor, defined according to 21st-century criteria" (p. 24).

Rigorous Curriculum Defined

My own definition of rigor as applied to standards, instruction, and assessment began with a focus limited primarily to the revised Bloom's Taxonomy of Educational Objectives (Anderson and Krathwohl, 2001).

In the process of "unwrapping" or deconstructing standards that I have continued to refine, educators match the skills (verbs) in the standards statements to one of the six cognitive processes in the revised taxonomy: *remember, understand, apply, analyze, evaluate,* and *create.* They then design assessment questions to reflect the approximate levels of the corresponding thinking skills (e.g., analyze: analysis question; interpret: interpretation question). Corresponding instruction intentionally provides students with opportunities to exercise each targeted skill at the appropriate level of rigor so they are prepared to answer the related assessment questions.

This was—and continues to be—a good starting place for making more rigorous, parallel connections between standards, assessment, and instruction.

However, when applied to curriculum design, I believe a broader definition of "rigor" must also include the *intentional inclusion of and alignment between all necessary components within that curriculum.* To design a comprehensive curriculum that intentionally aligns standards, formal and informal assessments, engaging student learning experiences, related instruction that includes a variety of strategies, higher-order thinking skills, 21st-century life skills, data analysis, and so on, is to indeed design a *rigorous* curriculum.

Keeping in mind my definition of curriculum—*the high-quality delivery system for ensuring that students achieve the desired end—the attainment of their designated grade- or course-specific standards*—along with my definition of rigor—*the reaching for a higher level of quality in both effort and outcome*, I put the two together to form a summary definition of a rigorous curriculum.

A **rigorous curriculum** is an inclusive set of intentionally aligned components—clear learning outcomes with matching assessments, engaging learning experiences, and instructional strategies—organized into sequenced units of study that serve as both the detailed road map and the high-quality delivery system for ensuring that all students achieve the desired end: the attainment of their designated grade- or course-specific standards within a particular content area.

The Student-Centered Curriculum

With all the focus up to this point on redesigning the curriculum to include all of the different components the *adults* in the system determine as being necessary, let us not forget the people for whom it is constructed—the students.

A rigorous curriculum must keep students at the center of its design. Although such a curriculum is based on a preset list of necessary components, in no way does this imply that rigor should be equated to rigidity. A rigorous curriculum must remain flexible, adaptable to the diverse and continuously changing learning needs of all the students it serves. By deliberately planning and creating *engaging* classroom learning experiences, the authors of a rigorous curriculum can provide the means for both new and experienced teachers to motivate reluctant, insecure learners as well as those students who have disengaged from learning out of disinterest or outright boredom. One of the ways rigorous curriculum design can help teachers address these challenges is by offering students precise learning targets, *meaningful and relevant* lessons and activities, and multiple opportunities to succeed.

Equally vital and often lacking sufficient emphasis in curriculum design is how to meet the learning needs of *advanced* students. When developing specific units of study, curriculum designers can consider the various ways to challenge and enrich high-achieving students so they can expand and deepen their understanding related to any unit topic.

Begin a Curriculum Glossary

As curriculum committees begin discussing the various elements related to curriculum design, participants nearly always ask for clarification about what a particular term or element means. The need to be "speaking a common language" with regard to curriculum development emerges early. Creating a glossary or lexicon of terms during the beginning stages of organizing the process will benefit everyone involved in the actual design of the curricula as well as the educators in classrooms and instructional programs who will be implementing those curricula. Such a glossary can be expanded throughout the process to include terminology used in conjunction with all relevant, standards-based practices in general.

Near the end of this book, I have included a curriculum glossary of the terms used throughout the rigorous curriculum design model. Feel free to expand upon this glossary of terms while creating your own glossary specific to your particular context and information needs.

Curriculum Development Needs Assessment

In the coming chapters, I propose a realistic approach for designing a curriculum model that achieves these ambitious—rigorous—outcomes. But first, you may want to consider conducting your own needs assessment to determine your current state of readiness for beginning this process.

Schedule an orientation session with those who will be involved in organizing the curriculum revision project to discuss the scope of the work. Conduct a corresponding needs assessment to determine your starting point. Such a needs assessment will help in clarifying why you are revising your curricula, what needs doing, and how you plan to author and implement the units of study.

Sample questions you may want to ask include:

- What is our curriculum philosophy? Does it reflect our school system's mission statement and provide the "ways and means" for fulfilling our educational mission?

- What is the current state of our existing curricula? Are all content areas in equal need of revision, or do we need to prioritize? Which ones must come first?

- Why should we consider revising or updating these curricula now?

- Do we have the necessary resources (time, personnel, budget) and the committed support of leadership (system-level and school-level) to begin the work and see it through to completion?

- What do we want our revised curricula to be and do? For example, if our curricula were indeed more rigorous, more engaging, and more relevant to *all* students, what would the impact be on their day-to-day motivation and achievement?

- What should the various components of our curricula include?

- What do we want to retain from our existing curricula? What do we want to add?

- What kind of structure, template, or framework will we use? Should it be content-area specific, or more universal, to promote consistency across the school system?

Answering these and other group-generated questions *before* beginning the actual creation of curricular units of study will provide a helpful and realistic look at current conditions and various viewpoints that organizers are wise to consider in advance of launching the project.

CHAPTER 2
How This Model Came to Be

Throughout the remainder of this book, I showcase educators and leaders from the school systems I have had the good fortune to assist in redesigning their existing curricula. To provide readers with a background context for this approach to rigorous curriculum design, here is a brief story of how this model came to be.

Herbert Lehman High School, Bronx, New York

Herbert Lehman High School, located in the Throg's Neck area of the Bronx, New York, straddles the commuter-packed Hutchinson River Parkway. Opened in 1971, this comprehensive high school has a school population of 4,300 students, grades 9–12, and more than 250 educators.

Karen Andronico, Assistant Principal, oversees the large English department of approximately 30 teachers. A guiding coalition of about 10 of these educators met with me repeatedly over many months beginning in December 2007 to redesign their English department's 9–12 curricula. Beginning with the prioritization and vertical alignment of the New York language arts standards, which included the input of the entire English department faculty, I facilitated the planning and production meetings of the guiding coalition's work in creating curricular units of study. Ms. Andronico and her colleagues continued developing the units between my visits.

What repeatedly made an impression on me about this group of dedicated English teachers was how they voluntarily gave up their own prep periods, again and again, to do this curriculum redesign work. Arranging coverage of each other's classes, three or four of these educators would come into our workroom in any given period while others would leave to teach a class. Those that left would return an hour or more later to continue working, while those present would again prepare to leave. This went on throughout each day I met with them over a two-year period. Even without benefit of school-designated professional development days, these professionals refused to let this lack deter them from doing the work they each saw as important and relevant to meeting the learning needs of their students. It was an inspiring demonstration of the extraordinary dedication and commitment of educators that the public rarely sees.

Hartford, Connecticut

I am indebted to the educators and leaders throughout the state of Connecticut who have also been among the first to embrace these ideas and implement them fully. Their real-world application of this "do-it-yourself" approach to curriculum design has provided great credibility to the worth of the model.

In January 2009, I was invited by Jennifer Allen, Director of Professional Development in Hartford, Connecticut, to present a morning and afternoon three-hour informational session to the curriculum writers of Hartford's system of schools. As preparation for writing standards-based curricula, I emphasized the need to first lay a solid, standards-based foundation that included these four interrelated practices:

- *Prioritizing* the state academic content standards
- "*Unwrapping*" those standards to pinpoint the concepts students needed to know and the skills they needed to be able to do
- Determining the foundational understandings or *Big Ideas* that students need to discover on their own from the "unwrapped" concepts and skills
- Creating *Essential Questions* to focus instruction and assessment and to spark students' interest in what they were about to learn

These established professional practices were already being implemented in school districts across the state as part of the Connecticut Accountability for Learning Initiative (CALI). CALI supports district efforts to improve student achievement in their underperforming schools as measured by the Connecticut Mastery Test (CMT) administered to students in grades 3 through 8 and by the Connecticut Academic Performance Test (CAPT) administered to grade 10 students. These assessments occur each year in March.

During the summer and fall of 2008, by invitation from James Thompson, Assistant Superintendent for Elementary Education, and Leon McKinley, Director of Elementary Education, I led a cohort of eleven Hartford pre-kindergarten through grade 8 schools through the prioritization and "unwrapping" of the state's math and English language arts standards. Therefore I knew that important groundwork for updating Hartford's district curricula in these two key content areas had already been accomplished.

In my presentation to the curriculum writers, I explained these four foundational practices as being the first in a recommended sequence of steps to develop a standards-based curriculum. These practices would be applied in a series of units of study delivered *prior to* the March state tests and then *continued* after those tests to the end of the school year. I described how to incorporate the other CALI professional practices—Common Formative Assessments, Data Teams, and Effective Teaching Strategies—into this curricular model. By using formative assessment results to diagnose student learning needs *before* and *during* each unit of study, teachers could differentiate their instruction to help students achieve measurable success by the *end*-of-unit post-assessment.

The feedback from everyone in attendance was positive and validating. Yet because the length of the session didn't allow time for participants to actually *apply* the information, it wasn't until a couple of months later that I learned the Hartford curriculum writers were following my recommended model, and that the process was working well.

West Haven, Connecticut

As I continued to present these ideas in New York and Connecticut, one Connecticut school system in particular quickly emerged as the real pioneer in the full development of this curriculum design model—West Haven Public Schools.

Neil Cavallaro and Anne Druzolowski, the district's new Superintendent and Assistant Superintendent, respectively, invited me, as a representative from The Leadership and Learning Center, to begin a long-term partnership with them to create new curricula in all content areas. At this time, they did not have a cohesive and consistent Pre-K–12 structure or framework for developing curricular units that incorporated all of the CALI practices.

The work began with approximately one hundred pre-kindergarten through grade 12 classroom teachers in the first cohort of content areas: English language arts, science, math, and social studies. Under the leadership of their respective content area supervisors, Amy Jo Palermo (math), Ann Valanzuolo (English language arts), Raffaela Fronc (science), and Mark Consorte (social studies), these combined teams of participating teachers learned how to prioritize and "unwrap" their state standards for individual units of study. Because there were no district-designated units of study at that time, I encouraged the teachers to select a unit topic of their own choosing that was relevant to their respective content area, grade level, and/or course just so they could learn the process.

The logical next step for West Haven was to identify and "map out" a comprehensive list of curricular units for each grade level and content area. These were to be paced from the beginning of the school year up to the CMT and CAPT testing in March and continued *after* state testing, so that students would acquire the grade- or course-specific district Priority Standards by the end of each school year.

By the fall of 2009, the district had posted an impressive number of curricular units on their Web site. Although a section for formative and summative assessments was included on the planning organizer for each unit, the curriculum writers had not yet received that professional development information. In my next workshop sessions with them, they began creating common formative assessments directly aligned to their "unwrapped" Priority Standards for the individual units of study they had created.

Owing to the scope of the work, district leadership scheduled subsequent "production days" with me present to offer technical support and guidance as needed while the curriculum writers continued to create and refine their curricular units and corresponding common formative assessments. Participating teachers reported success in "road testing" the units they had created in their own classroom and instructional programs.

In the fall of 2009, the work expanded to a second cohort of educators that included fine arts, health and physical education, early childhood education, world languages, career and technology education, and library media technology. These educators are all following the same road map and successfully making the process applicable to their own content areas.

Seeing this curriculum design process go from a conceptual "good idea" to a very doable, working model in West Haven convinced me that this model can be replicated in any school or school system. What is necessary for success is a shared readiness to begin the work coupled with a strong commitment to see it through to completion over a period of several years.

East Hartford, Connecticut

In January 2010, Debbie A. Kaprove, Assistant Superintendent of East Hartford Public Schools, invited me to present my curriculum model to the district's English language arts and math curriculum writers. Because we had a full two days allocated for beginning this work, participants had sufficient time to apply the first steps of the process. Led by their respective content area coordinators, the participants first organized themselves into two content area groups and then further subdivided themselves by grade spans: primary, upper elementary, middle school, and high school.

I had facilitated East Hartford's prioritizing and "unwrapping" of the state standards in previous years, so the assembled group of curriculum writers had the advantage of being able to build upon these two foundational steps and move quickly into the actual design of their district curriculum templates and creation of their first-draft units of study.

What impressed me most was the immediate level of engagement and the stimulating conversations that took place as the groups got down to work. One of the most gratifying comments I heard during the two days was this one spoken by one of the participating high school English teachers: "It's so great to feel validated and respected as a professional by being able to contribute to a process that makes sense and is relevant to our day-to-day work in the classroom."

The curriculum design project continues at different stages of development and implementation in these school systems. What the Herbert Lehman High School English department colleagues, and the curriculum writers in Hartford, West Haven, and East Hartford, have all done in such a relatively short amount of time has set the pattern that other school systems will surely follow in the coming years. What an honor and a privilege it has been to work with such dedicated professionals!

CHAPTER 3

Connecting Curriculum Design to the "Big Picture"

The Need for a Systems Approach to Curriculum Design

W. Edwards Deming (2000) defined a *system* as "a network of interdependent parts or components working together to accomplish the aim of the system."

Fred Kofman and Peter Senge (1995) wrote that "the defining characteristic of a system is that it cannot be understood as a function of its isolated components."

Mike Wasta, former Superintendent of Bristol Public Schools in Connecticut, sums up what he realized from his own personal experience in building such a system: "It is essential for everyone to understand that powerful instruction and assessment practices are not separately functioning 'good ideas' but are all part of an *intentionally aligned and whole system.*"

A *Process*, Not an Event

One of the real challenges facing educators and leaders in our schools today is the feeling of being overwhelmed. There are so many moving parts to constantly manage effectively in a system as complex as education that it can often seem as if we are novice jugglers, attempting to keep a hundred balls in the air simultaneously.

These moving parts include the many new professional practices we expect our educators and administrators to be learning rapidly and implementing immediately in their daily work. It's no wonder that the result is "initiative overload," and it takes real fortitude in heart and mind to keep smiling and striving under the weight of so many demands that the job of educating youth places upon each of us every day.

Yet the good news is that building such an integrated system is not only possible, it is absolutely doable—as long as everyone understands and frequently reminds one another that it is a *multiple-year process*, and not a one-year event. The key to success is to carefully plan and carry out the process in *incremental steps*.

But it also requires something else—something that can do much to lift the weight of that burden we often feel: understanding *why* we are implementing these new practices and how they fit in with what we are *already* doing.

Getting Buy-In

A question I hear regularly from educators and leaders attending my professional development sessions is, "How do we get 'buy-in' from colleagues who are resistant to adding anything more to their plate?"

In reply, I talk about the necessity of first seeing the "big picture." When we can see how everything is intentionally connected to everything else, and why each component needs to be a part of the whole—*before* we expect people to buy in—then things start to make much more sense to those whose initial reaction to anything new may understandably be resistance.

Of course this does not automatically guarantee buy-in; fully accepting a new idea or practice is a gradual process. But what the big picture does do is provide a clear purpose and logical rationale for investing time, thought, and energy into something *else*. When the why makes sense, people are more receptive to learning the how. Outward compliance changes more quickly to inner commitment, even though real buy-in only takes place when those learning a new practice have had sufficient chance to apply it and determine for themselves its merit.

To promote the first stage of buy-in—understanding the why—several years ago I created a big picture diagram to illustrate the intentional connections between powerful practices educators and leaders are implementing to improve student achievement. I selected only a handful of proven beneficial practices related to standards, instruction, assessment, and data to include on the diagram, because I wanted a reasonably simple, uncluttered visual that showed the purposeful connections between the ones selected. This diagram, represented in Figure 3.1, has served as a great focal point for professional discussions.

The simple description of the diagram reading from the bottom to the top is this: Beginning with the full list of academic content standards for all content areas, prioritize the full list of the standards to those *essential* for student success at each grade level and in each course. Next "unwrap," or deconstruct, these Priority Standards to pinpoint exactly what students need to know (key concepts) and be able to do (key skills). Then determine the educational Big Ideas relative to the "unwrapped" concepts that students are to discover on their own. Write corresponding Essential Questions to establish a learning focus for the duration of the unit. Students will respond to the Essential Questions with Big Ideas in their own words by the conclusion of the unit.

With this foundation in place, create a series of conceptual units of study that include classroom performance tasks and scoring guides (rubrics). "Bookend" each unit with a common formative pre- and post-assessment followed by Data Team analysis to diagnose student learning needs and select effective teaching strategies to meet those needs.

FIGURE
3.1   **Standards-Assessment Alignment Diagram**

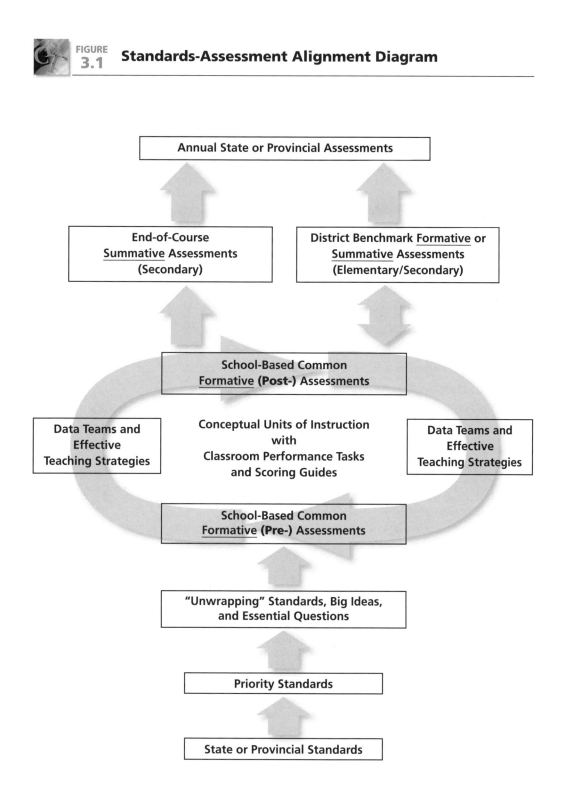

Align those in-school assessments *for* learning to district or school division benchmark assessments and high school end-of-course assessments *of* learning. Extend the alignment to external state or provincial standardized assessments. In this way, each level of assessment should provide teachers with predictive value of how students are likely to do on subsequent assessments *in time* for them to provide students with what Tom Guskey calls "corrective instruction." This represents the best use of data—to diagnose student learning needs in order to make appropriate instructional changes.

Updating the Diagram

In preparing to update the original standards-assessment diagram to emphasize curriculum design and its interdependent practices, I realized the need to expand the number of elements appearing on the diagram while retaining the relative simplicity of the original graphic. To do that, I first identified and grouped these added elements into four broad categories: standards, instruction, assessments, and data analysis, as shown in Figure 3.2, recognizing that certain elements, such as instructional strategies, overlapped more than one category.

Then I considered how best to organize all of these numerous elements into a cohesive whole for the updated diagram that would accomplish two primary objectives: (1) showcase curricular units of study as the nucleus of intentionally connected standards, instruction, assessment, and data practices; and (2) place each of the elements on the diagram in a specific location to indicate a linear progression, or order, of recommended implementation.

Such a comprehensive diagram would hopefully serve as a big picture road map for educators and leaders to:

- preview the eventual destination of a comprehensive curriculum as the centerpiece of a fully aligned standards, curriculum, instruction, assessment, and data system;

- see where they currently are on the journey of implementation; and

- show the specific sequence of signposts to follow to complete the journey.

Figure 3.3 is the result of this vision. Even though every single element in the table does not appear on the diagram, the associations between those that do appear and the few that do not should become apparent in the description that follows the diagram.

FIGURE 3.2   Specific Components of a Rigorous Curriculum Model

Standards	Instruction	Assessments	Data Analysis
State or Provincial Standards	Curricular Units of Study	State or Provincial Assessments	Instructional Data Teams Process
Priority Standards	Engaging Learning Experiences	Common Formative Pre-Assessments	Analysis of Data to Diagnose Student Learning Needs
Supporting Standards	Performance Tasks and Culminating Projects with Scoring Guides (Rubrics)	Common Formative Post-Assessments	Different Performance Levels of Student Subgroups
"Unwrapped" Priority Standards (Key Concepts and Skills)	Research-Based Instructional Strategies	Selected-Response and Constructed-Response Question Formats; Performance-Based Tasks	Instructional Strategies Matched to SMART Goals
Levels of Thinking Skill Rigor	Differentiation, Enrichment, and Intervention Strategies	Informal Progress-Monitoring Checks	Results Indicators for Adults and Students Matched to Instructional Strategies
Big Ideas and Essential Questions	Print and Tech-nology Materials and Resources	Traditional Diag-nostic Assessments: DIBELS (Dynamic Indicators of Basic Early Literacy Skills); DRP (Degrees of Reading Power); Running Records; etc.	Differentiation Strategies (Additional Supports for All Students Plus Enrichment Strategies)
Academic Vocabulary	District or Provincial Curriculum	District or School Division Benchmark Assessments	Intervention Strategies (Tiers 1, 2, 3)
Interdisciplinary Standards	Curriculum Scope and Sequence with Unit Pacing Calendar	Accommodations/ Modifications for Special Education Students and English Language Learners	Mid-Unit Evaluation of Targeted Strategies
21st-Century Learning Skills	Weekly and Daily Lesson Plans	End-of-Course/End-of-Grade Summative Assessments	Monitoring Effectiveness of Strategies and Evidence of Implementation

FIGURE 3.3   Rigorous Curriculum Design Alignment Diagram

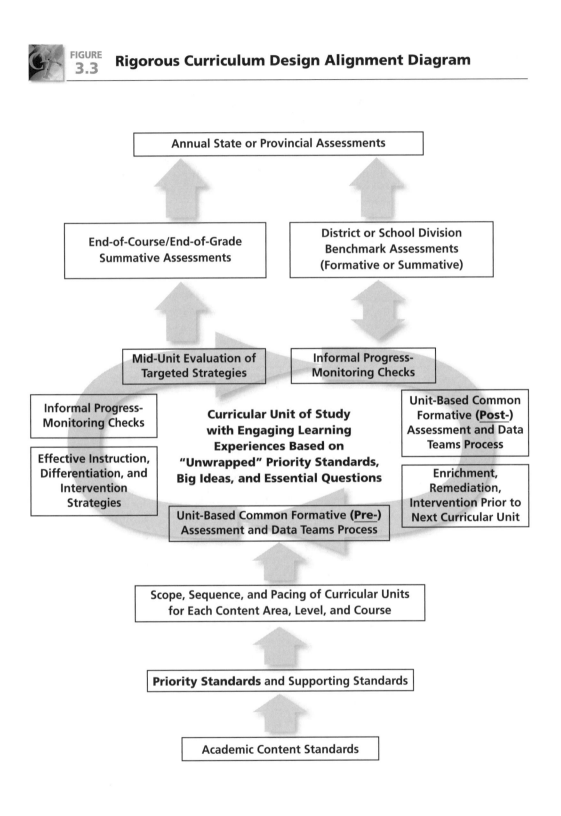

Putting It All Together

Presenting the detailed *sequence of steps* for creating rigorous curricular units of study that intentionally align standards, instruction, assessment, and data practices is the essential purpose of this book. The alignment diagram represents much of the curriculum design and implementation process visually.

For example, the foundational steps necessary for creating the units include the prioritization of standards, assigning them to units of study, and determining a pacing calendar. The actual design of the units includes "unwrapping" of the standards, writing Big Ideas and Essential Questions, creating unit assessments, planning engaging learning experiences, and selecting appropriate instructional strategies to meet the learning needs of all students. All of these key components appear on the alignment diagram and will be presented sequentially in the coming chapters.

The diagram also shows the sequence of steps educators will eventually follow to implement each of the units with colleagues who are part of an instructional Data Team, using ongoing assessments throughout the unit to gauge the effectiveness of the targeted instructional strategies. Even though the Data Teams process is not the focus of this book, it is indispensable to curriculum *implementation*. Again, the purpose of this chapter is to show the connections between all of the interdependent components of a fully aligned system in order to set curriculum design within the larger educational context.

The Updated Diagram Explained

In the following explanation, I have underlined the elements that appear on the updated alignment diagram as well as those that appear only in Figure 3.2. I divided the explanation into two parts—the first addressing the elements related to *constructing* the curricular unit, and the second to *implementing* that unit.

As with the original diagram, look first at the bottom and then at the top of the updated diagram. The same intentional alignment between the state or provincial academic content standards and the corresponding state or provincial assessments remains as the starting and ending points. This intentional alignment then extends to the internal, school-based assessments *for* learning and to the summative end-of-course and end-of-grade assessments and external, district or school division benchmark assessments *of* learning.

Constructing the Curricular Unit

The heart or center of the alignment diagram is the <u>curricular unit of study</u> with <u>engaging learning experiences</u> based on the "<u>unwrapped</u>" Priority Standards, <u>supporting standards</u>, and related <u>Big Ideas</u> and <u>Essential Questions</u>. This unit focus also includes specific <u>academic vocabulary</u>, relevant <u>interdisciplinary standards</u>, and <u>21st-century learning skills</u>.

Before planning any instruction and related learning activities for the unit in focus, the grade-level or course-specific educators first "begin with the end in mind" by creating a <u>common formative *post*-assessment</u> to administer at the *end* of the unit. This assessment typically includes a blend of both <u>selected-response and constructed-response questions and/or performance-based tasks</u> matched directly to the concepts, skills, and <u>levels of thinking skills</u> in the "unwrapped" Priority Standards. The educators next write the <u>common formative *pre*-assessment</u> aligned or "mirrored" to the post-assessment so they can determine growth in student learning from the pre- to post-assessment. They consider whether or not to include other <u>traditional diagnostic assessments</u> that may help them in their instructional decision making.

At this point, the teachers are ready to review their <u>instructional resources</u> and plan <u>engaging learning experiences</u> *directly matched to* the "unwrapped" <u>Priority Standards</u> concepts, thinking skill levels, <u>supporting standards</u>, unit-specific <u>academic vocabulary</u>, and the end-of-unit post-assessment. Such learning experiences need to include <u>authentic performance tasks</u> and/or <u>culminating projects</u> with accompanying <u>scoring guides (rubrics)</u> that provide evidence that the standards have been met.

With their learning activities in mind, the teachers can next consider which <u>instructional strategies</u> (<u>research-based</u>, <u>differentiation</u>, <u>enrichment</u>, and <u>intervention</u>) to use during instruction and related learning activities so they can <u>plan their weekly and daily lessons</u> accordingly.

Keeping in focus their end-of-unit common formative post-assessment, the teachers may then decide to collaboratively plan and design <u>informal progress-monitoring checks</u> (short, formative "checks for understanding") aligned to the post-assessment that will help them diagnose student learning needs *during* the unit of study. Alternatively, they may choose to wait and individually or collaboratively plan those quick assessments *for* learning once the unit is under way.

The unit of study with all of its key components is now ready to use.

Implementing the Curricular Unit

Around the diagram's center appears a clockwise progression of closely related practices applicable to each unit of study and carried out by the members of an instructional Data Team, a grade-level or course-specific group of educators who are teaching the same unit of study at the same time that also includes special educators, English Language Learner educators, and other instructional specialists and student support staff. After introducing the unit to students in their respective classrooms or programs and administering the common formative pre-assessment, the instructional Data Team will follow the established process for using the assessment data to improve student achievement.

First they will chart the students' assessment results according to levels of proficiency (step 1) and then analyze those results (step 2) to diagnose student learning needs. They will next set a SMART goal (Specific, Measurable, Achievable, Relevant, and Timely) (step 3) for student learning gains to achieve by the end of the unit. They will select research-based instructional strategies (step 4) to meet the goal for each of their different performance levels of student subgroups, including accommodations and modifications for special education students and language acquisition strategies for English Language Learners, and determine results indicators (step 5) to show whether or not the strategies are working for the educators and their students. Finally, they will decide how and in what ways they will *monitor* the effectiveness of the targeted strategies (step 6).

As part of the process, the team will also consider how they will differentiate and enrich instruction for individual students, small groups, and/or the entire class. They will decide which Tier 1 intervention strategies to use with all students and which Tier 2 and Tier 3 intervention strategies to use to assist students who are near to or far from achieving proficiency as defined by the SMART goal. They will create a comprehensive action plan for the intentional monitoring of the targeted strategies throughout the unit of study and for documenting evidence of implementation.

The team of teachers will schedule a mid-unit evaluation of their targeted teaching and differentiation strategies to determine if the strategies are producing the desired results indicators, and make whatever changes are needed. At the end of the unit, they will administer the common formative *post*-assessment and again repeat the Data Teams process. They will consider how to enrich proficient and advanced students, remediate almost-proficient students, and intensively intervene using Tier 2 and Tier 3 strategies for at-risk students before moving on to the next curricular unit.

After reassessing these latter two subgroups of students, the teachers will be ready to implement the next unit of study listed on their designated curriculum scope and sequence pacing calendar.

A Vision to Achieve Over Time

Remember, this is a "big picture" vision of an integrated standards-curriculum-instruction-assessment-and-data system to be achieved *over time and in incremental steps*. Its purpose is to help curriculum designers see the panoramic view, not to overwhelm anyone with the thought of how much time and effort will be needed to turn that vision into reality. I think the concept of "baby steps" is a good one to keep in mind here. We can only achieve big things in small steps that continually move us in the right direction. But isn't it better to know where we are heading rather than to be taking steps that may not carry us where we want to go? That is the fundamental purpose of the updated alignment diagram and accompanying explanation.

Many school systems are already well under way with the redesign of their curricula and with the implementation of these various system components. Despite their best efforts, it is not unusual for school systems to become temporarily sidelined or sidetracked in the process, particularly since this is a process in which there are so many intricate parts to manage and keep in sight. My hope is that this book will help maximize implementation efforts by offering practical guidance and a clear pathway for continuing the journey. No matter what your starting point may be, at the very beginning of the trip or somewhere farther along, the detailed road map presented in these pages should prove helpful.

In the next chapter, I present a synopsis of each of the sequenced steps to achieve the big picture vision of an aligned system of standards, curriculum, instruction, assessment, and data analysis.

Reader's Assignment

Beginning with this chapter and continuing in each subsequent chapter, there is a reader's assignment related to the particular information presented within the chapter. Each assignment will likely prove most beneficial when completed collaboratively by those who are organizing the rollout of curriculum development/revision. Many of the questions will prove relevant to those who will be creating the actual units of study.

1. Referring to Figure 3.2—Specific Components of a Rigorous Curriculum Model—decide if the various components are all relevant and applicable to your particular school system. Use this table as is, or create a similar table that represents what you determine to be the essential components necessary for constructing curricular units and implementing those units in your instructional programs.

2. Referring to Figure 3.3—Rigorous Curriculum Design Alignment Diagram—decide whether to use this graphic representation of an aligned curricular system, or whether to create your own version.

3. Determine where your school system currently is in terms of implementation of each of these interdependent practices. Which of these practices are already in place? Which ones should you focus on implementing next?

4. Draft a plan that includes the *order* you will implement each of the practices listed on the table and diagram you use.

CHAPTER 4
Overview of Curriculum Design Sequence

With this "systems approach" to curriculum design in mind, we are ready to think about a logical, step-by-step implementation sequence that will include all of the elements discussed in the previous chapter. What should that sequence look like?

Here is a preview of the rigorous curriculum design road map and its sequenced set of milestones. In subsequent chapters, I will present each of these milestone steps in detail. To promote shared ownership and in-depth understanding of each of these interconnected steps, it is important that all of them be done collaboratively, and not in isolation by any one individual.

BUILD A STRONG CURRICULAR FOUNDATION

Before constructing the curricular units of study, it is necessary to first build a strong foundation. Otherwise, curriculum design teams are erecting a superstructure upon an uncertain base. Here is a brief description of each of the five foundational steps:

1. **Prioritize the Standards.** Prioritize and vertically align from grade to grade and course to course the academic content standards or learning outcomes (grade- or course-specific learning expectations) for selected content areas. These represent the "assured competencies" that students are to know and be able to do by the end of each academic school year so they are prepared to enter the *next* level of learning.

2. **Name the Units of Study.** Name all of the specific units of study for each grade level and course in those selected content areas. Through these units of study, implemented during the year or course, students will learn and be assessed upon their understanding and application of the particular standards or learning outcomes in focus.

3. **Assign Priority Standards and Supporting Standards.** Assign Priority Standards *and* supporting standards to each unit of study, taking into account "learning progressions"—those building blocks of concepts and

skills that students need to learn before they can learn other ones. Confirm that every Priority Standard is assigned to one or more units of study that will be scheduled for administration *up to* and *following* state or provincial exams.

4. **Prepare a Pacing Calendar.** Referring to the school district or school division master calendar, create a curriculum pacing calendar for implementing the units of study to ensure that all Priority Standards will be taught, assessed, retaught, and reassessed throughout the school year—*prior to* state or provincial tests and then to the end of the school year. Adjust the number of days or weeks designated for each unit of study so that all units with the heaviest concentration of Priority Standards can be completed during the months leading up to the high-stakes tests. Factor in a "buffer" week *between* units for the purpose of reteaching and reassessing close-to-proficient students, intervening and reassessing far-from-proficient students, and enriching proficient and above students.

   Extend the pacing calendar to schedule the remaining units of study during the weeks or months following the state or provincial tests. Again, adjust the length and/or duration of each unit of study so that it can be implemented before the end of the school year.

5. **Construct the Unit Planning Organizer.** Brainstorm a list of elements to include on the unit planning organizer that will be used to create each unit of study. Draft a sample template that includes all of these elements. Revise the template as needed while designing the curricular units.

DESIGN THE CURRICULAR UNITS, FROM START TO FINISH

With the standards foundation in place, design each curricular unit of study, from start to finish. Here is a synopsis of each of the twelve sequential steps for doing so. Be sure to include all of these elements (except the weekly and daily planners) on the agreed-upon unit planning organizer.

1. **"Unwrap" the Unit Priority Standards.** "Unwrap" the assigned Priority Standards for each specific unit of study to determine the specific, teachable concepts and skills (what students need to *know* and be able to *do*) within those standards.

2. **Create a Graphic Organizer.** Create a graphic organizer (outline, bulleted list, concept map, or chart) as a visual display of the "unwrapped" concepts and skills, organized into two parts: one that lists related concepts under headings and the other that lists each skill, related concept, and *approximate*

level of Bloom's Taxonomy. Matching each skill and related concept with a thinking skill level reveals the skill's degree of *rigor*.

3. **Decide the Big Ideas and Essential Questions.** Decide the topical Big Ideas (foundational understandings, student "aha's") derived from the "unwrapped" concepts and skills for that unit of study. Write Essential Questions that will engage students to discover for themselves the related Big Ideas and state them in their own words by the end of the unit.

4. **Create the End-of-Unit Assessment.** Create the end-of-unit assessment (either individual classroom or common formative *post*-assessment) directly aligned to the "unwrapped" Priority Standards. Align the concepts, skills, and format of the end-of-unit assessment with district or school division benchmark assessments (K–8) or midterms and finals/end-of-course exams (9–12).

5. **Create the Unit Pre-Assessment.** Create the pre-assessment aligned or "mirrored" to the post-assessment. "Aligned" means the questions are directly matched to those on the post-assessment but may be fewer in number. "Mirrored" means the pre-assessment will include the exact number and type of questions that will appear on the post-assessment.

6. **Identify Additional Vocabulary Terms, Interdisciplinary Connections, and 21st-Century Learning Skills.** In addition to the vocabulary of the "unwrapped" Priority Standards concepts, identify other specific academic or technical vocabulary from the supporting standards and text materials that students will need to learn during the unit. Identify any interdisciplinary connections and 21st-century learning skills to emphasize when planning engaging learning experiences and related instruction.

7. **Plan Engaging Learning Experiences.** Design meaningful learning activities directly based upon the "unwrapped" concepts and skills and representative of additional vocabulary terms, interdisciplinary connections, and 21st-century learning skills. Plan engaging learning experiences—authentic performance tasks and/or culminating projects or performances with real-world applications—that challenge students to utilize deep thought, investigation, and communication. Create accompanying scoring guides (rubrics) as the means for obtaining objective evidence of student learning relative to the standards in focus. Confirm that the planned learning experiences will give students the

conceptual and procedural understanding of the "unwrapped" concepts and skills represented on the end-of-unit post-assessment.

8. **Gather Resource Materials.** Gather print materials and seek out technology resources that support the planned learning experiences for the unit. Select the most appropriate instructional resources and materials available that will assist students in learning and applying the "unwrapped" concepts and skills and discovering the Big Ideas.

9. **Select High-Impact Instructional Strategies.** Select high-impact instructional strategies (research-based, differentiation, enrichment, intervention, special education, English Language Learner) to use during instruction and related learning activities with the whole class, with small groups, and with individual students that have specific learning needs.

10. **Detail the Unit Planning Organizer.** Determine what additional details are needed to supplement the generally worded information on the unit planning organizer. For example, an instructional pacing and sequence of the "unwrapped" concepts and skills based on "learning progressions" (the sequence of concepts and skills students need to know and be able to do as prerequisites for learning the next set of concepts and skills); a listing of specific instructional strategies for specific students based on their learning needs (advanced students, at-risk students, special education students, English Language Learners) with suggested ways educators can use those strategies.

11. **Create Informal Progress-Monitoring Checks.** Find, design, or suggest quick checks for student understanding (exit slips, short-answer questions, thumbs up/down, etc.)—*aligned to the end-of-unit assessment and administered in conjunction with "learning progressions"*—for educators to use during the unit of study in order to gauge student understanding and adjust instruction accordingly.

12. **Write the Weekly Plan; Design the Daily Lessons.** Write the weekly lesson plan to implement the unit of study in weekly "installments," using it to guide and focus instruction of the targeted "unwrapped" concepts and skills and engage students in the planned learning experiences and assessments. Design the daily lessons to align with the related weekly plan.

IMPLEMENT EACH UNIT OF STUDY

When the unit planning organizers are completed and ready to use, implement each of the units according to the scheduled pacing calendars. Here is a brief description of the fourteen steps for doing so:

1. **Introduce the Unit of Study to Students.** Present the unit's Essential Questions to students and explain that they will be able to respond to these questions in their own words by the end of the unit. Preview for students the "unwrapped" concepts and other academic vocabulary terms they will be learning and applying.

2. **Administer the Unit Pre-Assessment.** Set the stage by first explaining to students the purpose of a pre-assessment (not for a grade, but to find out what they already know and don't know about the upcoming unit of study so that the teacher can plan instruction accordingly). Then administer the common formative pre-assessment (or individual classroom or program pre-assessment, if not part of a collaborative team).

3. **Score and Analyze Student Data.** Score and analyze student pre-assessments individually or with colleagues in grade-level or course-specific instructional Data Teams to diagnose student learning needs.

4. **Decide How to Differentiate Instruction.** Referring to the unit details provided with the unit planning organizer, decide how to differentiate instruction for specific students based on assessment evidence—including the enrichment of any students who are already proficient prior to unit instruction.

5. **Begin Teaching the Unit.** Begin teaching the planned unit of study, flexibly grouping students according to their learning needs and using identified instructional strategies.

6. **Administer Progress-Monitoring Checks.** Administer frequent, informal progress-monitoring checks aligned to the end-of-unit assessment—that coincide with the building-block progression of "unwrapped" concepts and skills—in order to make accurate inferences regarding students' understanding. These informal checks will assist individual educators and instructional Data Teams in monitoring the effectiveness of their targeted teaching strategies for the unit.

7. **Differentiate Instruction Based on Progress-Monitoring Checks.** Modify and adjust instruction for individual students, small groups,

and/or the entire class based on the results of the informal checks for understanding.

8. **Schedule Mid-Unit Evaluation of Instructional Strategies.** Schedule a mid-unit evaluation of the targeted teaching and differentiation strategies to determine their effectiveness. During this meeting, participating teachers will share effective use of the targeted strategies and may decide to change any strategies that are not accomplishing their intended purpose. Individual educators who are not part of an instructional Data Team will reflect on the effectiveness of their own selected strategies and make any needed changes.

9. **Continue Teaching the Unit.** During the remaining weeks of the unit, continue teaching the "unwrapped" concepts and skills in the pre-determined "learning progressions" sequence for specific learning activities and engaging learning experiences (authentic performance tasks). Continue using the targeted instructional strategies with all students, different groups of students, and individual students as planned.

10. **Continue Modifying and Adjusting Instruction.** Continue modifying and adjusting instruction as needed for individual students, small groups, and/or the entire class based on evidence derived from ongoing progress-monitoring checks.

11. **Administer End-of-Unit Assessment.** Administer the common formative post-assessment (or individual end-of-unit assessment if not part of a collaborative team).

12. **Score and Analyze Student Data.** Score and analyze student data individually or with colleagues in grade-level or course-specific instructional Data Teams. Celebrate successes! Plan how to address students' identified learning needs during the "buffer" week.

13. **Enrich, Remediate, and Intervene.** During a "buffer" week (or shorter period of time) scheduled between the unit of study just completed and the next one scheduled, reteach *differently* those students who are still not proficient; use Tier 2 and 3 intervention strategies and other appropriate strategies for at-risk students. Reassess all nonproficient students. Enrich those students who are proficient and advanced.

14. **Reflect and Begin Again.** When the unit is officially completed, reflect individually and/or with colleagues about what worked well and what, if

anything, should be changed the next time the unit is implemented. Take a deep breath, direct your focus to the next unit of study, and then repeat the process with that next unit.

Once again, keep in mind that this comprehensive set of steps for designing and implementing rigorous curricular units of study represents the *big picture*, a vision that cannot be accomplished overnight or even in a year. Rather, it is a carefully constructed road map with designated milestones to reach *over time*—a marathon, not a sprint.

This preview of the three sets of steps for building the curricular foundation, designing the actual curricular unit of study, and implementing the unit concludes Part 1. In Part 2, you will learn how to immediately apply the *details* associated with each of the steps summarized in the first set: building a strong curricular foundation.

Reader's Assignment

1. Referring to the above steps for *building a strong curricular foundation*, which ones, if any, have you already completed? Gather all related documents available for reference as you begin reading the related chapters in Part 2 in order to determine whether or not there is need for any revisions.

2. Following the same procedure for the steps related to *designing the curricular units*, determine which steps, if any, have already been accomplished. Begin gathering those documents for reference during Part 3 of the book.

3. Review the related steps for *implementing each unit of study*. Which of these steps related to collaborative analysis of student assessment data is your school system already implementing? Which ones are solidly in place, and which ones need further refinement?

PART TWO

Building the Foundation for Designing Curricular Units

CHAPTER 5
Prioritize the Standards

Background and Terminology

Since Douglas B. Reeves first introduced the concept of Power Standards to the education community in his 1997 book *Accountability in Action*, a huge majority of educators in school systems across North America continue to openly acknowledge that there are simply too many academic content standards or learning outcomes that educators are expected to teach and assess within the fixed number of instructional days available to them each academic school year.

In 2003, Dr. Reeves generously encouraged me to write and publish the book *Power Standards: Identifying the Standards that Matter the Most*, which I based on my own experience leading educators and leaders through the prioritization process he had originated. In 2006, Donald Viegut and I devoted a chapter in our book *Common Formative Assessments: How to Connect Standards-Based Instruction and Assessment* to the subject of Power Standards and the foundational role they play in designing common formative assessments.

Prioritizing the standards remains as relevant and necessary today as ever. Educators and leaders who are working to implement the big picture vision presented in the previous two chapters understand that all of the interrelated practices that make up that big picture are dependent upon a solid Priority Standards foundation.

Before addressing the topic of prioritizing the standards, or learning outcomes, it helps to first clarify standards terminology. I am defining *academic content and performance standards*, often used interchangeably with the term *learning outcomes*, as the general descriptions of knowledge and skills that students need to acquire in a given content area. *Grade-level expectations (GLEs)* or *course-level expectations (CLEs)* are *specific* descriptions of standards, or learning outcomes, for particular grade levels and courses, respectively. Terms for these grade-specific and course-specific standards vary by state and province.

Power Standards, or the more self-explanatory terms that are often used synonymously, *Priority Standards* and *Essential Outcomes*, represent a carefully selected *subset* of the total list of the grade-specific and course-specific standards within each content area that students must know and be able to do by the end of each school year in order to be prepared to enter the *next* grade level or course.

Priority Standards must meet three essential selection criteria: endurance, leverage, and a readiness or prerequisite for the next level of learning (Reeves, *Accountability in Action* and *Making Standards Work* 1996–2004). Based on the research of Robert Marzano (2001), this subset of standards typically represents approximately one-third of the total number of grade- or course-specific standards for a given content area. Initially selected for each individual grade level and course within a content area, they are then vertically aligned from one grade level and course to the next, pre-kindergarten through grade 12.

One of the greatest benefits to identifying essential, or prioritized, standards is that they counteract the long-standing "coverage" approach to teaching that persists when there are simply *too many learning outcomes*. Priority Standards provide educators with a sharp and consistent focus for *in-depth* instruction and related assessment. They provide *students* with multiple opportunities to learn those standards as opposed to a one-time instructional exposure to them.

The Problem is the Quantity

Standards serve a fundamental purpose: they provide educators with a complete listing of *what* they are expected to teach their students. The problem is not that there are standards; the problem is simply that there are *unrealistic numbers* of grade- and course-specific standards that educators are supposed to teach, assess, reteach, and reassess within a finite number of days each academic school year.

The high quantity of standards is not a problem limited to just a few individual states or provinces; it is a challenge facing educators across the United States and Canada. Not to single out any one state in particular, I randomly selected three representative samples of state standards, one each from the western, eastern, and central parts of the United States to illustrate my point.

Figures 5.1, 5.2, and 5.3 represent the numbers of *grade-specific* and *course-specific* standards in the identified content areas and grades along with the grade-by-grade totals. Not only do these sizeable numbers represent instruction and assessment challenges for the educators, but imagine the challenges these numbers mean to students, who must learn *all* of the grade-specific and course-specific standards *each year*. For students needing any kind of ongoing specialized instruction (remediation, intervention, special education, English Language Learners), the challenge for them becomes even greater.

FIGURE 5.1 **Number of State Standards by Grade Level and Course (Example 1)**

Grade	English Language Arts	Math	Science	Totals
Pre-K	56	22	18	96
K	73	35	20	128
1	90	39	23	152
2	93	42	21	156
3	91	43	23	157
4	91	44	25	160
5	79	49	31	159
6	66	45	36	147
7	61	46	26	133
8	62	46	29	137

FIGURE 5.2   **Number of State Standards by Grade Level and Course (Example 2)**

Grade	English Language Arts	Grade/ Course	Math	Grade/ Course	Science	Grade/ Course	Social Studies	Totals
K	71	K	35	K	31	K	38	**175**
1	99	1	39	1	30	1	51	**219**
2	95	2	40	2	29	2	51	**215**
3	100	3	43	3	32	3	59	**234**
4	80	4	42	4	31	4	79	**232**
5	94	5	38	5	39	5	87	**258**
6	87	6	39	6	41	6	73	**240**
7	90	7	43	7	40	7	79	**252**
8	63	8	43	8	43	8	108	**257**
9	81	Algebra I	42	Integrated	42	World Geography	66	**231**
10	84	Geometry	37	Biology	48	World History	81	**250**
11	81	Algebra II	44	Chemistry	49	U.S. History	92	**266**
12	84	Pre-Calculus	23	Physics	35	Government	81	**223**

FIGURE 5.3 **Number of State Standards by Grade Level and Course (Example 3)**

Grade	Math	English Language Arts	Science	Social Studies	Sub-Total	Arts	Physical Education	Health	Grand Totals
K	21	60	9		90				90
1	32	76	13		121				121
2	61	78	11		150				150
3	57	96	16	18	187	12	7	16	222
4	62	106	15		183				183
5	58	110	16	80	264	12	8	18	302
6	70	107	15		192				192
7	64	105	16		185				185
8	66	104	17	108	295	12	13	24	344
9–12	85	142	35	116	378	12	14	40	444

The equivalent term for standards in the Canadian provinces I have visited is *general learning outcomes*. Like the generally worded standards statements in the United States, these general learning outcomes represent the knowledge, skills, strategies, and attitudes that students are expected to demonstrate with increasing ability from kindergarten through the final year in secondary school.

The good news is that at each grade level there may be only a relatively small number of general learning outcomes students are to acquire. However, these general learning outcomes are accompanied by *grade-specific* learning outcomes that describe in detail what students are expected to demonstrate by the end of a particular grade. Depending on the province, the terms for these will vary, but typically they are referred to as either *outcome indicators* or *specific outcomes* that, when prioritized, become "Essential Outcomes."

Figure 5.4 shows the relevancy of prioritizing the standards in provincial school systems. This is a grade 4 example from one of the provinces that identifies only *five* general outcomes for English language arts, but *fifty-seven* specific outcomes. When these are added to the specific outcomes for the other subject matter areas, the total number of *specific outcomes* that students must learn is considerable.

FIGURE 5.4 Example of Number of Specific Outcomes Required in Grade 4

Subject Area	Grade 4
Social Studies	98
Science	66
Math	25
Visual Arts	46
Basic French	45
Physical Education/Health	59
English Language Arts	57
Total	**396**

The reality is that Canadian and U.S. educators are faced with the daunting challenge year after year of trying to teach, assess, reteach, and reassess their students on far too many grade-specific and course-specific learning outcomes. I present these examples for no other reason than to support my assertion that educators must be able to determine—through a thoughtful, collaborative process—the Priority Standards or Essential Outcomes they consider necessary for their students to know and be able to do. Until there are fewer standards, the need to prioritize will remain.

A Research-Supported Rationale

Not only does prioritizing the standards make sense from a logical and practitioner's perspective, the concept is supported by the published research and writings of Robert Marzano, Douglas Reeves, W. James Popham, and other highly respected education thought leaders. Here is a representative sample of compelling statements in support of prioritizing the standards:

Robert Marzano: "The sheer number of standards is the biggest impediment to implementing the standards" (Sherer, 2001, pp.14–15).

Douglas Reeves: "Because of the limitations of time and the extraordinary variety in learning backgrounds of students, teachers and leaders need focus and clarity in order to prepare their students for success. Power Standards help to provide that focus and clarity" (Reeves, 2001, p. 167).

W. James Popham: "Teachers need to prioritize a set of content standards so they can identify the content standards for which they will devote powerful, thoroughgoing instruction, and then they need to *formally and systematically* assess student mastery of only those high-priority content standards" (Popham, 2003b, p. 36).

W. James Popham: "Reduce the number of eligible-to-be-assessed curricular aims so that (1) teachers are not overwhelmed by too many instructional targets, and (2) a student's mastery of each curricular aim that's assessed can be determined with reasonable accuracy. Teachers who can focus their instructional attention on a modest number of truly significant skills usually can get their students to master those skills—even if the skills are genuinely challenging" (Popham, 2004, p. 31).

Two Persistent Misconceptions

The most persistent misconception about Priority Standards that I have encountered over the last decade is the idea that prioritizing, or "powering," the standards is synonymous with *eliminating* certain standards in favor of others. Nothing could be further from the truth. The word "priority" infers by definition that there are *other* standards students need to learn—but *in relation to* those designated as essential. I refer to these other standards as *supporting standards*.

Supporting standards, as the term implies, are those standards that *support, connect to, or enhance* the Priority Standards. They are taught *within the context* of the Priority Standards, but do not receive the same degree of instruction and assessment emphasis as do the Priority Standards.

For example, in one state's current English language arts standards document there are several sixth-grade standards listed under the reading substrand "Developing an Interpretation." Two of those standards appear below. The first standard is bolded to indicate that it has been identified as a Priority Standard. The second standard *supports, connects to, and enhances* the first, but it does not carry an *equal weight of importance* in terms of endurance, leverage (applicability to other content areas, i.e., interdisciplinary connections), and readiness for the next level of learning.

- **Explain how characters deal with diversity (e.g., culture, ethnicity, and conflicts of human experience), relating these to real-life situations.**

- Explain the use of flashbacks to convey meaning.

Certainly there is value in students recognizing and understanding how flashbacks help convey the author's meaning. This is a literacy device that could be used to *enhance* the portrayal of a person dealing with adversity in a story and in real life. However, if there is not sufficient time to emphasize both of these standards *equally*, then the educator must decide which of the two will *serve students the most*. Between this particular pair of standards, I believe most educators would agree that the first one should receive greater instructional focus and application. The second standard could be taught *in relation to* the first, but without the same degree of instructional emphasis.

A metaphor I frequently use to illustrate the interdependence of Priority Standards and supporting standards is that of a fence made of both posts and rails. Like fence *posts*, Priority Standards provide curricular focus in which teachers need to "dig deeper" and assure student competency. Like fence *rails*, supporting standards are curricular standards that *connect to and support* the Priority Standards. Without both the posts and the rails, there is no fence.

To illustrate the fence metaphor, consider a mathematical example—the relative importance of two geometric shapes: the rectangle and the rhombus. In my own first year as an elementary math teacher, I struggled to give reasonably equal time and attention to *all* geometric shapes (the "coverage" approach to instruction). As a result, my students rarely received enough time and practice in finding the area of any one geometric shape to become really proficient at that skill. In my second year, I thought it was more important for all students to really understand how to find the area of a rectangle rather than to try and rush them through finding the area of all the other shapes (i.e., rhombus, parallelogram, trapezoid, etc.), so I spent regrettably little time teaching the others. In subsequent years, it finally dawned on me that if students really understood *conceptually and procedurally* how to find the area of a rectangle, I could then show them how to apply that understanding in determining the area of a rhombus (and other geometric shapes)—even though they did not receive the same amount of instruction and hands-on practice with the rhombus as they had received with the rectangle.

With regard to the fence metaphor, in this instance the rectangle is decidedly a fence *post*, and the rhombus a fence *rail*.

The other frequent misconception is that prioritizing the standards means "dumbing down" or lowering to the minimum what we expect students to learn and how we expect educators to teach. Even though Priority Standards in the United States usually become those standards most heavily represented on state tests, this does not mean that classroom instruction and assessments should be *reduced* to only those tested standards. Prioritizing the standards has nothing to do with "lowering the bar," and everything to do with focus. It's about "less" being *more*.

Careful selection of a subset of grade-specific and course-specific standards that are deemed essential for students to know and be able to do only identifies the "what." From there, teachers must teach for *depth of understanding*, not coverage of content, by enriching, expanding, and building upon foundational concepts and skills. Priority Standards actually make it possible for teachers to be *more* creative and use *more* of their expertise because they are not continually "running on the standards treadmill," trying in vain to get everything in.

Common Core State Standards

The Common Core State Standards Initiative is a state-led effort coordinated by the National Governors Association Center for Best Practices and the Council of Chief State School Officers to ensure that U.S. students receive a world-class education and the preparation necessary to succeed in the 21st century global marketplace.

In 2009, governors and state commissioners of education from forty-eight states, two territories, and the District of Columbia committed to developing a common core of state standards in English language arts and mathematics for grades K–12 to prepare students for college and careers. This commitment also included the development of literacy skills and understandings necessary for students in grades 6–12 to apply to their study of history/social studies, science, and technical subjects.

The resulting Common Core State Standards (CCSS):

- align with college and work expectations;
- include rigorous content *and* application of knowledge through higher-order thinking skills;
- represent evidence- and/or research-based decisions; and
- build upon strengths and lessons learned from current state standards.

A significant feature of the CCSS is that they have been internationally benchmarked to high-performing nations in order to prepare students to be educationally and economically competitive in our global economy and society.

Finalized and released to the public in June 2010, these sets of standards define the knowledge and skills students should have to succeed in entry-level, credit-bearing, academic college courses and in workforce training programs.

Source: www.corestandards.org.

States are *not required* to adopt the Common Core State Standards. However, with Kentucky leading the way, forty-three states and the District of Columbia have now voluntarily chosen to do so.

This rapid adoption of the CCSS by nearly every state represents a historic shift away from the nation's tradition of *state-determined* standards. This will dramatically impact how new educators in participating states are trained and certified, how veteran educators will transition from state standards to national standards, how the new standards will be merged with the extensive standards-based reform work that has taken states years to accomplish, and how each participating state will guide and direct its districts to implement the Common Core.

Another significant challenge is assessment. Even though two major assessment development consortia—SMARTER Balanced Assessment Consortium (SBAC) and Partnership for the Assessment of Readiness for College and Careers (PARCC or Partnership)—are working to create national assessments aligned to the CCSS that will be first administered online in 2014–15, states that adopt the new standards will have to continue administering their existing *state* assessments until 2014–15. These assessments will not align as closely with the national standards as do their current state standards, especially if those standards are not as rigorous as the Common Core.

Fewer, Clearer, Higher

In 2008, Sir Michael Barber, onetime chief advisor to former British Prime Minister Tony Blair, stated: "The question of national standards is inescapable. The U.S. needs *fewer, clearer,* and *higher* national standards" (Klein, 2008, p. 24).

If *fewer* equates to "less than what we have now," if *clearer* is synonymous with "specific," and if *higher* signifies "rigorous," then the Common Core State Standards should make it more doable for U.S. educators to adequately teach, assess, reteach, and reassess *all* of them within an academic school year. This will certainly be welcome news to educators who have tried valiantly for years to teach their students such unrealistic numbers of existing standards.

As I prepared to read through the final versions of the English language arts and mathematics standards, one question naturally came to mind: if there are indeed *fewer* standards, will prioritization of these common standards even be necessary? I was naturally hopeful that the answer might be no—for the sake of educators and students—and then I found out that adopting states can also add *up to fifteen percent* of their existing state standards to the Common Core State Standards. This meant more standards, not less! Still, I remained optimistic.

Counting Them Up

The Common Core State Standards do indeed represent a commendable body of work: thoughtfully and logically organized, comprehensive in its scope, and articulately communicated to a wide audience. Of special significance are two sections in both the English language arts and mathematics documents that specifically address the need for English Language Learners and students with disabilities to receive *equal access* to these standards.

What I found immediately impressive about the Common Core State Standards is their overall specificity (*clearer*), their inherent rigor (*higher*), and their intentional organization by vertical progressions from grade to grade. Still to be determined, however, was the criterion most relevant to the issue of prioritization— *fewer*. The only way to determine this was to actually count them.

The English language arts core standards are organized by individual grades in kindergarten through grade 8 and by grade bands for grades 9–10 and 11–12. Classified according to the familiar language arts strands of reading, writing, speaking, listening, and language development, each strand presents College and Career Readiness (CCR) *anchor standards* (broad statements) along with *grade-specific standards* (additional specificity) that together define the knowledge and skills that students must know and be able to demonstrate by the end of each grade. The reading standards are organized by the substrands of literature, informational text, and foundational skills (K–5 only).

Figure 5.5 shows the numerical breakdown of the standards by grade levels and grade bands. I have listed the number of standards within each strand in separate columns and then added the columns together to show the total number of standards for each of these grades. I believe the totals speak for themselves in terms of whether or not prioritization is still needed—and these numbers do not take into account the *additional* standards states will be allowed to include from their existing state standards.

FIGURE 5.5   Common Core State Standards—English Language Arts

Grade Level(s)	Literature	Informational Text	Foundational Skills	Writing	Speaking & Listening	Language	Total
Kindergarten	10	10	17	7	8	21	73
Grade 1	10	10	19	7	9	27	82
Grade 2	10	10	11	7	9	25	72
Grade 3	10	10	9	21	10	31	91
Grade 4	9	10	6	25	10	26	86
Grade 5	9	10	6	25	10	24	84
Grade 6	9	10	—	28	10	22	79
Grade 7	9	10	—	28	10	19	76
Grade 8	9	10	—	28	10	21	78
Grades 9–10	9	10	—	28	10	18	75
Grades 11–12	9	10	—	28	10	17	74

 FIGURE 5.6   Common Core State Standards—Literacy Standards to Emphasize in History/ Social Studies, Science, Technical Subjects, and Interdisciplinary Writing

Grade Bands	History/ Social Studies	Science and Technology	Interdisciplinary Writing	Totals
Grades 6–8	10	10	20	40
Grades 9–10	10	10	20	40
Grades 11–12	10	10	19	39

Note: These literacy standards are not intended to replace existing content standards in those areas, but rather to *supplement* them.

Fewer Common Core State Standards in Mathematics

For years, studies of mathematics education comparing the United States to high-performing countries have led to the conclusion that the mathematics curriculum in the United States needs to be much more focused if the country is to ever see a real improvement in student achievement. Yet it is important to acknowledge that fewer standards written as broad, general statements are not synonymous with *focused* standards. The CCSS in mathematics aim for clarity and specificity.

The K–5 math standards provide students with a solid foundation in whole numbers, addition, subtraction, multiplication, division, fractions, and decimals so that students can do hands-on learning in geometry, algebra, probability, and statistics. The middle school standards are "robust" and designed to prepare students for algebra in grade 8 and for high school mathematics. The high school standards emphasize application of mathematical ways of thinking to real-world issues and challenges; they prepare students to think and reason mathematically in both college and career.

The Standards for Mathematical *Content* balance and blend conceptual understanding with procedural understanding. Students who lack conceptual understanding of a math topic typically overrely on procedures. Without a strong knowledge base of mathematical understanding from which to begin, students are less likely to apply math to practical situations, think and reason mathematically, use technology as a tool to expedite their work, explain their thinking, and reflect on their process.

The Standards for Mathematical *Practice* describe ways in which students engage with the mathematical content throughout their elementary, middle, and high school years. These eight standards, applicable to every math strand, are: (1) Make sense of problems and persevere in solving them. (2) Reason abstractly and quantitatively. (3) Construct viable arguments and critique the reasoning of others. (4) Model with mathematics. (5) Use appropriate tools strategically. (6) Attend to precision. (7) Look for and make use of structure. (8) Look for and express regularity in repeated reasoning.

The Common Core State Standards in math are potential "points of inter-section" between the Standards for Mathematical Content and the Standards for Mathematical Practice.

Source: www.corestandards.org.

Figures 5.7–5.9 show the numerical breakdown of the math standards by strands for grades K–5, 6–8, and 9–12, respectively. Again, I have listed the number of standards within each math strand in separate columns and then added the columns together to show the total number of standards for each of these grades.

FIGURE 5.7 **Common Core State Standards— Grades K–5 Mathematics**

Grade Level	Counting & Cardinality	Operations & Algebraic Thinking	Number & Operations in Base Ten	Number & Operations in Fractions	Measure-ment & Data	Geometry	Totals
Kindergarten	10	5	1	—	3	6	25
Grade 1	—	8	9	—	4	3	24
Grade 2	—	4	11	—	10	3	28
Grade 3	—	9	3	9	14	2	37
Grade 4	—	5	6	14	9	3	37
Grade 5	—	3	9	14	10	4	40

FIGURE 5.8 **Common Core State Standards— Grades 6–8 Mathematics**

Grade Level	Ratio & Proportional Relationships	Number System	Expressions & Equations	Geometry	Statistics & Probability	Functions	Totals
Grade 6	7	15	12	4	9	—	47
Grade 7	7	11	6	6	13	—	43
Grade 8	—	2	13	12	4	5	36

Even though the totals for mathematics are noticeably less than those for English language arts, the questions concerning prioritization still remain:

　• Are all of the Common Core State Standards in the elementary, middle, and high school mathematics strands *essential* for students to acquire in order to be ready for the standards at the *next* level of learning?

　• Will the length of the school year afford teachers the time needed to adequately teach, assess, reteach, and reassess students on *all* of the CCSS?

The issue of whether or not to prioritize the standards—in the Common Core, in existing state standards, or in provincial learning outcomes—should never be reduced simply to a "numbers" game. Certain standards may contain *increased rigor* that will require more instructional time and learning opportunities for students to

FIGURE 5.9 Common Core State Standards— High School Mathematics

The high school math core standards are not organized by grade level or course. Instead, they are categorized according to six conceptual categories: Number & Quantity, Algebra, Functions, Modeling, Geometry, and Statistics & Probability. Under each of these categories appear substrands of mathematical practices or topics with corresponding standards.

Conceptual Categories	Totals
Number & Quantity	32
Algebra	34
Functions	45
Modeling	Integrated throughout all strands
Geometry	45
Statistics & Probability	36

fully grasp them. Such standards should be identified as *priorities*, even if the total number of standards is not that large.

An objective way to resolve this issue and make these determinations is to decide whether or not each of the content area standards meets the *selection criteria* for prioritization.

Criteria for Priority Standards Selection

Left to their own professional *opinions* when faced with the task of narrowing the voluminous number of learning outcomes, educators naturally "pick and choose" those they know and like best, the ones for which they have materials and lesson plans or activities, and those most likely to appear on state or provincial tests. But without the benefit of *specific criteria* for prioritization, everyone is likely to make certain choices that are different from those of their colleagues.

Priority Standards are collaboratively decided, so there is an absolute need for *objective* selection criteria. These criteria, briefly introduced earlier in this chapter, are:

• *Endurance* (lasting beyond one grade or course; life concepts and skills)

- *Leverage* (cross-over application within the content area and to other content areas, i.e., interdisciplinary connections)

- *Readiness for the next level of learning* (prerequisite concepts and skills students need to enter a new grade level or course of study)

A second set of selection criteria, often used interchangeably with the first, looks at the standards through the "lens" of students and also considers standardized state or provincial assessments, college entrance exams, and career and technical education competencies—an important criterion for selecting Priority Standards that cannot be ignored in the current climate of high-stakes testing:

- *School* (what students need to know and be able to do at each level of learning)

- *Life* (what students will need to know and be able to do to be successful after the conclusion of formal schooling)

- *Tests* (those concepts and skills that are most heavily represented on external, high-stakes assessments)

Figure 5.10 illustrates the importance of these selection criteria that educators keep in mind when prioritizing the standards and learning outcomes. Two of the circles, "school" and "life," incorporate the criteria of endurance, leverage, and readiness for the next level of learning. The third circle, "external exams," adds a new criterion to consider.

The standards that meet all of the criteria mentioned in Figure 5.10 and in the preceding paragraphs will provide a clearly defined subset of Priority Standards or Essential Outcomes that *all* students need to learn by the time they leave each grade, each grade span, and the last year of high school.

The Power of Vertical Alignment

During the initial selection process, the conversations continually revolve around the key question: "What do students need to know and be able to do by the *end* of each school year or course of study in order to be successfully prepared to enter the *next* grade level or course of study?" Often I overhear someone say to the other members of the group, "But is this standard a fence post or is it a rail?"—a reference to the metaphor for prioritizing described earlier in the chapter.

After the Priority Standards are identified for the separate grade levels, they must then be vertically aligned with the Priority Standards selected for the grade levels above and below. To do this, participants write their selections on large chart

FIGURE 5.10 **Priority Standards Selection Criteria**

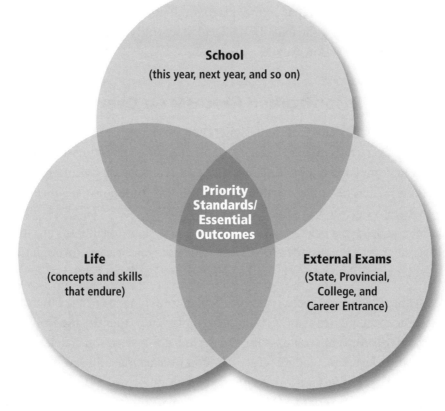

Priority Standards Selection Criteria:
What do students need to be successful in these three key areas?

School
(this year, next year, and so on)

Priority Standards/ Essential Outcomes

Life
(concepts and skills that endure)

External Exams
(State, Provincial, College, and Career Entrance)

paper and post them side-by-side on a wall, in grade-level progressions. As a group, they then take a collective look at the vertical "flow" of the selections from grade to grade *within* a grade span (Pre-K–2, 3–5, 6–8, 9–12) and then *between* grade spans (2–3, 5–6, 8–9). They keep alert for what Heidi Hayes Jacobs (1997) refers to as "gaps, overlaps, and omissions," removing unnecessary repetitions of certain standards and adding others where needed to correct conceptual or skill-based gaps or omissions. When they are finished, educators have a comprehensive alignment of standards from pre-kindergarten all the way through grade 12.

Having led educators and leaders through the prioritization process for more than ten years, I think the greatest benefits of the process are the animated, thoughtful, and truly collaborative discussions that take place while the groups of participants are *vertically aligning* the standards or outcomes. They may not always agree with one another, but they "agree to disagree." At such times, I am always reminded of Douglas Reeves' words of advice to educators facing this situation: "Forget the myth of getting 100 percent agreement; aim for a 'super majority' consensus. Ask yourselves, 'What *can* we agree on that all of our students need to know and be able to do by the *end* of each level of learning in order to be prepared to enter the next level?'" (Ainsworth, 2003, p. 97)

The Prioritization Process: An Overview

Since the units of study curriculum designers create will be based on the foundation of a solid set of vertically aligned Priority Standards and supporting standards (Essential Outcomes and supporting outcomes), it is absolutely essential to invest the time, energy, and resources needed to establish this foundation *before* moving on to the other steps I previewed in the previous chapter.

To that end, here is a brief overview of the process steps for identifying your Priority Standards. For assistance in guiding educators and leaders through this process, you may wish to contact The Leadership and Learning Center.

Step 1: Begin with *one* section of a particular content area (i.e., geometry, life science, making text connections, geography, etc.). Identify the Priority Standards for that section using the agreed-upon selection criteria (endurance, leverage, readiness for next level of learning, and standardized test emphasis). Limit selections to *approximately* one-third of the total for *each* section of the standards. (Note: The fractional count varies by section. Some sections may have fewer and others more. The idea is to collectively identify about a *third* of the total number of grade-specific standards as priorities. When prioritizing the Common Core English Language Arts standards, the fraction is closer to one-half. For the CCSS math standards, the fractional norm varies.)

Step 2: Reference state or provincial test requirements and school system data to determine and/or confirm whether or not selections reflect standards or outcomes most heavily emphasized on high-stakes external tests.

Step 3: Chart your initial selections, labeling the Priority Standards you have identified by number (1.1; 1.3; 1.4.b; etc.) and copying the *full text* of the proposed Priority Standard after each number. Include a fraction representing your number of choices for that particular section (approximately one-third).

Step 4: Post your charts in Pre-K–12 sequence and vertically align the selections. Compare one grade's selections to the grade above and the grade below *within that same grade span* (Pre-K–2, 3–5, 6–8, or 9–12). Identify gaps, overlaps, and omissions. Make adjustments as needed in standards selected to ensure the vertical "flow" *within* that grade span. Then make connections between the grade spans (2–3, 5–6, 8–9) until you have a completely aligned, Pre-K–12 "flow" of essentials. Repeat the process with the remaining sections of the content areas.

Step 5: Acquire educator feedback from all school sites to promote ownership by the full faculty within the school system. First explain the rationale for prioritizing the standards. If at all possible, conduct a mini-experience of the process for those educators who were not involved initially so they have the opportunity to better understand and realize the value of prioritization. Then invite feedback on the initial drafts that were created.

Step 6: Incorporate the collective feedback and input into a *second* draft. Publish, for each content area, a document containing all of the standards, with the Priority Standards bolded and the supporting standards in regular print.

Step 7: For each prioritized content area, identify *interdisciplinary* Priority Standards that all teachers in all grades can help students learn *through their own individual content areas.*

If your school system has identified Priority Standards in the past but has not reviewed and updated those selections, schedule a time to do so. I recommend conducting this review annually, after the state or provincial test results arrive. To reiterate, this is especially important to do *before* creating all of the curricular units of study. The Priority Standards form the very foundation of those units; therefore, they need to be verified in advance of authoring the units.

The document in Figure 5.11 will help in completing this review. If your school system has yet to identify the Priority Standards, the document may also prove helpful during the selection process. I am indebted to Lisa Almeida of The Leadership and Learning Center for creating the initial version of this document.

FIGURE 5.11 Priority Standards Confirmation Guide

Priority Standards Confirmation Guide

Content Area: _____   Grade Level: _____   Section: _____

Reviewed By: _____   Date: _____

Priority Standard/ Essential Outcome (Number and Brief Description)	Readiness for Next Level (School)	Endurance (Life)	State/Provincial/ College Test Correlation	Leverage/ Interdisciplinary Connections	Pre-K–12 Alignment	Selection Confirmed Y/N Notes/Comments

To Postpone Prioritization—Or Not

U.S. school systems located in states that have adopted the Common Core State Standards may rightfully question whether or not to postpone the prioritization of the CCSS until it is known whether or not their state is going to do this work. Even though the process of prioritizing can be accomplished in a matter of days, it still requires a great deal of thought and work by many people. If such prioritization by the state is imminent, or is on the very near horizon, it certainly makes sense to wait.

Those school systems that are unsure as to when, or if, the Common Core State Standards are going to be prioritized by their own state should, by all means, proceed in prioritizing as soon as possible. The benefits to educators and students of identifying the essential standards outweigh any possible benefits of delay. Should the CCSS be prioritized after the work is completed, everyone will already have had experience with the process and will likely be able to compare their selections with those chosen by the state, and make needed adjustments in less time than the process took initially.

Important: Whether or not your state has already prioritized the Common Core, or is about to do so in the near future, find out which of the state's current standards represent the allowable *fifteen percent* that are to be added to the CCSS. Collectively, these existing state standards along with the Common Core need to be prioritized.

When the Priority Standards are decided, curriculum designers will be ready to begin the next foundational step: naming the instructional units of study. These units will "house" both the Priority Standards *and* the supporting standards.

Reader's Assignment

1. Determine where your school system is with regard to prioritizing the standards or learning outcomes. If Priority Standards are already in place, discuss how long ago the selection process took place and whether or not the selections need to be reviewed and possibly revised *before* authoring the new curricular units of study. Use the Priority Standards Confirmation Guide (Figure 5.11) to assist you in this review.

2. (For U.S. school systems) Discuss whether or not to postpone the prioritization of standards if your state is intending to soon prioritize the Common Core Standards.

3. (For U.S. school systems) If your state has already adopted the Common Core Standards, apply the Priority Standards selection criteria (endurance, leverage, readiness, standardized test emphasis) to determine for yourselves

whether or not prioritization is necessary. As part of this discussion, determine whether educators have adequate time in the school year to teach, assess, reteach, and reassess *all* of the Common Core Standards so that *all* students are prepared to enter the next level of learning with those standards understood conceptually and procedurally.

4. If your school system is ready to prioritize the standards or learning outcomes at this time, follow the guidelines for doing so that have been provided in the seven-step overview of the process.

CHAPTER 6

Name the Curricular Units of Study

With the Priority Standards/Essential Outcomes identified in the selected content areas, the next foundational step in the rigorous curriculum design process is to "name" the different units of study for each elementary and middle school grade level and each high school grade and/or course of study. Through these units of study, implemented over the course of the year or semester, students will learn and be assessed upon their understanding and application of the particular standards or learning outcomes in focus.

The Curricular Unit of Study

The most commonly used structure for organizing instruction and assessment—the one that educators understand and use consistently—is the unit of study. A unit of study can be defined as a series of specific lessons, learning experiences, and related assessments based on designated Priority Standards and related supporting standards for a topical, skills-based, or thematic focus that may last anywhere from two to six weeks.

Some units naturally last longer than others depending on the complexity of the particular standards or learning outcomes assigned to that unit. However, the units should neither be too lengthy (seven to eight weeks) nor too short (five days), since they will, in most instances, be implemented in conjunction with common formative assessments and the corresponding instructional Data Teams process. Both of these related practices are most effective when the unit lasts anywhere from three to four weeks, the average length of most units of study. I will address this topic at greater length in Chapter 8.

The unit framework is the perfect structure for "housing" the many curricular components identified and described in earlier chapters. When all of the units of study for a specific content area are eventually sequenced in a "learning progression" continuum for each grade level and course, the combined result is a *rigorous curriculum* with its corresponding scope and sequence.

To begin the process of naming the units of study for a particular grade level or course, there are three approaches to consider. Some school systems name their units of study to correspond to the category headings of the state standards or provincial learning outcomes. For example, units of study for the subject of writing can be named to match the broad headings of the English language arts writing standards (i.e., writing conventions, writing genres, writing traits). Units of study for the content area of library media technology can be named to correspond with the titles of its standards (definition and identification of information needs, information strategies, information processing, application, and technology use). Physical education units can be organized according to specific sports (i.e., the basketball unit, the volleyball unit, the soccer unit, the field hockey unit, etc.). Science units can be named according to scientific concepts and processes (i.e., properties of matter, heredity and evolution, science and technology in society, forces and motion, etc.).

A second approach is to simply use the names of unit topics within existing curricula. This is often the approach many curriculum committees take when beginning the redesign of their curricula. They believe it is easier to just use the same organizational structure that people are accustomed to or familiar with and build from there. However, rather than just "reuse an old title with a new book," consider a different method.

The third approach, and the one I am recommending for use when implementing this rigorous curriculum design model, is to identify the particular units of study according to their *purpose and dominant focus throughout the unit* and then to name them accordingly. Such units of study can be broadly categorized into one of three types: topical, skills-based, or thematic.

The Three Types of Units

The *topical* unit of study focuses on a specific portion of a larger subject or discipline. For example, topical units in science might include: solids and liquids, sound, kinetic energy, the cell, photosynthesis, enzymes and metabolic functions, and so on. Topical units in math often are smaller sections of mathematical strands: place value, equivalency, and estimation (number sense); two- and three-dimensional shapes (geometry); and linear equations and inequalities (algebra). Possible topical units in English language arts could be: literary devices, character traits, narrative writing, and so on.

Skills-based units of study emphasize application. Skills-based units in math include: regrouping, converting fractions to decimals, estimating, telling time to the nearest quarter hour, and so on. Skills-based units in English language arts include:

developing an interpretation, applying before-during-after reading strategies, capitalizing and punctuating a piece of writing, interpreting the author's intent, and so on.

Thematic units of study are broader in nature and emphasize connections to other topics within the same discipline or to completely different disciplines. Examples of thematic units in science can be: life cycles, transformations, ecology, and global warming. Social studies thematic units might include: human movement, cultures, family ancestry, early civilizations, colonization, territorial expansion and its consequences, and so on. Thematic units of study in visual and performing arts might include: history of dance, musical theatre, composition and creativity, virtuosity, and art and multimedia, to name but a few.

A rigorous curriculum does not have to be limited to only one of these three basic types of organizational structures; in fact, it often includes a combination of all three. Different units of study within that curriculum may need a different emphasis. When considering how best to categorize each unit of study, first determine the *purpose and dominant focus* of the unit. What is the unit mainly supposed to accomplish? Then decide which type—topical, skills-based, or thematic—will best enable the educator who implements that unit to accomplish its purpose and focus. A phrase used in the field of architecture is relevant here: "Form should follow function."

Naming Units of Study in English Language Arts

Because concepts and skills in English language arts are so interdependent, deciding how to organize and name specific units of study in this content area can be especially challenging. In the school systems I have worked with to develop language arts units of study, the approach to naming units has differed from primary to upper elementary to middle to high school grade spans.

The overall consensus among language arts educators—and one that has resulted in major paradigm shifts in the minds of many—is to base English language arts units of study upon literacy skills and literary elements as opposed to particular stories, books, a prescribed anthology, or a basal reader. The units themselves may be topical, skills-based, or even thematic, but *the foundation for each of them is based upon specific literacy skills and literary elements.*

I remember an in-depth conversation I had years ago with a thirty-five-year veteran high school English teacher in the midwestern United States. After listening very respectfully to my recommendation to create high school English units of study based on literacy skills rather than particular literary works, he asked me, "But how does this fit in with my short story unit? The short stories I have my students read are classics. You're not suggesting I get rid of those stories, are you?"

I replied, "Not at all. I'm asking you to identify the particular literary skills *or* literary elements that these short stories illustrate and emphasize."

He thought for a moment and quickly named several literary elements: "theme, conflict, author's purpose, figurative language, inferences—there are lots of them."

"Would you regard all of the ones you've just named as *priority* literary elements that you want your students to know and be able to do?" I asked.

"Absolutely," he replied.

"Then all I'm suggesting is that you make those elements your primary focus and then choose short stories that best illustrate them. Make your selected short stories the 'delivery system' for helping your students appreciate and understand those literary elements."

This career educator looked at me silently for a couple of moments and then said, "You know, I never thought of it in that way before."

Naming English Department Units at Herbert Lehman

In Chapter 2, I introduced Karen Andronico, Assistant Principal of Herbert Lehman High School, who oversees her large English department of approximately thirty teachers.

Since the department already had a curriculum map in place, Karen and her team members decided to reorganize that map into *standards-based units* rather than to retain the existing map that was based on the grade-assigned novels. This shift of emphasis gave the individual grade-level team members greater freedom in the selection of instructional resources while at the same time keeping a consistent grade-level focus on the Priority Standards and supporting standards of each unit.

Karen writes, "In the past, we always referred to a particular unit by whatever book we used to teach that unit. Now we have renamed our units by *literacy topic*. For example, what we used to refer to as the *Of Mice and Men* unit, we now call 'Critical Thinking or Literary Elements.' Teachers may still continue to use that classic work of literature as their primary source during the unit, but our instruction and emphasis is based on the particular *literacy skills* we want to teach through our study of *Of Mice and Men*. When naming our new units, we referenced the curriculum we already had in considering what those specific names would be."

One of Karen's English department team members, Anibal Bruno, writes: "Topics for the four grade-level groups were decided in consideration of factors such as the needs of the students with respect to their specific grades, and the scaffolding of knowledge obtained as they move on to the next grade. For example, there was a general consensus regarding the importance of introducing incoming freshmen to the 'Lehman Approach to Writing' (a school-based writing program). By doing this, we hoped to set the foundation by which they are able to become accustomed to writing so that by their junior year, they will be [better] prepared for the Regents Exams [the New York state assessments]."

Here are the names of the six major topical units of study for each of the four English courses at Lehman High School:

Freshman English

Unit 1: Lehman Approach to Writing
Unit 2: Memoir
Unit 3: Mythology
Unit 4: Critical Thinking
Unit 5: Shakespeare (Drama)
Unit 6: Research

Sophomore English

Unit 1: Persuasive Writing
Unit 2: Nonfiction Reading
Unit 3: Reading Comprehension
Unit 4: Literary Analysis
Unit 5: Nonfiction Writing
Unit 6: Research

Junior English

Unit 1: Writing Process
Unit 2: American Poetry
Unit 3: Drama/Performance
Unit 4: American Short Fiction/Nonfiction
Unit 5: American Novel
Unit 6: Literary Analysis (Regents' Review)

Senior English

Unit 1: The College Application Process
Unit 2: Literary Research Paper
Unit 3: Literary Analysis of Classics and Contemporary Literature
Unit 4: Shakespearean Unit
Unit 5: Poetry Unit
Unit 6: Twentieth Century Literature—Existentialism

Karen concludes, "By organizing the units to convey the prioritized literacy skills, we reorganized our overloaded curriculum maps into standards-based units with literacy topics rather than book topics. The focus then became *students meeting standards and learning the unit's Big Ideas, concepts, and skills, rather than teachers teaching a particular book.*"

Naming English Language Arts Units in West Haven

Ann Valanzuolo is the K–12 District Supervisor for English Language Arts in West Haven, Connecticut. She leads the 44-member Language Arts Curriculum Committee comprised of two or three educators from each grade in all elementary schools, both middle schools, and the high school. Ann personally selected the committee members based on the quality of their teaching, their years of experience, their ability to work collaboratively, and their observable level of motivation.

Every elementary grade team includes a reading consultant, as well as at least one classroom teacher. Some middle school teams include a special education teacher. There are middle school teams at each grade level for both reading and English (writing/grammar). The grade 9 team includes a reading consultant, as well as two classroom teachers. The secondary department head and Ann work with all the teams to problem solve and suggest improvements.

At the beginning, the teams worked in larger groups (K–2, 3–5, 6–8 reading, 6–8 English, 9–10, and 11–12). However, most of the work has since been done by individual grade levels with collaboration between grades at different times, as needed.

Ann describes how the various teams named their units of study: "In most grades, particularly grades 3–10, we determined that our units were to be *skills-based,* named to correspond with the reading comprehension strands of our state tests (Forming a General Understanding, Developing an Interpretation, Making Reader/Text Connections, and Examining the Content and Structure) *or* with the writing process learner outcomes (writing, editing, and revising)."

Ann goes on to say, "The units occurring *after* state testing were named according to the *topical* focus of the unit—novel, speech, formal essay, etc. In grades 11–12, the units were named *thematically*—the hero; triumph over adversity; dystopia; men, women, and love; diverse cultures; etc."

An important part of the English language arts curriculum redesign work included the writing of special education units for grades 9–12. These units were named according to the following literacy topics and related skills: vocabulary, reading comprehension, general understanding, developing an interpretation, making reader/text connections, and writing.

Naming West Haven Mathematics Units

Amy Jo (A.J.) Palermo is West Haven's K–12 Math Supervisor. Her Core Mathematics Team consists of approximately 32 teachers and the district's two newly hired K–6 math coaches. The elementary team is made up of 16 elementary teachers, including one special education teacher and one English Language Learner teacher. The secondary team is made up of eight middle school teachers, seven high school teachers, and the 6–12 department head. Every one of the 11 district schools (eight elementary, two middle schools, and one high school) has had representation at some point during the curriculum writing process. The team members typically work separately in grade-span configurations (elementary, middle, and high school). Often the elementary team further subdivides so that the K–2 teachers and the 3–5 teachers can work together.

In describing how the math grade-span teams named their units of study, A.J. writes: "In naming our units of study, grades 6–12 mathematics core members typically used the same chapter names from the textbook series that they were currently using. However, the elementary team based their unit names on our Priority GLEs (grade-level expectations, Connecticut's term for grade- and course-specific standards). The Priority GLEs naturally seem to fit into categories, if you will, like Patterns, Measurement, Estimation, etc. So it seemed only logical to name our units accordingly."

Naming West Haven Science Units

The West Haven School District K–10 Science Curriculum Team is composed of nine K–5 teachers representing the different elementary schools, six middle school teachers (two from each grade, 6–8, with equal representation from the two middle schools), and eight teachers for grades 9–10 (half of the groups worked on the biology course and half on the chemistry course).

Raffaela Fronc, K–12 Science Supervisor, describes how her curriculum writers approached the naming of their science units:

"Based on the review of our Connecticut Grade-Level Expectations in science, our district had adopted the FOSS Program for grades K–5 prior to the start of the curriculum writing process. We used the FOSS kit titles to name most of the new curricular units, since those titles closely link to the state GLEs. For example, in grade five, 'Physics of Sound' is a FOSS kit title that closely aligns with fifth-grade Priority GLEs. In grades 6–8, our unit titles were derived from a mix of Priority GLEs and common topics. For instance, the unit title 'Simple Machines' addresses a number of our Priority GLEs."

Raffaela explained that in grades 9–10, the science curriculum writing team used a *blend* of textbook chapter titles, Priority Standards, and common topics to name their units. For example, the following high school Priority Standards are for a unit in their integrated science course:

- Explain why carbon forms so many different compounds based on its structure.

- Describe the combustion reactions of hydrocarbons and identify resulting by-products.

- Investigate carbon-based polymers and explain their general formation and structure.

- Explain how the chemical structure of polymers influences physical properties.

The common topic in these four Priority Standards is *carbon*—the focus of the entire unit. Consequently, the unit was aptly named "Carbon Chemistry."

Naming West Haven Social Studies Units

The West Haven K–12 Social Studies Curriculum Team consists of seven K–5 teachers representing the different elementary schools, six middle school teachers (two from each grade, 6–8, with equal representation from both of the district's two middle schools), and two teachers from each core course at West Haven High School (grade 9 Global Studies; grade 10 U.S. History; and grades 11 and 12 Issues in Government).

Mark Consorte, secondary Social Studies Department Head, describes how his group of K–12 curriculum writers approached the naming of their social studies units.

"We basically took the units that we already had in place, analyzed the new draft of the Connecticut state standards for social studies, and developed the individual units from there. Each grade-span group (elementary, middle, and high school) had a great deal of discretion in deciding the units. I served as both 'sounding board' and 'go-between' to relay the ideas back and forth between those teachers at every grade level who were *not* on the curriculum writing team and those who were.

"The teachers on the curriculum team decided the exact names for all of the unit titles. In one instance, I personally wanted one of the tenth-grade U.S. history units to simply be called 'The Civil War,' but two of my committee members and teaching colleagues wanted something more creative, such as 'Saving the U.S. From Itself.' I figured that since they were the ones doing all of the hard work of designing the unit, they should have the final say on what to call it."

Other Examples of Unit Names

The information and examples presented in this chapter, along with the specific directions in the Reader's Assignment, should be sufficient for curriculum designers to begin naming their units of study. However, if you wish to see a more representative listing of unit names within the content areas of English language arts, math, science, and social studies, look ahead to Chapter 8, in which the various unit titles are paced and sequenced.

After the units of study for each content area, grade level, and course have all been named, the next foundational step in the process of rigorous curriculum design is to "assign" to those units specific Priority Standards/Essential Outcomes and supporting standards/supporting outcomes. These will provide the instruction and assessment focus for each of the units. In the next chapter, the curriculum supervisors explain how their curriculum redesign committees accomplished this.

Reader's Assignment

1. With design-team colleagues, consider how you plan to name the different units of study for each elementary and middle school grade level and for each high school grade and/or course of study.

2. Decide the approach you will use to name the units:
   - Use the same category headings of the state standards or provincial learning outcomes
   - Use the names of unit topics within existing curricula
   - Identify the units according to their *purpose and dominant focus,* and then name them accordingly (recommended)
   - Incorporate a blend of all three approaches, if there is a good reason for doing so

3. Draft the names of the various units of study for each grade level and course within a specific content area; revise as needed.

4. Classify the named units of study by type: topical, skills-based, or thematic.

CHAPTER 7
Assign the Standards— Priority and Supporting

If the unit structure can be thought of as the solid "chassis" upon which to assemble all of the curriculum vehicle's working parts, then the Priority Standards and supporting standards* are the *engine* that powers the unit vehicle.

With the individual units of study named, the next task is to assign specific Priority Standards and supporting standards to each of them. When doing so, there are three relatively simple steps to follow:

1. Make the initial assignments of the Priority Standards to each of the units by matching the standards to that unit's main focus—whether topical, skills-based, or thematic.

2. Select the *supporting* standards that connect to and enhance the Priority Standards, ones that should be taught in conjunction with the selected Priority Standards and/or closely match the unit topic.

3. Distribute the Priority Standards across *more than one unit of study*. Doing this will enable students to have *more than one opportunity* to experience the Priority Standards in different learning situations and applications, thus helping them transfer and extend their comprehension of a particular Priority Standard from one context to another and reinforcing their understanding of the related Big Ideas.

Whereas the first two of these steps are fairly straightforward and self-explanatory, the third one needs further clarification.

---

*From this point forward, I am using the terms Priority Standards and supporting standards to also represent Essential Outcomes and supporting outcomes.

Distributing the Priority Standards

By distributing the Priority Standards, I do not mean the traditional practice of "spiraling" concepts and skills. A spiraling curriculum or textbook program often advocates moving on to subsequent lessons or chapters, even if students have not comprehended the concepts and skills of the current one. The rationale used to justify this practice is that those same concepts and skills will repeat and reappear in subsequent lessons and chapters; therefore, it is not necessary for students to stay with a particular standard until they get it. However, educators who have been told to "trust the spiral" have often commented to me how difficult it is, and how illogical it seems, to move ahead to the next lesson that focuses on *different* concepts and skills when students clearly have not grasped those being taught in the current lesson.

The ultimate goal for any given unit of study is that students will be able to demonstrate proficient attainment of the targeted Priority Standards on the end-of-unit assessment. However, student comprehension of any Priority Standard may be too shallow after only one unit's exposure to it. Many students need repeated practice with certain standards to gain a reliable understanding of them. If there are no subsequent opportunities for them to learn those Priority Standards in other units, gaps in student learning are likely to occur that may prove difficult to close as those students move ahead into other grades and other courses.

Even students who demonstrate a more advanced level of proficiency on an end-of-unit assessment may not thoroughly understand a particular Priority Standard in one unit's time only. Experiencing that same Priority Standard again in a *different* context within a *different* unit of study will give these students a greater chance of gaining and demonstrating deeper understanding of that standard.

Distributing the Priority Standards across multiple units of study enables *all* students to reinforce their understanding of those critical learning outcomes in each succeeding unit and provide evidence of increasing understanding through multiple assessments.

Now to qualify my recommendation: distributing the Priority Standards across multiple units is not a hard and fast rule. Educators in different disciplines may convincingly argue that certain standards belong in certain units of study *only* and to artificially distribute them to other units would not make sense instructionally. Professional judgment determines whether or not a Priority Standard *can or should be* reinforced in other units following the initial one in which it appears. The bottom line is this: students need to be able to enter the next level of learning with a solid understanding of each Priority Standard from the level before it. If this cannot be achieved during one unit of study only, then assigning that Priority Standard to one or more additional units is necessary.

Deciding How Many Priority Standards to Include in Each Unit

While assigning Priority Standards and supporting standards to the units of study, the question often arises: "How many Priority Standards should be included in each unit?" There is no required minimum or maximum number. The average seems to be three or four, but that depends on how cognitively challenging particular Priority Standards are, and whether or not students will encounter them in subsequent units.

Educators often include too many Priority Standards in one unit. One reason this occurs is simply because there are several Priority Standards that closely relate to a particular unit topic, and it only makes sense to assign them to that unit. Or the concern arises that there may still not be enough time in the school year to adequately teach, assess, reteach, and reassess all of the Priority Standards, so it is better to assign several to each unit as a safeguard that all of them will be included.

Distributing the Priority Standards can effectively resolve both of these situations. (1) If there are too many Priority Standards to include in one particular unit of study, consider splitting that larger unit into *two* units and allocate the Priority Standards accordingly. (2) If educators know that certain Priority Standards will reappear in other units, they will not feel they must address them all in one individual unit. Creating a pacing calendar (the subject of the next chapter) that carefully maps out the amount of time needed to teach and assess each unit of study can alleviate this concern.

To ensure that all of the Priority Standards are both included and distributed across the various units of study, many curriculum designers create a chart that indicates the unit(s) of study to which each Priority Standard is assigned. They then tally the number of times each Priority Standard appears within the various units. In this way, they can see where they need to make adjustments to ensure that each Priority Standard receives sufficient emphasis during the school year.

Fidelity of Implementation

In the following sections of this chapter, I again share real-world examples of implementation of this curriculum design model from those who are working through the process in their respective school systems. Many of these examples follow my recommended guidelines "to the letter." Other examples do not reflect these guidelines as closely. At times, some may even seem to contradict them. This in no way violates the fidelity of implementation of these guidelines and recommendations that I personally presented to the educators and curriculum directors in these school systems.

When introducing any new professional practice to educators, I always use the phrase, "for your professional consideration." My role is to point the way and recommend a series of steps to accomplish a desired end. I believe that even if educators make different choices than the ones I have recommended, it is essential that they "own" their process and their products. Their approach may work just as well or even better for their specific purposes than the one I am advocating.

Curriculum design must be regarded as a continual "work in process." It is in the actual in-school implementation of these units that curriculum writers/educators will find out whether their curricular units improved student achievement or not. And if the units do not accomplish this primary purpose, then educators will be more than willing to revise them so that the next time the units are implemented, they do. Such a "process of understanding" cannot take place if curriculum writing teams do not have the freedom and flexibility to experiment and make changes as they proceed.

Assigning Standards to Units at Lehman

Herbert Lehman High School's Assistant Principal, Karen Andronico, reported that her English Department members simply followed the guideline I had suggested of choosing three or four Priority Standards from their grade-level lists to directly match the focus of each unit of study.

Her teaching colleague, Mr. Bruno, introduced in the previous chapter, elaborated with his own explanation. Note his emphasis on the vertical progression of student learning and on helping students make interdisciplinary connections.

He writes: "Priority Standards were matched with the needs of the students uppermost in our minds. As with the naming of the units, our decisions around assigning Priority Standards to those units were based primarily on 'scaffolding.' We also decided to include other standards in our units that represent the basic canon of knowledge and understanding applicable not only to English but also to other content areas. This reflected our belief that students should be able to transfer and apply literacy skills from one curriculum to another (inter-curricular studies). Also, since some Priority Standards overlap across the grades, such as those related to research and writing, we assigned those standards *vertically*, across the 9–12 units of study."

Assigning Standards to English Language Arts Units in West Haven

Ann Valanzuolo (District Supervisor for K–12 English Language Arts) summarizes here the process she and her English language arts curriculum writers followed to assign standards to their units. She uses the term Priority GLEs as the short form of Priority Grade-Level Expectations, a Connecticut term synonymous with Priority Standards in grades Pre-K–8 only. In grades 9–12, Connecticut educators typically use the term Priority Standards.

"For units based on the state-tested strands or objectives, the assignment of Priority GLEs to those units was pretty self-evident. The grade-span teams looked at the different learning objectives listed under each strand on the state testing framework and selected the Priority GLEs that matched. The units of study that were *not* based on state-tested objectives were assigned Priority Standards to coincide with the specific material that would be taught in a particular unit (speech, essay, hero, dystopia, etc).

"Some Priority GLEs were assigned to multiple units, especially those aimed at making reader-text connections, because, district-wide, this is a 'weak strand' in terms of our state test score results. Also, Priority GLEs associated with reading comprehension skills in grades 1–2 were repeated in several units because of our students' need for more understanding of those skills.

"The teams double-checked to make sure that every Priority GLE or Priority Standard was assigned to one or more units by referencing a chart of all the designated Priority Standards and supporting standards for each grade. By looking at the chart, the teachers could make sure that all standards were included by checking them off as they were assigned to their respective units.

"One further note: the development of K–1 units of study has required a somewhat different approach from that which we used in grades 2–12, and that team's work continues to evolve. Originally, they decided to continue using the units of their commercial reading program because those units aligned well with the order of phonics instruction. Since prioritizing the GLEs for those grades, the K–1 teachers have made sure that those priorities are being taught within the basal program's units. As the K–1 teachers have continued to learn and apply the other components of this curriculum design approach, they are now creating new units of study based on the Priority GLEs."

I think two points that Ann makes are especially noteworthy: (1) they assigned certain Priority GLEs that *students particularly struggle with* to more than one unit of study so students would have multiple opportunities to learn those essential standards, and (2) they referenced an *organizational chart* to make certain that all Priority GLEs were included in the units. I encourage curriculum designers to follow this same procedure when assigning standards to their own units of study.

Assigning Standards to Math Units in West Haven

In determining the specific standards for the West Haven math units of study, A.J. Palermo (District K–12 Math Supervisor) describes the process she and her team followed. Their use of a "landscaped document" seems particularly effective in "housing" the Priority GLEs.

A.J. writes: "To be sure that each prioritized math standard was assigned to a unit, the team first created a document entitled 'Priority GLEs K–5 and Priority GLEs 6–8.' This landscaped document was very helpful because it provided a place where teachers could see the vertical alignment of the Priority Standards they chose right through the grades. This document made it easy to see if we had too much overlap or too many gaps within or across the different grade spans and across all of the grades together.

"After we 'housed' each Priority Standard in a particular unit, we went back through the supporting standards and found the unit where each one fit the best. We did not, however, assign the Priority Standards or supporting standards to multiple units. We felt that because our teachers regularly include a 'spiral review' approach as a natural part of delivering quality math instruction, the major concepts and skills in our Priority Standards would naturally reappear and be retaught from unit to unit."

Assigning Standards to Science Units in West Haven

Raffaela Fronc (District K–12 Science Supervisor) and her science teams assigned the Priority GLEs to units of study according to science content areas. "In grades K–5," Raffaela writes, "each of our units focuses on one of three specific content areas of science—life, earth, or physical. So our process was simply to match the particular Priority GLEs in those content areas to the corresponding units.

"At the middle school level, grade 6 is earth science, grade 7 is life science, and grade 8 is physical science, so we assigned our Priority GLEs according to specific topics within each of those three corresponding grades.

"At the high school level, we focused our initial efforts on the two grades of science content represented on the CAPT state exam: grade 9 life science and grade 10 integrated science. Integrated science includes physics, chemistry, and earth science, each lasting approximately two months. In both of these grades, we assigned our Priority Standards to matching units of study within the courses. We are in the process of developing units for grades 11 and 12."

When I asked Raffaela about distributing the Priority GLEs and Standards across multiple units, she replied: "Throughout the process of prioritizing the K–10 science standards (grades 11–12 to be added), our primary focus was on aligning all of the standards from grade to grade in a vertical progression of science concepts. Because we intentionally repeated those concepts from grade to grade in order to deepen student understanding of them, we did not think it necessary to assign the Priority GLEs and Standards to more than one unit of study. Certainly we will revisit this idea after we finish implementing all the units and determining the results in student learning."

Assigning Standards to Social Studies Units in West Haven

Lastly, I asked Mark Consorte (grades 6–12 Social Studies Department Head) to describe how his social studies curriculum writers assigned the different Priority Standards and supporting standards to each of their social studies units. Mark writes:

"Each grade-span team (with input from me and from the other social studies teachers assigned to our committee) discussed and decided into which units to place the Priority GLEs and supporting ones. Sometimes the same GLEs were put into multiple units. For example, in kindergarten and grades 1 and 2, we purposely put overlapping standards pertaining to national holidays and heroes and community helpers into several units of study because our new draft of state social studies standards also contained overlap in these areas. We also decided to do this because we felt that those lessons are very important and that young children need repetition for lessons to 'stick.'

"There was no process we followed to ensure that *every* state GLE was included somewhere. To be honest, assigning *only* the Priority GLEs to different units of study was sometimes all we felt teachers of social studies had time to teach, especially in the elementary grades, where this content area often has to take a 'back seat' to those that are state-tested. Even in the secondary grades, 6–12, we agreed that we must move away from the customary instructional emphasis on 'coverage of material' to a focus on the key concepts we felt students needed the most. One major change we made to accomplish this was to split U.S. history into both grades 8 *and* 10, so we can teach 'depth over breadth.'"

As Mark points out, even when a school system does prioritize its standards, instructional time constraints coupled with the challenges of teaching and assessing *all* of the standards—Priority and supporting—are considerable. Sometimes the best that educators may be able to do is to make sure that students receive in-depth instruction and learning opportunities of a Priority Standard within *one* unit of study, even if that is the only opportunity students have to learn that particular standard. This is not to be misconstrued as endorsement of that position, but rather the honest acknowledgement of instructional reality.

When assigning Priority Standards to different units of study, the subject of pacing inevitably comes up. In the next chapter, I offer suggestions and examples for appropriately pacing the units of study to ensure that both *breadth* and *depth* of the standards can be successfully accomplished within the time frame of the school year or course. Effective pacing calendars reassure educators that they can reasonably stay "on track," implementing all of their units within the fixed parameters of time without sacrificing student understanding to do so.

Reader's Assignment

Make an initial assignment of Priority Standards and supporting standards to all of your curricular units:

1. Identify three or four Priority Standards that directly match each unit's main focus or purpose. Consider the cognitive challenge of each Priority Standard when assigning them to the units. As a general rule, the more challenging the rigor, the fewer selections there should be.

2. Select the *supporting* standards that connect to and enhance the Priority Standards, ones that should be taught in conjunction with the selected Priority Standards and/or closely match the unit topic.

3. Distribute the Priority Standards to more than one unit of study unless there is an instructionally sound reason for not doing so.

4. Create a grid to show the correlations between the Priority Standards and the units of study. Tally the number of times each Priority Standard appears in all of the units together to confirm that all Priority Standards are assigned and assured of the needed degree of emphasis.

5. Redistribute or reassign to other units any Priority Standards that are not sufficiently represented.

CHAPTER 8
Prepare a Pacing Calendar

Simply defined, a pacing calendar is a yearlong or course-long schedule for delivering all of the planned units of study for a designated grade level or course, *not* the instructional materials used within those units. Ideally, a pacing calendar helps educators ensure that students learn all of the grade- or course-specific Priority Standards and their related supporting standards *in the right order* through a sequenced implementation of the units.

For many educators, a pacing calendar can seem to be either a friend or a foe. When it is helping an educator "stay on track" to accomplish all the units of study by the end of a course or school year, the pacing calendar is a real help. When it causes panic in the mind of an educator who is not able to "keep up the pace," it becomes a real hindrance.

I remember Douglas Reeves speaking years ago on the topic of pacing guides: "A pacing guide is exactly that—a *guide*. It is not a mandate. In no state's standards have I ever seen the words, 'learns algebra quickly.'"

Learning Progressions

Learning progressions suggest the order in which particular concepts and skills "should" be taught. Educators usually determine themselves the order in which they will teach particular concepts and skills when planning their own units of study, most commonly sequencing concepts and skills from simple to complex. This building-blocks approach helps students develop their understanding of those concepts and skills in a way that makes sense to them.

Learning progressions do need to be considered when pacing curricular units, both horizontally and vertically. An ideal pacing calendar provides *suggested* horizontal learning progressions *within* grades and courses and *suggested* vertical learning progressions *between* grades and courses. Notice the emphasis on the word "suggested."

W. James Popham (2007) points out that "with few exceptions, there is no single, universally accepted and absolutely correct learning progression underlying any given high-level curricular aim" and that "any carefully conceived learning progression is more likely to benefit students than teachers' off-the-cuff decision-making" (p. 83).

Because these developmental learning progressions are not likely to be self-evident in vertically or horizontally aligned curricula, curriculum designers need to think through what the logical order might be when presenting the units to students within one grade or course and between other grades and courses. My recommendation is to have an initial discussion in terms of learning progressions and then make a "first-pass" sequence of how the group thinks the units ought to be sequenced.

Learning progressions are not only important for curriculum designers to consider when preparing the pacing calendars for the units of study. They are also important to think about when planning informal "progress-monitoring checks" of student understanding during a unit of study and when pacing weekly and daily lesson plans, two topics I address in Chapters 12 and 15, respectively.

Here is how the English Department members at Lehman High School in the Bronx, New York, did this. I asked them to write the name of each of their grade-level units on large index cards. After doing so, each grade-level team posted its cards on different sections of the windows and began discussing among themselves which units they thought should come first, second, and so on, based on the idea of learning progressions. Needless to say, they did not immediately reach unanimous agreement on what those learning progressions should be. But they did eventually arrive at a consensus of what the order of their *units of study* should be.

It seems to be true that certain subject matter areas lend themselves more naturally to this sequencing of units based on learning progressions than others do. In math, science, and even social studies, it is typically much easier to organize the instruction of concepts and skills into a linear or chronological sequence or hierarchy. English language arts, however, is endlessly recursive. Nearly everything is interwoven and interdependent. However, when laying out a sequence of units of study, these learning progressions need to be discussed and decided, even if there is uncertainty about what the "ideal" or "correct" order should be.

For now, just be mindful of the need to discuss the horizontal and vertical "flow" of units within and between each grade and course in terms of learning progressions. In Part Three, I will explain learning progressions in more detail as they apply to the planning of engaging learning activities and the sequencing of instruction within each individual unit of study.

The Challenge of Pacing Instruction

Pacing instruction is one of the challenges educators face on an almost daily basis, and it presents educators with two problematic choices: (1) spend extra class periods or lessons to make sure all students "get it" before moving on to the next unit of study; or (2) stick to the prescribed schedule for administering the units of study and keep moving from one to the next, even if students have not had enough time and sufficient learning experiences to understand the standards within those units.

The downside to the first choice, especially if it is repeated several times during the school year or course, is that educators will have to continually play "catch-up" in order to quickly teach and assess the remaining units of study, or they will have to abandon them altogether because they have simply run out of time. The downside to the second choice is superficial "coverage" of standards that students may never have the opportunity to learn in depth.

Compounding this dilemma in the United States is the amount of instruction and assessment that needs to take place *before* the state tests, particularly in those states that administer their high-stakes assessments as early as March of each year. Since one of the selection criteria for Priority Standards is the identification of those standards that are most heavily represented on the state test, this makes it imperative for educators in those states to have sufficient time to teach their Priority Standards in depth *prior to* the state assessments.

Ideally, a pacing calendar would guarantee a viable curriculum for every student. Robert Marzano (2003) explains the relationship between viability and time: "In the current era of standards-driven curriculum, viability means ensuring that the articulated curriculum content for a given course or given grade level can be adequately addressed in the [instructional] time available" (p. 25).

The "Buffer" Week

Even by distributing the Priority Standards across one or more units of study and providing students with multiple opportunities to deepen their understanding of those standards, the reality is that certain students will not always demonstrate proficiency on the end-of-unit assessment. When planning the pacing calendar for any particular grade level or course, curriculum designers need to build into the schedule short intervals *between* the units of study. This interval between units is called the "buffer" week, a term I attribute to Tommy Thompson, Principal of New London High School and former Assistant Principal of Bernie Dover Middle School in New London, Connecticut.

The "buffer" week can last anywhere from a couple of additional class periods or lessons to as long as a week. Think of the buffer week as "scheduled breathing room" that gives the educators extra time to further remediate students who are almost proficient (as demonstrated on the end-of-unit assessment), or intervene for students who are far from proficiency. Proficient and advanced students also benefit from these buffer weeks by receiving *enrichment* lessons and activities. The buffer week provides educators with another opportunity to more specifically differentiate instruction and learning activities to meet the diverse learning needs of *all* students, thus reducing resistance to the tight adherence of following a preset schedule.

Creating a pacing calendar that addresses all of the factors and issues described above is not easy, but it is doable. When a grade- and course-specific pacing guide is designed to include realistic time frames, take into account learning progressions, and provide for some flexibility when needed, educators will be much more likely to see the pacing calendar as a professional aid rather than a detriment.

Recommended Length of Units

The recommended number of weeks for a unit of study is typically three to four, determined by several factors:

- The age of the students (i.e., younger students, shorter units; older students, longer units)
- The complexity of the content
- The standards assigned
- The learning experiences planned

If the topic is large, with challenging Priority Standards and supporting standards in it, the unit will naturally have to be longer. If the topic is not as large and the related standards are not as cognitively demanding, the unit can be shorter in duration. One unit of study may require four weeks, followed by a unit that needs only two or three. The length of units should not be standardized, but should depend on how much time the educators need to implement them as planned. Again, form should follow function.

Many educators often plan units of six weeks or even much longer. They may want to consider subdividing units scheduled longer than four weeks into two *separate but related* units of shorter duration. There are several reasons why I am offering this suggestion:

1. Educators may find it difficult to maintain a sharp instructional focus during longer units that contain too many Priority Standards and supporting standards.

2. Students may lose track of what they are supposed to be learning and have difficulty determining the Big Ideas of the unit when the unit is too long and complex.

3. Longer units with numerous standards may make it difficult for educators to assess student understanding frequently enough to diagnose student learning needs and respond effectively. Educators may find out too late into the administration of a longer unit that many students have not learned all of the targeted standards. Even with the extra time provided by the end-of-unit buffer week, this may still not be enough time for them to help non-proficient students achieve proficiency.

For these reasons, I am recommending shorter units of study. Shorter units enable educators, whether or not they are members of an instructional Data Team, to analyze student learning needs from ongoing formative assessment results more quickly and to differentiate instruction accordingly.

Resource-Suggested Units of Study

One of the problematic issues that surfaces when curriculum writers are preparing their pacing calendars has to do with learning materials and existing resources. Often, educators teaching the same grade or course in the same school are unable to implement a unit of study at the same time as their colleagues due to a shortage of instructional materials and resources.

For this reason, the units of study may need to be "resource-suggested" rather than "resource-required" (with the possible exception of certain classic works). They should not be dependent upon all educators having simultaneous access to specific teaching resources and materials. Even though such a recommendation will require more ingenuity and creative thinking on the part of the educators, this may alleviate the persistent problem of acquiring equitable resources when budgets are tight. Another factor for U.S. school systems to consider is that different state agencies conducting curriculum audits of school systems' existing curricula are strongly advising that curricula not be resource-dependent.

On a brighter note, when funding *is* available for purchasing instructional materials and multimedia resources to help implement the curricular units, the pacing calendar's sequenced listing of units of study for each grade and course will help leaders, curriculum designers, and educators make informed decisions regarding which instructional materials and resources to acquire and require.

"Finding the best textbooks for standards-based teaching and learning is possible only after the district has determined the grade levels and sequence in which critical standards are to be taught" (O'Shea, 2005, p. 37).

How to Create the Pacing Calendar

To create the first-draft pacing calendar, have on hand the school system's master calendar for the academic school year. Reference the following guidelines to outline a first-draft schedule of the instructional units for each grade and course.

1. Discuss the *approximate* amount of time needed to implement each unit of study. Questions to help make these determinations include:

   • Based on the complexity of the content, about how long should this unit be?

   • Do we know from experience how long this unit typically takes to implement?

   • About how long will it likely take educators to teach and assess the assigned Priority Standards and the supporting standards in this particular unit?

   • About how much time will the majority of *students* need to learn these particular standards?

   • Are the Priority Standards in this unit also assigned to *other units*, so that less time might be needed to teach these standards in this particular unit?

2. After answering the preceding questions, decide and record next to the name of each unit the *approximate* number of weeks allocated to deliver it.

3. Discuss the *order* in which Priority Standards are sequenced within a continuum of units at each grade level and in each course (horizontal learning progressions).

4. Related to this sequencing, discuss which units need to be delivered *prior to* the state or provincial assessments, especially if these assessments occur one to three months prior to the end of the school year. Make sure that the units with the greatest concentration of Priority Standards are scheduled during the months leading up to these high-stakes assessments. This will require careful planning with regard to the Priority Standards that need to be taught in a learning progressions sequence, such as certain math or literacy skills that students need to know and be able to do before they are ready to learn others.

5. If the school system administers quarterly or trimester district or school division benchmark assessments, consider which units of study need to occur in the weeks prior to those benchmark tests so there is alignment between them.

6. Look at all of the units of study for a particular grade level and course and create a first-draft sequence of those units leading up to the state or provincial assessments.

7. Extend the pacing calendar *after* the state or provincial assessments to the end of the school year to ensure that all students will be prepared to enter the next grade or course with the Priority Standards as "assured competencies."

8. Schedule "buffer" weeks between the units of study.

9. "Do the math" to make sure all of the units of study and buffer weeks fit within the total number of available instructional weeks as shown on the school system's master calendar.

10. Just as the Priority Standards are vertically aligned from one grade to the next, the units of study should be as well. Look for the learning progressions of units *between* grades and courses. This will help determine if students will be able to build upon and extend their understanding of the Priority Standards and supporting standards from one grade and course to the next. Make adjustments as needed so that these progressions are both accurate and apparent.

Pacing Calendar Examples

After creating the initial pacing calendar, educators will have a schedule for delivering their sequenced grade- or course-specific units of study. However, only after they actually *implement* each unit will it be clear whether or not the time allotted and sequence indicated worked as planned. For this reason, it will most likely be necessary to revisit the pacing calendar and make any needed adjustments based on the "field-tested" feedback received before the pacing calendar's *second* year of implementation.

The pacing calendar examples that follow reflect this "work-in-progress" approach to creating and implementing a scope and sequence for several different content areas. These are initial drafts for the first year of curricular implementation, examples that serve as excellent starting points to illustrate the ten process steps for preparing the pacing calendar.

Pacing the Lehman High School English Units

Summarizing the process the English Department at Herbert Lehman High School in the Bronx, New York, followed to pace their grade-specific units of study, Mr. Bruno again explains: "You will recall that we planned six units of study for each of the grades, 9 through 12. We numbered the six units for each grade, and listed them in a particular order, to *suggest* an implementation sequence. However, as far as the *actual* order in which the units are taught, we had to allow for a bit of autonomy, since we are not yet at the point where every grade-level teacher is going to be teaching the same unit at the same time. One of the contributing factors to this decision is that we may not have the necessary quantity of books for everyone in a particular grade to be using at the same time. The 'Lehman Approach to Writing' unit, on the other hand, is something that can be taught without relying upon certain books, which, in my opinion, makes it an ideal unit for the start of the school year."

Pacing the West Haven English Language Arts Units

Addressing the process that the West Haven English language arts curriculum teams followed to pace their units of study, Ann Valanzuolo (K–12 English Language Arts Supervisor) wrote, "There was a scope and sequence of units, including a pacing calendar, included in the curriculum binder provided to each grade-level teacher at the beginning of the year. In some grades, that calendar has already been revised as our units of study are examined and changed. Grade 2 units are all six weeks in duration, which includes five weeks of teaching and one week of assessment and reteaching [buffer week] before beginning the next scheduled unit."

Figures 8.1 and 8.2 contain two of West Haven's sample pacing calendars, one for first grade and the other for ninth grade.

Pacing Units Prior to the State Test

Ann Valanzuolo next addresses the deliberate pacing of certain units prior to state testing in March: "We made sure that in grades 3–8 and in grade 10 the units of study focused primarily on those Priority GLEs (Grade-Level Expectations) that most addressed the skills students needed for success on the state assessments. For example, the first four units in grades 3–7 focus heavily on the four reading comprehension strands represented on the Connecticut Mastery Test. The teachers finish teaching Unit 4 approximately two weeks before the CMT, so they can then review all strands during that time. The same planning holds true for grades 6–8 English units which focus on all tested writing, editing, and revising skills prior to the CMT, and in the reading comprehension units for grades 8 and 10."

FIGURE 8.1 Grade 1 English Language Arts *Suggested* Pacing Guide

Note to Teachers: For units two through six, a week has been built in between each unit, for reteaching and additional assessment time. During this time, you can continue post-assessing for the previous unit and begin pre-assessing the next unit.

Unit 1
- Begin week of August 31, 2009, first full week of school.
- End week of October 5, 2009.

Unit 2
- Begin week of October 13, 2009.
- End week of November 16, 2009.
- Reteaching and assessment week—November 23, 2009.

December report card—December 16, 2009.

Unit 3
- Begin week of November 30, 2009.
- End week of January 18, 2010.
- Reteaching and assessment week—January 25, 2010.

Unit 4
- Begin week of February 1, 2010.
- End week of March 15, 2010.
- Reteaching and assessment week—March 22, 2010.
- Additional unit review week if needed—March 29, 2010.

March report card—March 31, 2010.

Unit 5
- Begin by week of April 5, 2010.
- Take 7–8 weeks to teach and assess the skills in Unit 5.

Unit 6
- You do not have to assess skills in Unit 6.
- Unit 6 is optional. Skills have either already been taught in first grade or will be taught in second grade.

June report card—June 17, 2010.

FIGURE 8.2 Grade 9 English Language Arts *Suggested* Pacing Guide

Unit 1	Elements of Literature	6 weeks
Unit 2	Human Nature	4 weeks
Unit 3	Life to Literature	4 weeks
Unit 4	Universal Theme	5 weeks
Unit 5	Writing Across the Disciplines	5 weeks
Unit 6	Supplemental Reading	5 weeks

Pacing the West Haven Math Units

A.J. Palermo (K–12 Math Supervisor) describes how the math curriculum writing teams paced their math units: "We created a document and pacing calendar that included the names of the units and the grades, as well as the suggested number of weeks that should be spent on each unit. We have made changes to this pacing calendar based on the feedback received from teachers *and* based on the instructional resources that some grades K–5 teachers are piloting now.

"What we are finding during this quality-control year is that many of the units spanned too long of a period of time, or that too much information was packed into one unit. The duration of some of the units has been adjusted. For example, one long unit on the topic of money is now *two shorter units*: counting money and estimating with money amounts.

"You will also notice when you look at the pacing calendar (Figure 8.3) that grades K–2 thought it would be a nice idea to keep the names of their chapters the same so teachers and students could see the progression of a topic through the grades and start making connections to previous learning.

"Also, the team members were very cognizant about completing certain units of study *before* state testing, particularly those units representing math concepts and skills that our test score results showed to be district-wide weaknesses. Two grades (3 and 5) went on to schedule specific units of study to implement in the remaining months of the school year *following* state testing."

FIGURE 8.3 Grades K–5 Mathematics Pacing Calendar

Kindergarten	Pacing	First Grade	Pacing	Second Grade	Pacing
Geometry	Sept.–Oct.; 5 weeks	Geometry	Sept.–Oct.; 5 weeks	Geometry	Sept.–Oct.; 5 weeks
Patterns and Sorting	Oct.–Nov.; 6 weeks	Patterns and Sorting	Oct.; 4 weeks	Patterns and Sorting	Oct.–Nov.; 5 weeks
Number Sense	Nov.–Jan.; 6 weeks	Number Sense	Nov.–Dec.; 6 weeks	Number Sense	Nov.–Dec.; 6 weeks
Addition and Subtraction	Jan.–Feb.; 5 weeks	Addition and Subtraction	Dec.–Jan.; 6 weeks	Addition and Subtraction	Dec.–Jan.; 6 weeks
Money	March; 4 weeks	Money	Feb.–March; 6 weeks	Money	Feb.–March; 6 weeks
Measurement	March–May; 5 weeks	Measurement	March–May; 6 weeks	Measurement	March–April; 6 weeks
Data and Graphs	May–June; 5 weeks	Data and Graphs	May–June; 5 weeks	Data and Graphs	May–June; 6 weeks
Third Grade	Pacing	**Fourth Grade**	Pacing	**Fifth Grade**	Pacing
Place Value Value of Numbers	2 weeks	Computation Number Sense	2 weeks	Place Value	13 days
Addition/ Subtraction 2-Digit Numbers	2 weeks	Place Value Estimation	2 weeks	Multiplication	12 days
Rounding (Numeracy)	2 weeks	Multiplication	3–4 weeks	Division	14 days
Estimation (Word Problems, Computation, Money)	1 week	Time and Calendar	1–2 weeks	Graphing	*
Money	1 week	Probability and Statistics	2–3 weeks	Geometry	*
Multiplication/ Division	2 weeks	Division	3 weeks	Fractions	*
Fractions	1–2 weeks	Fractions/Decimals and Percents	3 weeks	Measurement	*
Ratio and Probability	1–2 weeks	Geometry and Measurement	4 weeks	Division	Post CMT
Time	3 weeks	Patterns and Trends	2 weeks	Decimals	Post CMT
Graphing	2 weeks				
Geometry	2–3 weeks				
Measurement—1	1–2 weeks				
Algebra	2 weeks				
Algebra—Part 2	Post-CMT				

*To be determined.

FIGURE 8.4   **Grade 7 Mathematics Pacing Calendar**

Unit 1—Decimals	August 31–September 25
Unit 2—Fractions	September 29–October 23
Unit 3—Ratios, Proportions, and Percents	October 26–November 25
Unit 4—Equations, Expressions and Patterns	November 30–January 12
Unit 5—Measurement and Geometry	January 13–February 12
CMT Preparation and Administration of CMTs	**February 22–March 12**
Unit 6—Data and Probability	March 22–April 16
Unit 7—Integers	April 26–May 21
Unit 8—To Be Decided	May 28–End of School Year

The representative Grade 7 math pacing calendar in Figure 8.4 emphasizes the units of study that occur before and after the state tests in March.

Pacing the West Haven Science Units

Raffaela Fronc (K–12 Science Supervisor) summarizes the process her science curriculum teams followed to create their pacing calendar:

"We began designing the pacing calendar by keeping in mind the importance of having a *vertical* alignment for each of the science units. By the end of the process, we did achieve a K–10 vertical alignment. The final pacing calendar document includes the names of all the units, grades, and suggested time frames that should be spent on each unit. We have continued to make changes to this calendar based on the feedback from teachers. The timeline is based on the science areas to be covered from physical to life to earth science. Based on this year's implementation of the units, next year we will have to change some of the pacing for certain grades.

"In addition, state tests in science occur in grades 5, 8, and 10, so we did need to keep this in mind as we developed our sequenced pacing guide to include most of the tested topics *prior to* the March tests."

West Haven's pacing calendar for their K–10 science units of study is shown in Figure 8.5.

FIGURE
8.5 **West Haven Curriculum Unit Pacing Calendar for K–10 Science**

UNIT	PACING GUIDE	K	1	2	3	4	5
1	September ⬇ November	Senses (6 weeks); Weather (6 weeks)	Forces and Motion; Measurement GLE # 6 (temperature)	Solids, Liquids, and Gasses	Testing Properties of Matter	Forces and Motion and Change	Solar System: Earth, Moon, and Sun (* weeks); Sound (* weeks)
2	November ⬇ January	Properties of Matter; Heredity and Evolution	1.2 Structure and Function; Measurement GLE #5 (liquids)	Properties of Soils	Properties of Rocks and Minerals	Electrical and Magnetic Energy	Light (4 weeks); Senses (* weeks)
3	January ⬇ April	Science and Technology (Man-Made and Natural Materials)	Life Cycles; Measurement GLE #1 (length and weight)	Nutritional Needs of Humans	Conservation; Reusing and Recycling	Earth's Water and the Water Cycle	Enhancing vision; CMT review
4	April ⬇ June	Heredity and Evolution	Life Cycles; Measurement GLE #1 (length and weight)	Plant Life Cycle	Adaptation of Plants and Animals	Interaction of Living and Non-Living Things in Their Environment	Human Body

*To be determined.

PACING GUIDE	6	7	8
September ⬇ November	Unit 1: Meteorology	The Cell (Unit 1) Sept.–Oct.; Photosynthesis (Unit 2) Oct.–Nov.	Chemistry • Elements, compounds, mixtures • Atoms/molecules • Periodic Table
November ⬇ January	Unit 2: Groundwater	Cell Division (Unit 3) Nov.–Dec.; Heredity (Unit 4) Dec.–Jan.	Force and Motion
January ⬇ April	Unit 3: Astronomy	Living and Non-living Factors in Ecosystem (Unit 5) Jan.–Feb.; Good Stuff In, Bad Stuff Out (Unit 6) March–April	Energy and Simple Machines
April ⬇ June	Unit 4: Geology	Support and Movement (Unit 7) *; Microbes (Unit 8) May; Bacteria in Food (Unit 9) *	Bridges/ Technology

*Time frame to be determined.

FIGURE 8.5 **West Haven Curriculum Unit Pacing Calendar for K–10 Science** *(continued)*

PACING GUIDE	9	10
Sept.–Nov.	Units 1, 2: Cells; Cell membrane	Units 1, 2: Experimental Design (4 weeks); Periodic Table (4 weeks)
Nov.–Jan.	Units 3, 4, 5: Enzymes; Infectious Diseases and Bacteria; DNA/RNA	Units 3, 4, 5, 6: Carbon Chemistry (4 weeks); Polymer Resources (1 week); Global Interdependence (1 week); Global Warming (1 week)
Jan.–April	Units 6, 7, 8: Genetically Modified Foods; Genetics; Evolution (part 1)	Units 7, 8, 9, 10: Alternative Energy (1 week); Phase Changes (3 weeks); Electricity/Magnetism (2 weeks); Cycles (1 week)
April–June	Units 8, 9: Evolution (part 2); Ecology	Units 11, 12, 13, 14: Lunar Exploration (4 weeks); The Solar System (2 Weeks); The Atmosphere (2 weeks); Severe Weather (2 weeks)

Pacing the West Haven Social Studies Units

Mark Consorte (high school Social Studies Department Head) describes how the social studies curriculum writing teams paced their units of study:

"The units are sequenced according to the order in which they will be taught. Pacing is constantly being discussed among the curriculum committee teams, especially at the high school during our collaborative planning time that is now built into our daily schedule. On that point, I want to say that in my view, this has been the biggest positive change for West Haven High School. Teachers are 'talking shop' and sharing ideas and resources like never before, and working very well together. At the elementary and middle schools, pacing is discussed on the several release days that have been provided for us throughout the year.

"As far as pacing the units prior to the state test, grade 10 U.S. history teachers built in monthly practice essays so the students would be ready for the related sections of the state test by early March. Since social studies is not specifically tested on the grades 3–8 state tests, however, the scheduling of the elementary and middle school units has not been affected by this factor."

Pacing for West Haven social studies units is shown in Figure 8.6.

FIGURE 8.6 West Haven K–12 Social Studies Pacing Calendars

Social Studies Kindergarten
Kindergarten National Heroes—Ongoing
Kindergarten Transportation—Ongoing
Kindergarten Weather and Clothes—Ongoing
Kindergarten American Holidays—Ongoing
Kindergarten Culture—Ongoing
Kindergarten United States Symbols—February and March
Kindergarten Community Helpers—Ongoing

Social Studies Grade 1
Grade 1 Transportation—Ongoing
Grade 1 History-Related Holidays—Ongoing
Grade 1 Safety—Ongoing
Grade 1 Citizenship—Ongoing
Grade 1 Culture—Ongoing
Grade 1 Home—February and March
Grade 1 Neighborhood and Community—Ongoing
Grade 1 Family Ancestry—March and April

Social Studies Grade 2
Grade 2 Human Movement—September–October
Grade 2 Laws and Services of West Haven—September–October
Grade 2 Cultural Ethnic Groups—November–January
Grade 2 History-Related Holidays—Ongoing
Grade 2 Wants and Needs—February–March
Grade 2 Economic Systems and Resources—February–March
Grade 2 Local Historical Sites—April–June
Grade 2 Man-Made vs. Natural—April–June

Social Studies Grade 3 (Pacing not yet determined in all but first unit)
Grade 3 Map Skills, Geography—Exploring Where and Why Map Lessons—
    4 weeks, Daily Geography—Yearlong
Grade 3 Local Government and Citizenship
Grade 3 Historical Figures of the United States
Grade 3 Historical Events, Sites, and People of Our Local Region
Grade 3 Economics
Grade 3 Ethnicity and Culture

FIGURE 8.6 **West Haven K–12 Social Studies Pacing Calendars** *(continued)*

Social Studies Grade 4

Grade 4 Unit 1 Geography—September–October

Grade 4 Unit 2 Native Americans—November–January

Grade 4 Unit 3 Connecticut History—February–March

Grade 4 Unit 4 Connecticut Government and Current Events—April–May

Grade 4 Unit 5 Economics—May–June

Social Studies Grade 5

Grade 5 Unit 1 Exploration—First Marking Period

Grade 5 Unit 2 Colonization—Second Marking Period

Grade 5 Unit 3 American Revolution—Third Marking Period

Grade 5 Unit 4 The Constitution—Fourth Marking Period

Social Studies Grade 6

Grade 6 Unit 1 Geography Skills—10 days

Grade 6 Unit 2 Early Civilizations—25 days

Grade 6 Unit 3 Ancient Egypt—25 days

Grade 6 Unit 4 Ancient Greece—23 days

Grade 6 Unit 5 Ancient Rome—25 days

Grade 6 Unit 6 Middle Ages and Renaissance—25 days

Social Studies Grade 7

Grade 7 Unit 1 Introduction to Geography—10 days

Grade 7 Unit 2 North America—45 days

Grade 7 Unit 3 Latin America—25 days

Grade 7 Unit 4 Africa—30 days

Grade 7 Unit 5 Europe—20 days

Grade 7 Unit 6 Asia—35 days

Grade 7 Unit 7 Pacific Realm—15 days

Social Studies Grade 8

Grade 8 Unit 1 Colonization and Exploration—September

Grade 8 Unit 2 Revolutionary Era—October–November

Grade 8 Unit 3 Establishment of U.S. Government—December–January

Grade 8 Unit 4 Expansion—February–March

Grade 8 Unit 5 A Nation Divided—April–June

FIGURE 8.6 **West Haven K–12 Social Studies Pacing Calendars** *(continued)*

Social Studies Grade 9
Grade 9 Unit 1 Imperialism—Two weeks
Grade 9 Unit 2 World War I—Four weeks
Grade 9 Unit 3 Revolutions and Totalitarianism—Two weeks
Grade 9 Unit 4 World War II—Four weeks
Grade 9 Unit 5 Genocide—Five to Six weeks
Grade 9 Unit 6 Terrorism and Global Issues—Six weeks

Social Studies Grade 10
Grade 10 Unit 1 U.S. History Review—Two weeks
Grade 10 Unit 2 Saving the U.S. From Itself—Two weeks
Grade 10 Unit 3 Growth, Change, and Expansion—Two weeks
Grade 10 Unit 4 U.S. and World War I—Three weeks
Grade 10 Unit 5 The Roaring 1920's—Two weeks
Grade 10 Unit 6 Great Depression and New Deal—Two weeks
Grade 10 Unit 7 World War II—Four weeks
Grade 10 Unit 8 Cold War—Five weeks
Grade 10 Unit 9 Civil Rights Movement—Two weeks
Grade 10 Unit 10 Contemporary America—Two weeks

Social Studies Grades 11, 12 (MP = Marking Period)
Grade 11, 12 Constitution and Structure of Government—First MP (3 weeks)
Grade 11, 12 Bill of Rights—First MP (3 weeks)
Grade 11, 12 Discrimination—First MP (3+ weeks)
Grade 11, 12 Abortion—Second MP After Thanksgiving Recess (2 weeks)
Grade 11, 12 Physician Assisted Suicide—Second MP (2+ weeks)
Grade 11, 12 Life and Death Issues: Death Penalty—Second MP (last unit)
Grade 11, 12 Foreign Policy—Third MP (2 1/2 weeks)
Grade 11, 12 Immigration—Third MP (3 weeks)
Grade 11, 12 Drug Policies in America—Fourth MP (1 week)
Grade 11, 12 Poverty in America—Fourth MP (2 weeks)
Grade 11, 12 Contemporary Educational Issues—Fourth MP (2 weeks)

To conclude this chapter, let me share Mark Consorte's closing remarks about the value of the *ongoing* curriculum design process in West Haven.

Mark writes: "In summary, I would like to say that without these release days we have been given to produce and revise these units of study, I believe the entire initiative would have failed. Teachers would have seen this school reform initiative as just another passing fad. But being able to work together for entire days on a regular basis has really helped keep the momentum going. It also sends the message to all teachers that this curriculum redesign work is important and here to stay."

One final foundational step remains before curriculum designers begin the actual creation of the units of study: construction of the unit planning organizer, the focus of the next chapter.

Reader's Assignment

1. Refer to the ten recommended steps entitled, "How to Create the Pacing Calendar," presented earlier in this chapter.

2. In separate content area groups, select one grade or course of study and draft an initial pacing calendar for that grade or course.

3. Repeat the same steps with the other grades and courses.

4. While working through the process, record any issues or questions that need to be discussed and later resolved.

5. When finished drafting all of the grade-specific and course-specific pacing calendars for each content area, create a feedback form for educators to complete as they follow these calendars to implement the units of study. The feedback received will be useful for curriculum design supervisors/teams to refer to when deciding whether or not to revise the pacing calendars in future years.

CHAPTER 9

Construct the Unit Planning Organizer

The Priority Standards are identified and vertically aligned, the units of study have been named, all the grade- or course-specific standards have been assigned to the units, and an initial pacing calendar to ensure the implementation of each unit within its corresponding grade level or course has been created. What's next in the curriculum design process?

Now the design teams must construct a unit planning organizer that includes all of the components or elements deemed necessary for a rigorous unit of study. This final foundational step can certainly take place earlier in the process, but this is the most logical place for it to occur—just before creating the actual units of study.

Brainstorm the Unit Planning Organizer Components

The unit planning organizer is a blank template divided into several sections, each of which is "populated" with the specific information relative to that section. Because this organizer needs to be comprehensive, yet manageable for busy educators, curriculum designers need to first brainstorm the various elements or components necessary for it to include.

For example, on the first day I met with the curriculum writers in East Hartford, Connecticut, to redesign their district's Pre-K–12 English language arts and math curricula, we discussed what the unit planning organizer should include. The various teams first brainstormed what they thought those elements should be and then reported out to the whole group. As I facilitated the discussion, a volunteer typed the list on my computer so that it could be projected onto a large screen for all to see. The initial list included:

- Unit title

- Pacing: duration of units

- Aligned to East Hartford Priority GLEs/Priority Standards

- "Unwrapped" concepts and skills (derived from Priority Standards)

- Essential Questions and Big Ideas

- Key vocabulary

- State test correlations

- Bloom's Taxonomy
    — Explicitly linked to "unwrapped" skills
    — Embedded in learning and assessment tasks

- Assessments: pre-, post-, informal progress-monitoring checks administered throughout the unit

- Instructional practices (including differentiation)

- Research-based effective teaching strategies including SRBI (Scientific Research-Based Interventions—Connecticut's specific term for Response to Intervention)

- Instructional planning and sequencing

- English Language Learner goals

- Interdisciplinary connections

- Explicitly linked, modeled lessons (graphic organizers, electronic resources, etc.)

- Resources and materials (specific lists by grade level and course)

- Rubrics or scoring guides; progress-monitoring tools

- Recommendations for Tier 2, Tier 3 interventions required by SRBI

- Links to Scholastic Achievement Test (SAT) for grades 11–12

One Template or Several

After discussing and coming up with the initial list of elements or components to include on the unit planning organizer, curriculum designers need to address the issue of whether to create several *subject-specific* templates or one *universal* template to be used by all content areas. These three questions will help in making this decision:

1. Should we have one universal template representing all of the brainstormed components *to ensure consistency* across all content areas?

2. Do we want to have some flexibility in the template design, so long as all of the agreed-upon components or elements are included?

3. Shall we agree to try out different templates in different grade spans and different content areas in order to see which ones work best for achieving our aim?

Several issues are likely to surface during this discussion that have a direct impact on which one of the two approaches the curriculum writers may choose to take. For example, I frequently hear the initial concern that because the brainstormed list of elements or components is so lengthy, a template that includes all of these elements will be too unwieldy, too long, too complicated, and not user-friendly.

If there is no clear consensus of agreement at this early stage of the template construction process, I recommend giving the various design teams the freedom to construct a first-draft template that makes sense to *them*. Once the teams actually start designing their own template, initial ideas begin to change. And when the designers actually start filling in the various sections of their template with related information, their ideas can change again. Even if the first drafts of the unit planning organizer do not include all of the components brainstormed by the entire group, as people think more about what their template may be lacking, they begin to see the need to include those elements they might have initially rejected.

East Hartford's Choice

This issue of whether to construct one universal template for all content areas, or subject area-specific templates, surfaced right away with the East Hartford curriculum writers. After some discussion, they opted for separate templates for English language arts and mathematics. They also decided to create an elementary version and a secondary version for each subject area-specific template, believing this would give them more latitude to customize their unit planning organizer for their specific curricular needs. Since we were in the experimental phase, I whole-heartedly supported their decision to do so, saying, "Form follows function."

The results certainly justified their collective decision. When each of the four design teams (elementary English language arts, secondary English language arts, elementary math, and secondary math) began creating their first draft of a unit of study using the team-created unit planning organizer, they found they were able to modify the template as they went along to include everything they determined necessary for a comprehensive unit of study

At the end of our first day of design work, I asked someone from each of the four teams to share out with the large group their team's first-draft template and a

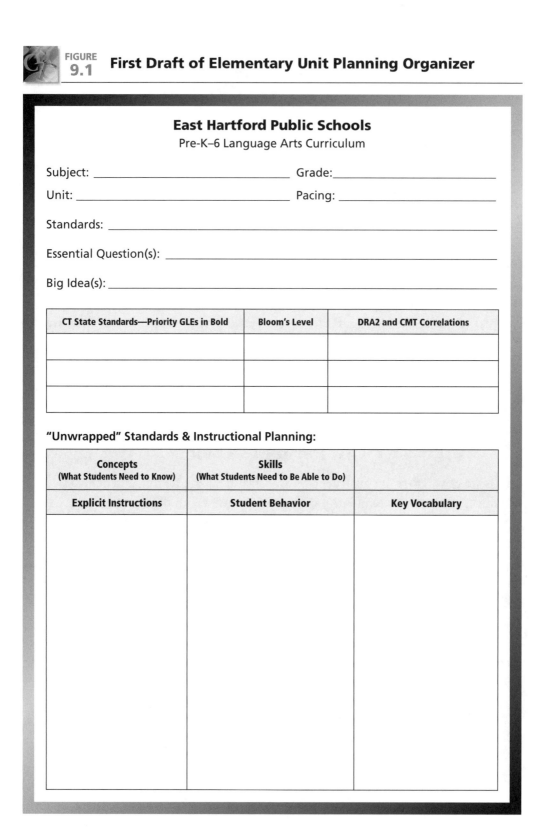

FIGURE 9.1   First Draft of Elementary Unit Planning Organizer

East Hartford Public Schools
Pre-K–6 Language Arts Curriculum

Subject: _____   Grade: _____

Unit: _____   Pacing: _____

Standards: _____

Essential Question(s): _____

Big Idea(s): _____

CT State Standards—Priority GLEs in Bold	Bloom's Level	DRA2 and CMT Correlations

"Unwrapped" Standards & Instructional Planning:

Concepts (What Students Need to Know)	Skills (What Students Need to Be Able to Do)	
Explicit Instructions	**Student Behavior**	**Key Vocabulary**

FIGURE
9.1 **First Draft of Elementary Unit Planning Organizer**
(continued)

Research-based Effective Teaching Strategies:

Assessments
- Common Formative Pre-Assessment (Followed by Data Team Analysis)
- "Dipsticks" (Informal Progress-Monitoring Checks)
- Common Formative Post-Assessment (Followed by Data Team Analysis)
- Rubrics

Instructional Resources

Prioritized Materials	Skills

Differentiation:

Tier 2	Tier 3

ELL Strategies	Enrichment

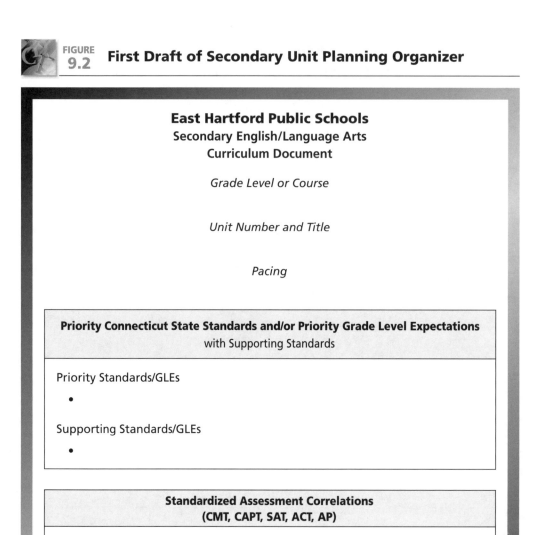

FIGURE 9.2 **First Draft of Secondary Unit Planning Organizer**

East Hartford Public Schools
Secondary English/Language Arts
Curriculum Document

Grade Level or Course

Unit Number and Title

Pacing

Priority Connecticut State Standards and/or Priority Grade Level Expectations with Supporting Standards

Priority Standards/GLEs
 	
    •
 	
Supporting Standards/GLEs
 	
    •

Standardized Assessment Correlations **(CMT, CAPT, SAT, ACT, AP)**
•

"Unwrapped" Priority Standards

Concepts (What students need to know)	**SKILLS** (What students need to be able to do)	**Bloom's** **Level**
• • • • • •	• • • • • •	

FIGURE 9.2 **First Draft of Secondary Unit Planning Organizer** *(continued)*

Essential Questions
(Student-Friendly Language)

-

Big Ideas
(Teacher-Friendly Language)

-

Unit Assessment Plan

Common Formative Pre-Assessment

- (Direct Live Link to Assessment with Scoring Guides)

Informal Progress-Monitoring Tools

- Collins Type 1 Activities
  — "To Do Now"
  — Exit Slips
  — Timed Writings

- Collins Type 2 Activities
  — Quizzes
  — Exit Slips with Specific Questions

- Other Informal Progress Monitoring Tools as determined by Data Teams and Teacher

Common Formative or Summative Post-Assessment

- (Direct Live Link to Assessment with Scoring Guides)

FIGURE 9.2 **First Draft of Secondary Unit Planning Organizer** *(continued)*

Instructional Planning Stage One

Required Resources and Materials

-

Recommended Resources and Materials

-

Required Key Vocabulary to Be Taught (Collins Vocabulary Cards)

-

Research-Based Effective Teaching Strategies

-

Instructional Planning Stage Two

*Differentiation Strategies for **Intervention***

-

*Differentiation Strategies for **Enrichment***

-

*Differentiation and Effective Teaching Strategies for **ELL Students***

-

brief explanation about the elements they included and whether or not they had made any changes to the template as they worked throughout the day. This proved to be an excellent forum for further discussion about the "separate but equal" approach the design teams had chosen to follow. Interestingly, as each team shared their work-in-progress, other teams incorporated ideas they particularly liked into their own unit planning organizers. This did much to promote a shared ownership of the process that respected the need for flexibility while holding to a common vision of what East Hartford's curricular units needed to include.

East Hartford Unit Planning Organizers

Blank versions of the elementary and secondary English language arts unit planning organizers created by the East Hartford curriculum design teams appear in Figures 9.1 and 9.2. The elementary and secondary versions of the math unit planning organizers are very similar, and so have not been included here.

The majority of elements that the East Hartford curriculum designers initially brainstormed are present on both the elementary and secondary English language arts unit planning organizers. As the designers continue designing curricular units of study, they may continue revising their templates to include elements not represented on these first-draft documents. Again, this reflects the "work-in-progress" approach to curriculum design that I believe is essential to developing truly functional curricular units of study.

West Haven's Unit Planning Organizer

Early in their process of curriculum redesign, the West Haven district leaders and curriculum supervisors decided upon one *universal* unit planning organizer to be used in all subject matter areas. Following this decision, design teams began drafting a unit planning organizer that would simultaneously accomplish two related goals: (1) provide a *consistent* template for use in all grades and content areas across the district, and (2) include all of the key components supervisors and designers considered important to a robust curriculum.

After several revisions, the teams agreed upon and later adopted for use district-wide the official West Haven unit planning organizer, shown in Figure 9.3.

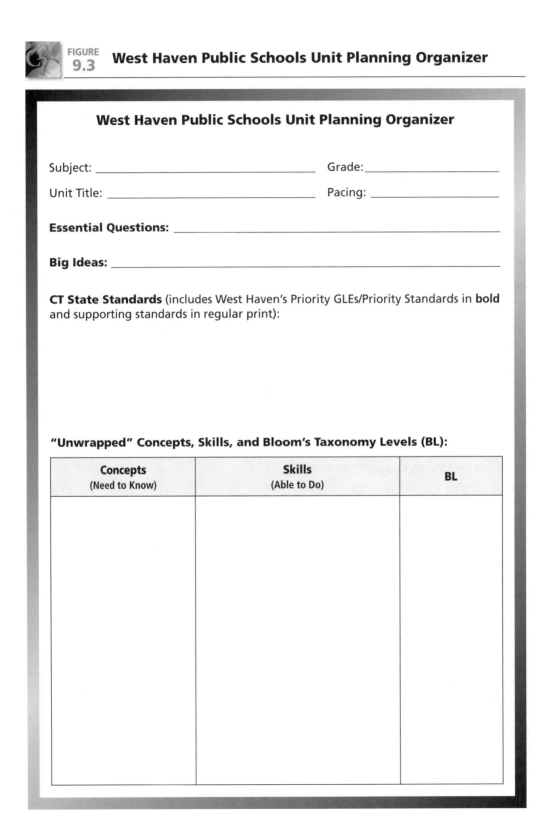

FIGURE 9.3 **West Haven Public Schools Unit Planning Organizer**

West Haven Public Schools Unit Planning Organizer

Subject: _____ Grade: _____

Unit Title: _____ Pacing: _____

Essential Questions: _____

Big Ideas: _____

CT State Standards (includes West Haven's Priority GLEs/Priority Standards in **bold** and supporting standards in regular print):

"Unwrapped" Concepts, Skills, and Bloom's Taxonomy Levels (BL):

Concepts (Need to Know)	Skills (Able to Do)	BL

FIGURE
9.3 **West Haven Public Schools Unit Planning Organizer** *(continued)*

Unit Assessments:

Common Formative *Pre*-Assessment (followed by Data Team analysis):

"Dipsticks" (Informal Progress-Monitoring Checks):

Common Formative *Post*-Assessment (followed by Data Team analysis):

Instructional Planning:

Suggested Resources/Materials:

Suggested Research-based Effective Instructional Strategies:

Vocabulary/Word Wall	Enrichment/Extension	Interdisciplinary Connections

Using this template, the curriculum groups began designing units of study during scheduled release time from their instructional programs. During the summer months of that first year of production, design team members received stipends to continue creating the curricular units of study for implementation in classrooms the following school year.

The West Haven template, constructed nearly a year before the East Hartford templates, incorporates many of the same brainstormed elements listed at the beginning of this chapter. Since multiple units of study have now been created in the first cohort of content areas (English language arts, math, science, and social studies) and also in the second cohort (health and physical education, library media technology, career and technical education, world languages, visual and performing arts, and early childhood education), the unit planning organizer has not been revised to include other elements. Instead, an *accompanying* document that provides additional information to assist educators in implementing the units of study is planned for distribution during the 2010–2011 school year.

Further Detailing the Unit Planning Organizer

As illustrated by the three sample templates presented in this chapter, the unit planning organizer needs to include important elements related to standards, instruction, and assessment. However, more details are needed for the templates to be fully useable by the educators who will implement the units of study in their own classrooms and instructional programs.

For example, within the broad category of instructional strategies, there are the specific types of specialized strategies to include as a helpful reference for educators: the many kinds of research-based teaching and differentiation strategies, the three tiers of intervention strategies, and the strategies particularly applicable to English Language Learners and special education students.

As another example, within the category of instructional planning, curriculum designers should make recommendations for using different types of standards-based engaging learning experiences that are not tied to textbooks, such as authentic performance tasks that incorporate 21st-century learning skills and interdisciplinary connections. Suggestions for instructional pacing and sequencing that take into account "learning progressions" are also necessary to include.

When first constructing the unit planning organizer, including this level of detail is premature. However, as designers move further into the process of creating the curricular units of study, providing this deeper level of detail will greatly enhance the overall quality of the units of study. In Chapter 15, I suggest time-saving, practical ways and examples in which design teams can add these details.

For now, the focus is on constructing the first draft of the unit planning organizer. When it is completed, design teams will be ready to use the template to create their first unit of study. In Part 3, you will learn how to immediately apply each of the steps for designing the rigorous curricular unit, from start to finish.

Reader's Assignment

1. With your curriculum design colleagues, brainstorm a list of the elements or components you believe essential to include on the unit planning organizer.

2. Discuss and decide whether to have one *universal* template that includes all of the brainstormed elements or *different templates* for different content areas and/or levels (elementary, middle, high).

3. In your design team groups, draft the layout of the unit planning organizer that includes the brainstormed elements or components.

4. Share the drafts created by the different design groups with the whole group.

5. Make any desired revisions to the template(s).

6. Add any new terms to your curriculum glossary that you began developing earlier in this process.

PART THREE

Designing the Curricular Unit of Study— From Start to Finish

CHAPTER 10

Select a Unit of Study and Identify Matching Standards

In the next six chapters, I present the specific steps for designing the curricular unit, from start to finish. These steps can be followed by all educators and leaders, regardless of whether or not they have completed all of the foundational prerequisites described in prior chapters. However, because of the importance of laying that curricular groundwork *in advance*, I want to again encourage designers to complete these steps before creating all of the units.

Depending on readers' individual situations, some will have already completed the first design step described in this chapter and be ready to skip to the next one, while others will need to complete a few preliminaries before they are able to complete this step.

The following five situations represent different stages of readiness for moving forward in the design process from this point. Identify the situation that most closely represents your own. Then read and follow only the corresponding "next steps" for that particular situation.

Situation #1: You are a school or school system leader, a curriculum supervisor, or a classroom educator in a school system that "started from scratch" to revise existing curricula using this curriculum design model. Together, you and your colleagues have *already* (1) identified and vertically aligned the Priority Standards, (2) organized and named units of study for each grade level and course within one or more content areas, (3) assigned the Priority Standards and supporting standards to those units, (4) created the pacing calendars, and (5) constructed the unit planning organizer(s).

Situation #2: Your school system has identified and vertically aligned the Priority Standards, but it has not yet begun the actual revision of curricular units in the targeted content areas. You and your curriculum committee members are gathered together at an orientation meeting to receive further direction.

Situation #3: Your school system leaders are discussing the need to update existing curricula, although none of the foundational steps for creating a system-wide curricular redesign have yet been completed. In your role as a school administrator, curriculum supervisor, literacy coach, or math coach, you may soon be asked to take part in this project. But first you want to try creating a unit of study on your own following the process described in this book.

Situation #4: As a classroom educator, you work in a school system that is not yet ready to organize and begin comprehensive curriculum design. You wonder whether you should wait until the entire school system is ready to revise the curricula before creating a unit of study following this model.

Situation #5: Your school system has recently redesigned *all* of their curricula, yet you are curious to know how this model's approach to creating curricular units of study compares to the process your school system followed.

The following five sets of "next steps" correspond to the five different situations described above.

Choose the Most Relevant Next Steps

Next Steps for #1: You have already completed this step and can skip to the next chapter. All your team members need to do next is select one of the units of study listed on the pacing calendar for any given grade or course. Then follow the Chapter 11 guidelines that explain how to "unwrap" the assigned Priority Standards.

Next Steps for #2:

1. Provide everyone with the "big picture" overview of the curriculum design process so they can all see how the many separate components are, in fact, integrated parts of a whole system.

2. Explain how the unit of study is the building block of a rigorous curriculum and is based upon the Priority Standards.

3. Discuss the fact that three foundational steps must be taken *before creating all of the curricular units of study* for the targeted content areas:
   • Naming the units of study for each grade level and course
   • Assigning the Priority Standards and supporting standards to each unit

• Preparing grade-specific and course-specific pacing calendars for all of the units

As a group, decide when these foundational steps will be taken.

4. Have the group experience the curriculum design process *prior to* completing these three foundational steps. To do so, break into content area and/or grade-span teams. Brainstorm the elements to include on the unit planning organizer and create a first-draft template.

5. In each of these design teams, identify a topical, skills-based, or thematic focus for a unit of study applicable to any grade or course within a particular content area, and list it on the template.

6. Refer to the school system's Priority Standards and select three or four of those grade- or course-specific essential standards that match the unit of study. Write them on the unit planning organizer in the space provided. Identify supporting standards that connect to and/or enhance the targeted Priority Standards and list them also.

7. When the groups are finished, turn to the next chapter to learn the "unwrapping" Priority Standards process.

Next Steps for #3:

1. Depending on your particular role, identify a topical, skills-based, or thematic focus for a unit of study:

    Administrator—choose a content area and grade level that you are most familiar with or have experience teaching, and then select a unit of study accordingly.

    Curriculum Supervisor—choose a unit of study for any grade or course within your particular content area that you think will help you most when later sharing this process with curriculum design team members.

    Literacy Coach—choose a unit of study for any grade or course in English language arts that represents important literacy skills for students to acquire.

    Math Coach—choose a unit of study for any grade or course in math that proves particularly challenging for students to learn.

2. Refer to the content-area standards for your selected unit of study, and select three or four related standards that *you consider to be extremely important (priority)* for students to learn during that unit. Identify supporting standards that connect to and/or enhance the standards you identified as priorities.

3. Design a unit planning organizer following the guidelines presented in Chapter 9, or choose one of the three provided. Record your selected standards in the Priority Standards and supporting standards respective columns, and then turn to the next chapter to learn how to "unwrap" the standards you have selected for your unit.

Next Steps for #4: You absolutely do not need to wait until your entire school system is ready to redesign the curricula before experimenting with this model. Since you are more than likely quite accustomed to planning units of study in your own instructional program, select an upcoming unit of study that you know you will be teaching soon and apply this model to it. When you eventually implement the finished unit in your own instructional program, you will be able to determine for yourself the value of this approach to unit construction. Even without the outer support of your school or school system, you can replicate the process *on your own* with future units of study you wish to create.

To create your unit, first choose one of the unit planning organizer templates from Chapter 9 or construct your own following those examples. Select three or four standards that closely relate to your selected unit of study and are critically important for your students to learn. Then identify two or three other standards that support the essential ones. Record all of the targeted standards on the template. When finished, turn to the next chapter to learn how to "unwrap" the standards you decided are essential.

Next Steps for #5: Select any one of your completed curricular units. Skip to the next chapter and read how to "unwrap" the standards. Apply the "unwrapping" process (including the writing of Big Ideas and Essential Questions) to the standards in your selected unit. Determine if the process provides you with greater clarity about the specific learning outcomes for that unit. Continue through the remaining steps of the model in a similar way. Use this book as a benchmark collection of ideas and examples to help you review and refine your existing units.

Reader's Assignment

1. Follow the "next steps" directions for whichever situation most closely mirrors your own, if you have not already done so.

2. Begin listing questions to ask, resources to acquire, colleagues to talk with, and so on, as you work through the above next steps that are most relevant to your particular situation.

3. Determine which preparatory steps still remain to be completed before design teams create *all* of the curricular units of study for each targeted content area, grade level, and course.

CHAPTER 11

"Unwrap" the Priority Standards; Write Big Ideas and Essential Questions

In many instances, standards lack clarity, degree of specificity, and explicit levels of rigor. Because the Priority Standards are the focal point in the design of a rigorous curriculum, they need to be carefully analyzed by educators to determine exactly what they mean. Only by examining the actual wording of a standard can educators decide for themselves what a standard signifies in terms of student learning outcomes.

"Unwrapping" the standards is a process that I first learned in the fall of 1999 from Donald Viegut, former Pre-K–12 Director of Curriculum and Instruction in the school district of Merrill, Wisconsin. Seeing the power of this method to help all educators demystify the meaning of their grade- and course-specific standards, I began incorporating it into the *Making Standards Work* performance assessment workshop originally developed by Douglas Reeves. Since that time, I have continued to develop and refine the "unwrapping" process through my work in school systems across North America. The rationale and process, as presented in my 2003 book *"Unwrapping" the Standards: A Simple Process to Make Standards Manageable*, continue to have real relevancy for Pre-K–12 educators in all content areas as they design common formative assessments and standards-based curricular units of study.

As applied to standards, there are many synonyms in use for the term "unwrapping." The one closest to what "unwrapping" really means in the standards-based context is "deconstructing," a term attributed to Grant Wiggins and Jay McTighe in *Understanding by Design* (1998). When deconstructing or "unwrapping" grade-level and course-specific standards for a unit of study, an educator analyzes the wording of a standard to determine exactly what students need to know (the concepts) and be able to do (the skills). Even though the initial task of "unwrapping" is to *separate* concepts from skills, the two remain interrelated. How each skill is *applied* to a particular concept determines its corresponding level of cognitive rigor. When educators "unwrap" standards, they reference a thinking skills hierarchy, such as Bloom's Taxonomy, to identify the approximate thinking level of each individual skill. They can then intentionally align both instruction and assessment to the "unwrapped" concepts, skills, and matching thinking-skill levels.

Two Early Problems Resolved

Two problems emerged in the early years of "unwrapping" the standards. Because educators collaboratively prioritized the standards, they logically thought that the next step would be to collaboratively "unwrap" *all* of the Priority Standards *and* supporting standards for each grade level and course. However, this proved to be a formidable undertaking for those who did the work. People wondered if there might be an easier way—especially since the promised benefit of "unwrapping" was, ironically, "a *simple* process for managing the standards."

Despite the challenge of "unwrapping" everything, educators persevered. They knew that this work, when finished, would provide a valuable resource. Everyone could simply reference the master list of "unwrapped" standards and select from it those concepts and skills to focus on during instruction. Yet the question remained of *when and in which instructional units of study* educators would actually teach and assess those "unwrapped" standards.

Another problem was that only those individuals who had actually done the work of "unwrapping" really understood what it meant. Those who had not been part of the initial effort wondered what all the fuss was about. Many thought that the standards, as written, were already "unwrapped." Others looked upon this practice as merely "rewriting" the standards, a task they did not see any point in doing!

The solution to both problems was to give educators a firsthand experience of "unwrapping" standards for a self-selected unit of study that was relevant to them, after which they would design a common formative assessment or curricular unit of study for their own grade level or course. If, after this, educators received from the school system common formative assessments or curricular units with the "unwrapped" *Priority Standards* included, they would understand what these elements meant.

Supporting standards in those units were not formally "unwrapped." Instead, educators reviewed the supporting standards relative to a particular unit on their own to identify related concepts or pertinent vocabulary. Because the educators had gained their own personal understanding of the "unwrapping" process, they could make these additions and then move right into the planning of engaging learning experiences and effective instruction to impart the targeted concepts and skills to their students.

The Four Parts of "Unwrapping"

Whether or not your particular school system has already provided the "unwrapped" Priority Standards in given units of study or whether you need to complete this part of the unit-design process yourself, this chapter will give you important information to further your understanding and application of the practice.

There are four sequential parts to the "unwrapping" the standards process:

1. "Unwrap" the Priority Standards.

2. Create a Graphic Organizer.

3. Write the Big Ideas.

4. Create the Essential Questions.

Included in the following sections are standards from *several different content areas* to illustrate the various aspects of the four-part "unwrapping" process.

PART 1: "UNWRAP" THE PRIORITY STANDARDS

This is the deconstruction step of the process. Read carefully each Priority Standard for a particular unit of study. Analyze the wording in each one to identify the embedded concepts and skills. Concepts are the important nouns or noun phrases, and the skills are the verbs. To "unwrap," underline only those nouns or noun phrases that represent *teachable concepts.* Circle only those verbs that represent what *students* are to do.

For example, in the science standard, "The student will identify the processes involved in weathering and the effect of erosion on rocks and the surface of the Earth," the teachable concepts are underlined and the only skill indicated for students to do is circled.

Here is a related "unwrapped" standard: "The student will identify how eroded materials are transported and deposited over time in new areas to form new features."

In this second standard, note that again, only the verb "identify" is circled. Even though there are other verbs included in it—"eroded, transported, deposited, form"—they have not been circled. They are descriptors of the teachable concepts, not skills that the students themselves are expected to do.

When "unwrapping" certain standards, it happens that almost every word is underlined, as shown in the above two science examples. In such instances, educators can rightly wonder what the point is of "unwrapping." The power of the practice reveals itself in the *physical doing* of it. By studying the wording of the standard to determine precisely what students need to know and be able to do,

FIGURE 11.1 **"Unwrapped" Grade 6 Mathematics Graphic Organizer (Example 1)**

Title of Unit of Study: Measurement (Units of Measure; Circles)

Priority Standards:

6.1—SELECT and APPLY <u>appropriate standard units and tools</u> to MEASURE <u>length, area, volume, weight, time, temperature,</u> and the <u>size of angles</u>.

6.4—KNOW <u>common estimates of Pi (3.14, 22/7)</u> and USE these values to ESTIMATE and CALCULATE the <u>circumference</u> and the <u>area of circles</u>. USE the <u>formulas</u> for the <u>circumference</u> and <u>area of a circle</u>.

Concepts (Need to Know About Measurement):

6.1—Standard Units and Measuring Tools for:
- Length
- Area
- Volume
- Weight
- Time
- Temperatures
- Size of Angles

6.4—Circles
- Circumference
- Area
- Estimates of Pi (3.14 and 22/7)
- Formulas
  — Circumference
  — Area

FIGURE
11.2 **"Unwrapped" Grade 6 Mathematics Graphic Organizer (Example 2)**

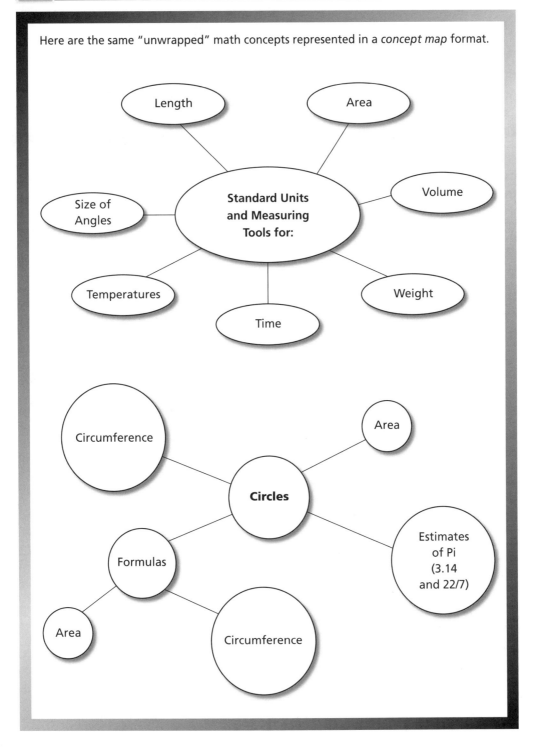

Here are the same "unwrapped" math concepts represented in a *concept map* format.

educators become acutely aware of what it is they are to teach and what they will
later assess.

PART 2: CREATE A GRAPHIC ORGANIZER

With the teachable concepts and skills from the Priority Standards clearly identified,
the next step is to represent all of these elements on a graphic organizer of one's
own choosing. The four types of graphic organizers educators use most frequently
are a bulleted list, an outline, a concept map, or a chart.

I always recommend listing the *concepts* on one section of the graphic organizer
and grouping like concepts under broader headings, whenever possible. For
example, in the "unwrapped" Priority Standards and bulleted list graphic organizer
for a sixth-grade math measurement unit of study (Figures 11.1 and 11.2), the
individual concepts are grouped under two broad headings: *Standard Units and
Measuring Tools*, and *Circles*. Notice that the skills in this example appear in
CAPITAL LETTERS and the teachable concepts are underlined.

The point to remember with regard to creating the graphic organizer is that the
specific format does not matter. What does matter is that *each and every teachable
concept* from the Priority Standards for a particular unit of study is represented on
the graphic organizer of choice in a way that makes organizational sense to the
educator.

The "Unwrapped" Skills

The second half of the graphic organizer represents the "unwrapped" Priority
Standards skills. In addition to listing each skill and its related concept(s) in
parentheses after it, an approximate level of Bloom's Taxonomy for each skill is
identified, depending on how that skill is used. To complete this part of the graphic
organizer, refer to the six levels of the revised Bloom's Taxonomy, provided in
Appendix A. Each of the six levels includes an alphabetized list of verbs associated
with that level in the revised Bloom's Taxonomy of Educational Objectives
(Anderson and Krathwohl, 2001).

Notice in the following English language arts example how the same skill is
assigned two *different* Bloom levels because of the concept in parentheses.

(2) INTERPRET (informational text)

(4) INTERPRET (**implied** information in text)

Interpreting informational text is not as cognitively demanding as interpreting
implied information. To *infer* is more challenging (rigorous) than to *interpret*. How

you *use* the skill with its corresponding concept(s) is what helps determine that skill's approximate level of rigor.

Another example is the skill, "identify." Typically, this is a level one, or knowledge classification, skill. However, if the English language arts skill "identify" appears with the concept "main idea," that pairing indicates a higher level in the thinking-skill hierarchy and needs to be represented as such on the graphic organizer.

Figure 11.3 shows the second half of the graphic organizer for the same sixth-grade math measurement unit of study. The approximate level of Bloom's Taxonomy appears in parentheses in front of each skill to indicate its level of rigor *as it applies to the related concepts.*

When identifying the *approximate* Bloom's Taxonomy level for each skill and related concept(s), certain skill-verbs may not appear in any of the lists. Decide which list of verbs comes closest and use that corresponding level number.

Listing the concepts on the top section of the graphic organizer and then again on the bottom section can *seem* needlessly redundant. However, my reason for advocating a clear separation between concepts and skills in this way is that each section has a distinctly unique purpose. Seeing the concepts by themselves, especially when grouped together under broader headings, makes it easier to

FIGURE 11.3 **"Unwrapped" Grade 6 Mathematics Graphic Organizer—Part 2**

Skills (Be Able to Do):

(1) KNOW (common estimates of pi)

(1) SELECT (appropriate units, tools)

(1) MEASURE (length, area, volume, weight, time, temperature, angles)

(2) ESTIMATE (circumference, area of circle)

(3) CALCULATE (circumference, area of circle)

(3) USE (formulas for circumference, area of circle)

(3) USE (common estimates of pi)

(3) APPLY (appropriate units, tools)

determine the Big Ideas during the next part of the "unwrapping" process, and provides educators with a standards-derived list of the key concepts—vocabulary terms—for the unit of study.

Many teachers are writing the "unwrapped" concepts on large chart paper and posting the chart in their classrooms to remain throughout the unit of study. Doing this keeps students focused on the specific standards vocabulary relevant to that unit. Such a chart can also become part of a larger "word wall" of additional key terms relevant to one or more units of study. The educators themselves keep their unit graphic organizer in their daily plan book to reference as they plan weekly and daily lessons. Some elementary educators have told me they are sending this list of key terms home to parents in a monthly newsletter to keep them informed of what their children will be learning during a particular unit of study.

The skills, with their approximate levels of Bloom's Taxonomy, provide a great reminder to educators when planning and delivering daily lessons to provide students with several opportunities throughout the unit to exercise the targeted skills *at the indicated levels of thinking-skill rigor.*

One important point to make here concerns the level of rigor in the "unwrapped" skills for any Priority Standard. Whenever educators make the unhappy discovery that certain skills are limited to lower levels of Bloom's Taxonomy, I always encourage them to add one or two more skills that *do* represent higher levels of rigor. This is not "rewriting" the standards. Instead, it is encouraging educators not to restrict or reduce the level of rigor during instruction to lower-level skills just because the Priority Standards in focus do not include higher-level skills.

West Haven's universal unit planning organizer represents all of these key elements of the graphic organizer in a slightly different, chart format. The graphic organizer for a grade 10 social studies unit entitled "Growth, Change, and Expansion" is shown in Figure 11.4. (Note: BL indicates Bloom's Taxonomy level.)

In Figure 11.4, each of the three skills and corresponding Bloom level is matched to *all* of the side-by-side concepts listed in the left-hand column. This works very well as long as there is only one skill for *multiple concepts* (although this may still indicate a need for a different Bloom level if the difficulty of those concepts warrants it).

If, however, the reverse is true and there are two or three different skills that all relate to the same concept, then each skill must be matched to a *different* Bloom level, as in the following example (Bloom's Taxonomy levels are in parentheses):

(2) INTERPRET (informational text)

(4) ANALYZE (informational text)

(5) EVALUATE (informational text)

FIGURE
11.4

**West Haven Unit Planning Organizer—
"Growth, Change, and Expansion"**

Concepts (Need to Know)	Skills (Able to Do)	BL
Impact of technology and scientific discovery on American society • new inventions • spread of industrialism • factory and city life • social Darwinism	EVALUATE	5
Significance of evolving heterogeneity of American society • immigration • culture • new ideas	ASSESS	5
Changing role of American participation and influence in world affairs • imperialism • colonialism • international police force	TRACE	4

How curriculum designers choose to represent their "unwrapped" concepts and skills on a unit's graphic organizer is a system-based or curriculum committee-based or individual educator-based decision. What should remain consistent and be included on the graphic organizer, regardless of format, are the following elements:

• Specific concepts, similarly grouped under broader headings (whenever applicable)

• Specific skills, each one matched to one or more concepts

• Approximate Bloom's level for each skill-concept match-up, determined by how the skill is used with that concept

A reminder about the supporting standards: Most educators do *not* "unwrap" the supporting standards assigned to a unit of study. This keeps instruction and assessment sharply focused on the "unwrapped" Priority Standards. Instead, they list on the graphic organizer *additional concepts* from the selected supporting standards and include those concepts in the Unit Vocabulary or "Word Wall" section of the unit planning organizer.

PART 3: WRITE THE BIG IDEAS

Those who are mechanically adept often say that the only way to really understand how something works is to take it apart and put it back together again. In the third step of the "unwrapping" process, educators can see if this holds true with regard to their work with standards. After deconstructing the standards to identify the separate concepts within them, the next step is to "put them back together again" in a way that shows the important connections between those concepts.

Big Ideas represent the three or four foundational understandings—main ideas, conclusions, or generalizations relative to the unit's "unwrapped" concepts—that educators want their students to discover and state in their own words by the end of the unit of study.

John Hattie (2009) writes: "Teachers are successful to the degree that they can move students from single to multiple ideas, and then relate and extend these ideas [so] that learners construct and reconstruct knowledge and ideas. It is not the knowledge or ideas, but the learner's *construction of the knowledge and ideas,* that is critical" (p. 37).

Written as *complete sentences* and not phrases, Big Ideas convey to students the benefit or value of learning the standards in focus. They represent what educators want students to remember long after instruction ends. These foundational understandings can be broad, topical, or both.

Broad or Topical Big Ideas

A *broad* Big Idea is a generalization derived from one area of study that can be equally applicable to other areas of study, such as this example: "We interpret information and draw conclusions both from what we read and from what we experience in real life."

A *topical* Big Idea relates clearly to one content area only, as in this example: "Mathematical formulas and estimates provide shortcuts for determining needed mathematical information."

A Big Idea can occasionally be both broad *and* topical, represented in this example: "Objects can be compared, classified, and sorted by their different attributes"—a statement that is true for a particular unit of study in both math and science.

Big Ideas—whether broad, topical, or both—help students scaffold their understanding so they can eventually make further generalizations and connections to other units of study within a discipline and to other disciplines.

Educators usually write their Big Ideas as adults would say them. However, some begin right away by thinking how students themselves might express the Big Ideas, and then "translate" their initial wording into student-friendly language. Here is a Big Idea for the subject of writing that emphasizes the importance of audience and purpose, represented two ways:

Adult version: "It is appropriate to use a variety of writing styles to communicate information for a variety of purposes and to a variety of audiences."

Student version: "Writers need to know how to write in different ways for different people."

Big Ideas can prove challenging to write, especially in the beginning. This is a *process*, and the quality of the Big Ideas improves with practice. I regularly say to educators when they are writing their first-draft Big Ideas: "Don't worry about getting them 'right'; just get them down; get them written. You can always go back later and 'wordsmith' them. Just keep thinking about what you would want the students to say in their own words regarding the *value or benefit* of learning those particular concepts."

PART 4: CREATE THE ESSENTIAL QUESTIONS

At the beginning of a unit of study, educators post, in a prominent location in the classroom or instructional space, two to four questions written in bold, colorful lettering. They explain to their students that these questions are a special type of question known as an "Essential Question," and that *by the end of the unit of study,* they want *all* students to be able to respond to each of these Essential Questions in their own words.

Essential Questions are engaging, open-ended questions that educators use to spark student interest in learning the content of the unit about to commence. Even though plainly worded, they carry with them an underlying rigor. Responding to them in a way that demonstrates genuine understanding requires more than superficial thought. Along with the "unwrapped" concepts and skills from the Priority Standards, educators use the Essential Questions *throughout the unit* to sharply focus instruction and assessment.

The Relationship between
Big Ideas and Essential Questions

The relationship between the Big Ideas and the Essential Questions, in its simplest form, is this: the Big Ideas are the students' responses to the teacher's Essential Questions.

It is important here to make a distinction between "answers" and "responses." The word "answer" may imply that there is only one correct reply, whereas the word "response" allows for more latitude and depth in the reply. Because the Big Ideas reflect students' personal insights developed over the course of the unit, the word "response" seems to capture more of that intent. It conveys the idea that there is not one single correct answer that all students must state verbatim, but rather reveals connections students have been able to make on their own in relation to the Essential Questions.

There are certainly exceptions. Often the Essential Question is so fundamental to student understanding within a particular unit of study that it needs to be directly (and correctly) *answered*. A two-part Essential Question provides an effective solution.

In two-part questions, the first question requires recall of important information, whereas the second question reveals the underlying rigor and requires a higher level of thinking to respond correctly. Notice, in the following example of a two-part English language arts Essential Question, how the Big Idea responds to the *second* of these two questions.

> **Essential Questions:** What are literary devices? Why do authors use them?
>
> **Big Idea:** Literary devices enhance and deepen fiction's impact upon the reader.

The first question is a recall of information question—students need to be able to correctly answer and give examples of what literary devices *are* through the asking of lower-level recall types of questions. Certainly this is important for students to be able to do, but the *second* Essential Question goes way beyond the first in terms of thinking skill demand.

Another related example is this pair of math Essential Questions:

> **Essential Questions:** What is estimation? Why do we need to know how to estimate?
>
> **Big Ideas:** Estimation produces a value that comes close to a problem's actual answer. Whether you estimate or need to calculate the actual answer depends on the situation.

The first Big Idea is a direct "answer" to the first part of the two-part Essential Question. Even though it does not appear to exemplify the usual definition of a Big Idea, it represents a prerequisite math understanding that students must acquire in order to be able to apply that understanding to problems or life situations requiring estimation. The second Big Idea is a "response" to the second part of the question. It indicates a generalization students have been able to make as a result of making connections between the concept of estimation and its application in many situations.

Essential Questions that begin with "how" and "why" require students to mentally reach beyond lower-level recall into the higher-level kinds of thinking represented in the upper levels of Bloom's Taxonomy: analyze, synthesize, evaluate. When educators present students with *seemingly* simple questions, such as the second ones shown in both of the preceding examples, the level of instruction, classroom learning experiences, and corresponding assessments rise to meet them.

Engaging Essential Questions

West Haven, Connecticut, science curriculum writers heard me challenge the teams to strive for more *creativity* in the wording of their Essential Questions so as to capture and hold their students' attention and interest. The following examples wonderfully represent the result of their efforts to do so. Notice how the wording of the matching Big Ideas in parentheses remains very straightforward, as it should.

- Why does the magnet stick to the refrigerator? (Like poles repel and unlike poles attract.)

- After a swim, would you rather dry yourself off with a napkin or a bath towel? (Some materials absorb more liquid than other materials.)

- Why should you eat a popsicle quickly on a hot day? (Change of temperature can affect the state of matter.)

- What would happen if I kept my plants in the closet over summer vacation? (Plants need sunlight, water, and nutrients.) *Source: Grade 2 science curriculum writers, West Haven, CT*

- Why would bowling be different if the lanes were carpeted? (Experimental results can be used to determine the effect that forces, such as friction, have on an object's motion.)

- What are the forces acting on a ball flying through the air that cause it to eventually fall to the ground? (Unbalanced forces cause accelerations, or unbalanced forces cause changes in motion.)

- What evidence can you cite to justify why it takes longer for an "18-wheeler" to stop than for a Ferrari to stop? (Inertia is a measure of how hard it is to change the motion of an object. Inertia affects the motion of objects.) *Source: Secondary science curriculum writers, West Haven, CT*

Here are several randomly selected matched sets of Essential Questions and parenthetical Big Ideas from several different grades and content areas. Some are more "engaging" than others, but all correctly represent the question-response relationship.

- How is one group of objects different from another? (Objects can be compared, classified, and sorted by their different attributes.)

- How can an author "capture" an audience? (Knowing who one is writing for is essential to engaging the readers.)

- Why learn mathematical formulas? How do estimation and formulas work together? (Mathematical formulas and estimates both provide shortcuts for determining needed mathematical information.)

- Where do "dog books" live in the library neighborhood? How do we find nonfiction books in the library? (The Dewey Decimal system is a map of the library neighborhoods.) *Source: Library Media Technology group, West Haven, CT*

- How do you know if your main idea is *really* the main idea? (Main ideas must be supported with evidence from the text and supporting details.)

- Why isn't a digit always worth the same amount? (The position of a digit determines its value in a number.)

- Why is teamwork a necessary life skill? (Teamwork promotes cooperation and a positive interaction among individuals.)

- Why do all civilizations—past and present—need organizational structures? (Geographic, political, cultural, and other structures work together to ensure the survival and advancement of all civilizations.)

- Should writers use transition words and phrases? Why or why not? (Writers should use transition words and phrases to make their writing flow smoothly and connect ideas.) *Source: Middle School English group, West Haven, CT*

- If you could read music like a pro, what would it allow you to do? (Reading music allows you to participate and communicate in the language of musicians.) *Source: Elementary music teachers, West Haven, CT*

The West Haven, Connecticut, middle school visual arts curriculum writers created the following three Essential Questions with matching Big Ideas listed below them. Notice how the Big Ideas, even though adult-worded, provide *additional information* than what is asked in the questions. This is important. Often educators unintentionally "give away" the Big Idea by including it as part of the Essential Question. Big Ideas should offer more than a mere restatement of the Essential Questions.

Essential Questions:

1. Why would an artist choose particular digital media concepts, techniques, and processes over others?

2. Which elements of art and principles of design will be the most dominant in a digital media project, and why?

3. Why is life experience a good source of inspiration for an artist?

Big Ideas:

1. Some digital media concepts have unique characteristics that may prove more effective for conveying the artist's vision in a particular project than others.

2. The specific elements of art and principles of design that are applied to digital media projects are based on the requirements and needs of the project, as well as on personal choices.

3. Life is all encompassing. Each day offers new experiences that add to the creation of new ideas and references to draw inspiration from.

Lastly, the East Hartford, Connecticut, pre-K–6 literacy curriculum team applied the student-friendly approach to the wording of their Big Ideas by writing them in a first-person format. Note also the emphasis on key vocabulary terms derived from the "unwrapped" standards.

Essential Questions:

1. How can you better understand the *characters* in the story?

2. How can you determine the *conflict* faced by the characters in the story?

3. How can you use *inferences* to help you understand the story?

Big Ideas:

1. I can understand the characters in the story by identifying the characters' physical and personality traits.

2. I can understand the conflict of the story by identifying what started it.

3. I can understand what the author means from his words and from what I already know.

Three Frequently Asked Questions

There are always many questions that educators ask when they are deeply engaged in the process of writing their Big Ideas and Essential Questions. Here are three of them:

1. Can the Essential Question be written before the Big Idea?

The answer is yes, but then you must still figure out the Big Idea response to that question. The reason for determining the Big Idea *first* is that it represents the desired *end* learning goal and is derived from the "unwrapped" concepts— the focus of the unit of study. The "unwrapping" process moves from the concrete to the abstract—from isolating the separate concepts to putting them back together as Big Ideas. One effective way of creating the Essential Question is to look at the Big Idea and think, "If that's the desired response, what's the question?"

2. Must there be a one-to-one correspondence between the Big Idea and the Essential Question?

No, but educators usually write them in matching pairs. It is certainly acceptable, however, to have one Essential Question that will yield two corresponding Big Idea responses. The converse is equally true. Sometimes only one Big Idea results from two Essential Questions. The recommendation is to write a matching Essential Question and Big Idea so that students are sure to communicate their specific understanding of each Big Idea by the end of the unit.

3. When students are reading multiple stories within a unit of study, should the Big Ideas stay the same while the Essential Questions change to fit a particular story or text?

I recommend that the Essential Questions and Big Ideas remain the same throughout the unit, since they are directly derived from the "unwrapped" Priority Standards for that unit. However, many educators write story-based or novel-based *focus questions* to help students make direct connections to the particular story or novel they are reading.

For example, the Big Idea for the unit of study might be: "Main ideas must be supported with evidence from the text and supporting details." A *focus question* related to the Essential Question, "How do you know if your main idea is really the main idea?" might be this one related to the story *Hattie's Birthday Box*: "Why was Hattie so happy and comforted by Granddaddy's gift, even though he thought she would be angry?"

If educators help students see the *connections* between the story- or novel-based focus questions and the unit's Essential Questions, students will be able to provide Big Ideas that represent generalizations applicable to more than one story rather than just specific answers to questions about only one story in particular.

Connect Each Day's Lesson to Essential Questions

The most powerful example of an educator's effective use of Essential Questions that I have personally seen and heard still remains that of Sue Sims, a southern California high school geometry teacher who posted Essential Questions around her classroom as guideposts for the unit of study.

Each day, in the final four minutes of a 42-minute instructional period, Ms. Sims asked her students to reflect upon what they had just finished doing that day in class and then respond to her closure question, "Which Essential Question did we work on today?" Not only did her heterogeneously mixed class of sophomores learn to answer this question orally, she also expected her students to respond in *writing* by including the Essential Questions on her end-of-unit test.

During my visit to her classroom, Sue showed me many samples of the unit assessment results from her students and concluded with this testimony: "In eighteen years of teaching high school math, I have never seen these kinds of scores and this level of student understanding on unit tests. This practice has changed the way I teach."

Readers interested in more information about all four parts of the "unwrapping" process (excluding the connections to Bloom's Taxonomy that I developed after the process was first published), may wish to refer to my book *"Unwrapping" the Standards*. It presents more than 85 examples of "unwrapped" standards with accompanying Big Ideas and Essential Questions in all four grade spans (K–2, 3–5, 6–8, and 9–12) in numerous content areas.

Reader's Assignment

1. For a selected unit of study, "unwrap" the Priority Standards to determine the specific concepts and skills (what students need to know and be able to do) within those standards.

2. Create a graphic organizer (bulleted list, outline, concept map, or chart) that lists identified concepts under major headings; list each skill with its related concept(s) in side-by-side parenthetical notation.

3. Determine the degree of rigor for each skill by identifying its approximate level (1–6) according to Bloom's Taxonomy.

4. Decide the topical and/or broad Big Ideas (foundational understandings) derived from the particular "unwrapped" concepts and skills for that unit of study.

5. Write the Essential Questions that students will be expected to respond to with their own Big Idea responses. The following questions may help in doing so:

   • What questions will not only lead students to discover the Big Ideas on their own, but also *engage* them?

   • Can we write our Essential Questions to be more open-ended, so that students can respond to them in more than one way?

   • Can we make our Essential Questions *two-part* questions: one that asks a lower-level recall question (who, what, where, and/or when) and another that asks a higher-level, thought-provoking question (how and/or why)?

6. Identify any additional concepts or vocabulary from the supporting standards to add to the unit planning organizer. Along with the "unwrapped" concepts from the Priority Standards and any other unit-specific vocabulary, these will become the collective "word wall" of standards-based terms for the unit.

CHAPTER 12

Create the Unit Assessments— Pre-, Post-, and Progress- Monitoring Checks

The one true purpose of educational assessment is to correctly determine student understanding of the standards in focus and then to use those assessment results to inform, modify, adjust, enrich, and differentiate instruction to meet the learning needs of all students.

No statement to date has had a bigger impact on my thinking about assessment's essential purpose than this one, written by W. James Popham:

> "Teachers use test [results] in order to make inferences about their students' cognitive status. Once those score-based inferences have been made, the teacher then reaches instructional decisions based (at least in part) on those inferences. *Educational assessment revolves around inference making*." (emphasis added, 2003b, p. 60).

When educators understand that the primary reason for assessing their students and then diagnosing the results is to *accurately infer* what students need next in terms of their learning, assessment becomes as important as, if not more important than, the particular standards and lessons they are teaching.

There are six fundamental steps to using assessment results to inform instructional decision making:

1. **Know your purpose.** All of the assessment literature points to this underlying first step in planning assessment. Determine exactly what it is you want to find out, what it is you want the assessment to do, and why you are administering the assessment in the first place.

2. **Determine the appropriate assessment that will accomplish your identified purpose.** In this context, "appropriate" means the specific format(s) most likely to tell you what you want to know. The major assessment formats and their related types include: *selected-response* (multiple-choice, true/false, matching, fill-in using a provided word bank),

constructed-response (short or extended writing), and *performance-based* (physical demonstration).

3. **Select or create a quality assessment.** Take great care in choosing questions from an external source and/or crafting the assessment questions yourselves. If a question is faulty in any way, and students answer it incorrectly, educators will later have to determine whether the question itself was the problem or whether students simply did not know the content upon which it was based. Decide whether the planned questions included in the assessment will enable you to make an *accurate* inference as to what students know and can do. When completing this step, refer to published guidelines for selecting or creating quality selected- and constructed-response questions.

4. **Administer and score the assessment; analyze the assessment results.** Look for evidence of student learning, specific to your purpose, in the student responses. Conduct an item analysis, determining which questions individual students answered correctly and which ones they did not.

5. **Make an accurate inference.** This will be possible only if the assessment questions that you selected or created in step three are of quality and provide valid and reliable data.

6. **Adjust instructional decisions in a timely manner.** Determine instructional "next steps" for students based on the inferences you have made.

Formative, Summative, or Both

Assessments can be broadly classified as summative (assessment *of* learning) or formative (assessment *for* learning), but they can also be both. In our book *Common Formative Assessments: How to Connect Standards-Based Instruction and Assessment* (2006, pp. 27–28), Donald Viegut and I explain how an educator's *use* of assessment results is what determines whether a particular assessment can be categorized as formative (in-process), summative (ended), or both.

For example, a mid-unit quiz or an end-of-unit test is usually considered to be summative, especially when student papers are graded and recorded. But if an educator (1) carefully analyzes student responses to each of the assessment items on a summative quiz or test in order to diagnose individual student learning needs and then (2) uses that information to inform instruction accordingly, either the next day or in the next unit of study, the assessment is both summative *and* formative—the summative *results* are being used formatively.

Any kind of assessment can be rightly considered formative whenever educators provide students with the opportunity to revise their work or performance after receiving teacher feedback. This "assessment *as* learning" approach benefits students by helping them clarify or deepen their understanding of a problem or question they initially misunderstood and answered incorrectly.

For example, the single greatest practice I ever instituted as a classroom educator in terms of its impact on student learning and motivation occurred when I began having my upper elementary and middle school students create *with me* a scoring guide for a major project or performance task. Because the students helped decide the specific wording for the performance criteria, they knew exactly what they needed to do to receive a particular score on the project or task. When I showed students how to continually refer to the scoring guide as they worked on the assignment, they understood what the criteria actually meant in terms of what they needed to do to correctly complete the task.

When students self-assessed their work and found they had forgotten to include something listed on the scoring guide, most of them were able to go back and fix it right away. For those who did not know how to fix what was not yet correct, I was there to explain or show them what they still needed to do. When I evaluated their work products at the conclusion of the assignment, students saw that I was using the very same criteria they had used to create those products. And when my evaluation of their work matched theirs—as it nearly always did—they realized the fairness of the process and the amazing power scoring guides gave them to achieve success.

Common Formative Assessments

As regards rigorous curriculum design, common formative assessments (CFAs) are a perfect fit. In this context, "common" simply means an assessment based on the "unwrapped" Priority Standards for a unit of study that grade-alike and course-alike educators collaboratively create and administer to all of their students at approximately the same time. These unit-based assessments *for* learning, when aligned to summative assessments *of* learning (whether school-based, district- or school-division-based, or state- or province-based), provide educators with predictive value of how students are likely to perform on those summative assessment measures *in time* for them to "change up" instruction as needed.

Common formative assessments provide "snapshots" of student understanding of the unit's Priority Standards *only*. Together with classroom assessments and student work products based on the unit's Priority Standards *and* supporting standards, they produce a "photo album" of student understanding.

In 2008, Douglas Reeves wrote me an e-mail in response to a question from one of my seminar participants regarding the *frequency* of classroom assessment:

> "Whatever the frequency, the assessments don't need to reflect *every* part of the curriculum, but should be focused on the Priority Standards. That's why more frequent assessments that are brief and focused are better than infrequent assessments that attempt to be comprehensive. Also, teacher-made assessments are more likely to be aligned with classroom instruction than the proliferating off-the-shelf assessments that may claim 'alignment' with standards but may or may not be linked to classroom instruction."

Common formative assessment items are deliberately matched to the level of rigor indicated in the "unwrapped" skills of the Priority Standards for that particular unit. For example, level 2 of Bloom's Taxonomy represents the cognitive process level of understanding. Related level 2 verbs such as *compare* and *contrast* indicate the need for corresponding assessment questions that ask students to compare and contrast.

The actual items or questions on paper-and-pencil common formative assessments typically include a *blend* of formats, both selected-response and constructed-response. However, if the specific purpose of a common formative assessment can best be accomplished by having students write, then educators may decide to use only the constructed-response format to achieve that particular purpose.

Educators who teach performance-based content areas (visual and performing arts, physical education, career and technical education, world languages, library-media technology, etc.) for the most part create unit-based common formative assessments that enable students to *physically* demonstrate their understanding of the "unwrapped" Priority Standards concepts and skills.

When creating the instruments to score student performance on assessments, curriculum teams or collaborative grade-level teams make an *answer key* for the selected-response format and create a *scoring guide or rubric* for constructed-response and performance-based formats. The scoring guide—when purposely written with *objective* criteria—enables educators and students to receive quick and accurate feedback on student performance.

Regardless of the assessment formats used on a common formative assessment, student results are analyzed in grade-level or course-specific Data Teams to guide further instructional planning and delivery. "Singletons," educators who alone teach a particular grade level or course within an individual school, are not able to create a *common* assessment unless they have the opportunity to collaborate with their counterparts in other schools. Certainly they can independently follow the same guidelines for creating a quality assessment as their colleagues who create common assessments. However, the more opportunities they have to meet with those who teach the same content area or course in other schools, the more they will be able to create *common* formative assessments that they can administer and score separately but later meet to discuss together.

Whether curriculum designers create the assessments for widespread use throughout the school system, or whether educators create their own common formative assessments for individual units of study, the relevancy and usefulness of the assessments become particularly apparent when educators have ongoing collaborative opportunities to discuss the assessment results. The 10-step process I created for The Leadership and Learning Center's *Common Formative Assessments* seminar shows educators how to create a quality formative assessment that includes a blend of selected- and constructed-response questions with accompanying scoring guides.

After summarizing a body of research on the impact of formative assessments, distilled from four thousand studies spanning 40 years, Dylan Wiliam concludes: "When well-implemented, formative assessments can effectively *double* the speed of student learning" (Wiliam, 2007–2008, p. 36). Note the beginning phrase, "When well-implemented." It is not enough just to *administer* formative assessments. To realize their full potential for improving student achievement, such assessments must be carefully constructed, student results must be thoughtfully analyzed, inferences must be accurately made, and subsequent instruction must be differentiated to meet student learning needs accordingly.

The Scoring Guide

Before presenting my recommended steps for creating the different curricular unit assessments, I would like to first showcase one of the most powerful tools educators can use to expedite the scoring process and gain *timely* feedback on student performance. This tool is the scoring guide, or, as it is more often referred to in education circles, the rubric.

Used in conjunction with constructed-response written assessments and performance-based assessments, the scoring guide is a written set of *specific* criteria describing different levels of student proficiency relative to those assessments.

The biggest challenge I see with scoring guides continues to be the vague and highly subjective language used to describe each performance level. Words like "some, few, many, most, little, generally, clearly, elaborately, appropriately" and so on can be interpreted in multiple ways, making it difficult—and time-consuming—for educators to be able to individually decide or collaboratively agree upon an accurate score for a student's work. Therefore, specificity in wording and format on a scoring guide is critical. Without it, there can be no reliability in terms of the scoring guide's consistency.

Key attributes of effective scoring guides include:

- Specific, measurable, observable, "student-friendly" language understood by students, teachers, and parents
- Task requirements and scoring guide criteria that fit "hand-to-glove"
- Models of student work matched to the scoring guide criteria so students can see how the criteria "translate" into actual work products
- Criteria provided *before* students begin task
- Student access to criteria *during* task
- Criteria used to evaluate student work product or performance *after* task

The first design step in creating a scoring guide is to determine the different performance levels. The designated names, labels, and/or numbers of these performance levels vary widely from location to location, but typically they include four and sometimes five distinct categories as follows:

- Advanced or Exemplary
- Goal and/or Proficient
- Basic or Progressing
- Below Basic, Beginning, or Not Yet Proficient

The most effective way to create a scoring guide that incorporates all of these attributes is to first decide the criteria for the "Goal" level, since those criteria represent the desired level of performance for all students to demonstrate. To create the criteria for this category, simply refer to the *details* of the assessment task instructions and underline the specific elements students are to include in their written product, performance, or demonstration. Write those elements as verb phrases in the goal section of the scoring guide (e.g., "identifies the attributes of one main character in the story").

Next, create the *advanced* or *exemplary* level that begins, "All 'Goal' criteria met *plus*:" and then add other criteria describing what those same goal criteria might "look like" at this higher level (e.g., "identifies the attributes of two main characters in the story, noting similarities and differences between them"). Spending the time to thoughtfully create criteria for this top level of the scoring guide is one of the most effective ways educators can enhance the rigor of an assigned learning task. This not only benefits the students needing enrichment and extension opportunities, but also provides a "ladder of success" for *all* students to climb—*if* the criteria are objectively worded. Words and phrases such as "elaborate, highly detailed, extensive use of engaging vocabulary" that are typically used in the top level of rubrics do not give students the specificity they need in order to produce a quality product that represents those criteria.

The third step in designing a scoring guide is to write the criteria for the *progressing* level. It is at this level where the difficulty in writing rubrics really shows up. For years, I would attempt to write one of the progressing-level criteria with a phrase such as this: "May not include all the attributes of the main character." Not happy with that, I would soon succumb to the easy way out of this dilemma by resorting to words like "includes some, few, many, or most of the attributes," and so on. Yet my students always wanted to know what those words meant in terms of a specific *quantity*. That led me to the solution that I have shared with Pre-K–12 educators ever since: include only *one* criterion for the progressing level that reads, "Meets _____ of the Goal criteria," with a quantity inserted in the blank. This approach to scoring guide design has repeatedly generated a positive reaction from educators everywhere.

For example, if there are five criteria for the "Goal" level, the *progressing* category reads, "Meets three to four of the 'Goal' criteria." Since the "Goal" criteria represent the main target for all students to hit, if all of those criteria are not yet met, then students are still *progressing* toward that level of performance and quality. Once those criteria *are* met (by allowing students the opportunity to revise their work), the evaluation changes from "progressing" to "goal."

This same idea can be applied to the final level of the scoring guide: "beginning" or "not yet"—words I prefer since they imply an optimistic belief that the student *will* achieve the "Goal" eventually. These terms are certainly more encouraging than the rubric I once saw that had the title "Why Bother?" for its lowest level!

Although that is an extreme example, almost invariably the wording in the bottom category of the scoring guide is negative and discouraging, with descriptors that begin with the word *no*: no character attributes; no details; no comparisons, no, no, no! The alternative to using this negative wording is to write two phrases: "Meets fewer than _____ of the 'Goal' criteria"; and "Task to be repeated after reteaching." The message to the student from the teacher is clear: you still have more work to do, and I am here to help you.

Creating the scoring guide in this way simplifies the entire process by eliminating subjective and negatively worded criteria for the below-"Goal" levels. Such objective wording makes *quick and accurate scoring* by educators (and students who self-assess) easy to accomplish. Equally important, the value of this streamlined approach is that it keeps students and educators focused on the specific criteria needed for *successful* completion of the task, product, or performance.

Two Performance-Based Scoring Guides

In the upcoming section, "The End-of-Unit Assessment," I explain how to apply this scoring guide design approach to a paper-and-pencil, constructed-response assessment question. Here, however, I present two sample *performance*-based scoring guides developed by West Haven, Connecticut, secondary physical education curriculum writers and middle school digital arts curriculum writers for their respective instructional programs (Figures 12.1 and 12.2). Notice how the scoring guide criteria in both examples are specific, objective, and focused on the desired criteria students are to demonstrate. The other performance levels provide descriptors *in relation to* those criteria. In keeping with their state's reporting of

 FIGURE 12.1 West Haven Physical Education Rubric

Advanced
- ☐ Arrives on time to class
- ☐ Is dressed appropriately
- ☐ Stays on task and actively participates
- ☐ Follows rules and safety practices
- ☐ Is courteous and cooperative and demonstrates sportsmanship

Proficient

Meets 4 of the 5 "Advanced" criteria

Average

Meets 3 of the 5 "Advanced" criteria

Needs improvement

Meets 2 of the 5 "Advanced" criteria

Needs Intervention

Meets fewer than 2 of the 5 "Advanced" criteria

student performance data on state tests, the educators have used *five* levels rather than four, even though the headings of those levels vary by content area.

The scoring guide in Figure 12.1 is a *behavioral* rubric, one that the physical education curriculum designers determined to be appropriate for use again and again with large numbers of students while they are learning and demonstrating the key skills specific to several different sports.

A Powerful Testimonial

Middle school fine arts educator Kathryn Shea, one of the authors of the scoring guide for a digital arts project shown in Figure 12.2, shared with me how powerful the results of using the scoring guide have been for her students—and for her.

"How could this one element—a *rubric*—change my classroom learning environment so dramatically? The answer is that it took away all the fear of the unknown, took away all the worry of failing, and opened up the students' minds to the joy of the creative process. . . . As an art educator, I have always prided myself in creating an environment where the students felt comfortable and open to experiment with the media, a place to relax and be creative. But this rubric brought things to a whole new level; it put all the control in the students' hands. Suddenly they knew *exactly* what they had to do to meet 'Goal,' as well as what to do in order to go 'above and beyond.'

"One initially doubtful student summed it all up. He told me he was not looking forward to my class because he felt he was not good in art. When we went over the scoring guide together, he stated: 'So let me get this straight. We do what the rubric says, and we earn an A? Hmm . . . You set this up so we really can't fail. If you are doing that, then I have to give it a shot. What would be the point not to?'

"Needless to say, I was floored. The students now 'get it'—they self-assess using the rubric I provide them with each major project; they answer the Essential Questions with their own Big Ideas; they ask meaningful questions without being prompted. The empowerment this process has given them has been literally life-changing, here in my little corner of the art education world!"

Creating the Unit Assessments and Scoring Instruments

With the standards-based foundation of the unit now set—the "unwrapped" concepts and skills with related Bloom's Taxonomy levels, the Big Ideas, and the Essential Questions—it seems only logical to next begin looking through resource materials and begin planning the corresponding instruction.

FIGURE
12.2   **West Haven Fine Arts Rubric**

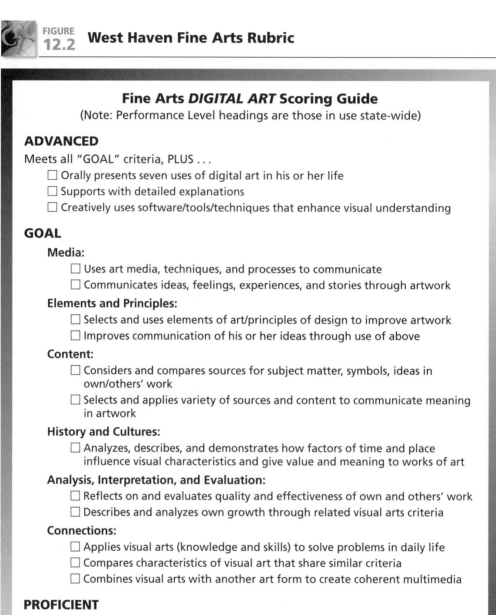

Fine Arts *DIGITAL ART* Scoring Guide
(Note: Performance Level headings are those in use state-wide)

ADVANCED

Meets all "GOAL" criteria, PLUS . . .

☐ Orally presents seven uses of digital art in his or her life

☐ Supports with detailed explanations

☐ Creatively uses software/tools/techniques that enhance visual understanding

GOAL

Media:

☐ Uses art media, techniques, and processes to communicate

☐ Communicates ideas, feelings, experiences, and stories through artwork

Elements and Principles:

☐ Selects and uses elements of art/principles of design to improve artwork

☐ Improves communication of his or her ideas through use of above

Content:

☐ Considers and compares sources for subject matter, symbols, ideas in own/others' work

☐ Selects and applies variety of sources and content to communicate meaning in artwork

History and Cultures:

☐ Analyzes, describes, and demonstrates how factors of time and place influence visual characteristics and give value and meaning to works of art

Analysis, Interpretation, and Evaluation:

☐ Reflects on and evaluates quality and effectiveness of own and others' work

☐ Describes and analyzes own growth through related visual arts criteria

Connections:

☐ Applies visual arts (knowledge and skills) to solve problems in daily life

☐ Compares characteristics of visual art that share similar criteria

☐ Combines visual arts with another art form to create coherent multimedia

PROFICIENT

Meets 9–11 of the "GOAL" criteria

BASIC

Meets 7–8 of the "GOAL" criteria

BELOW BASIC

Meets FEWER than 7 of the "GOAL" criteria

Lesson retaught differently. Student repeats task(s) until proficient.

Authors: Kelly Flynn, Bailey Middle School; Kathryn Shea and Julie Tomcheski, Carrigan Middle School, West Haven, Connecticut

However, since these foundational elements represent the end-of-unit learning goals for students to attain, I recommend that curriculum designers *first* create the end-of-unit assessment that will provide evidence of whether or not students have achieved those learning goals. *Then* design the means—the lessons and learning experiences—to prepare students for that culminating assessment. By aligning instruction and learning activities to the end-of-unit assessment, rather than the other way around, educators are better able to make all instructional decisions in relationship to students arriving successfully at the standards destination.

Beginning with the end in mind, curriculum designers or individual grade-level and course-specific teams of educators are now ready to construct the three different kinds of assessments that are part of each unit of study. Created in this order, these are:

- The end-of-unit *post*-assessment
- The start-of-unit *pre*-assessment
- The *during*-unit progress-monitoring checks

The End-of-Unit Post-Assessment

The following eight steps provide curriculum designers, "singletons," and collaborative teams of educators with a recommended sequence for designing the end-of-unit assessment:

Step 1: Since the purpose of the end-of-unit post-assessment is to accurately measure student understanding of the unit's "unwrapped" Priority Standards, first decide which of the three major assessment formats (selected-response, constructed-response, and/or performance-based) will best achieve the assessment's purpose.

Step 2: Reference the graphic organizer for the specific "unwrapped" Priority Standards concepts and skills upon which to base the assessment.

Step 3: Practice writing an assessment question—in any of the three major formats—to closely match *one* of the "unwrapped" skills and its corresponding level of Bloom's Taxonomy.

Step 4: For selected-response questions, make all of the distracters *plausible.* The traditional multiple-choice test question provides one correct answer choice and three distracters (incorrect answer choices). Of the three distracters, one is "almost right" and the other two are usually "out in left field." Students learn to eliminate the left-field wrong answers so as to have a fifty-fifty chance of selecting the correct answer from the remaining two choices.

When writing a selected-response question, try writing the distracters so they are *all* plausible and/or reflect common student errors or misconceptions. Doing so will increase the rigor of the question, lifting both the level of related instruction and the level of student thinking necessary to answer the question correctly.

As suggested by my colleague Tony Flach, two guiding questions to assist educators when determining the plausibility of distracters are: "What errors or misconceptions are students likely to make or have when working on this particular 'unwrapped' concept and/or skill?" and "What responses would result from those errors or misconceptions?"

Here is a summary of a short reading passage followed by an example of a related multiple-choice question that has one correct answer and two plausible distracters:

A BUCKET OF TROUBLE

An East Indian folk tale tells of two frogs on a farm that had the misfortune of jumping into a pail of fresh milk left near the barn by the careless son of the farmer. The frogs were unable to jump out of the pail and had no recourse but to paddle continuously around in the milk in order to stay afloat. The larger of the two finally gave up and sank beneath the white waves, while the other frog kept on, determined to keep on paddling as long as he had breath in his little body. At last, thoroughly exhausted and unable to swim another stroke, he began to sink to his demise, only to find himself resting upon something solid beneath him. With one final exertion, he jumped from the large pad of butter that he had churned by his incessant paddling out of the milk pail to freedom.

The "unwrapped" concepts, skill, and level of Bloom's Taxonomy in focus are these: Level 4—DRAW (inferences, conclusions, and generalizations). They are represented in the rigor of the following multiple-choice question:

This tale *best* illustrates which one of the following generalizations:
a. Danger can show up in the most ordinary places.
b. Events sometimes take a surprising turn if you refuse to quit.
c. Everyone fails some of the time.

The correct answer choice is "b." The two distracters, "a" and "c," are *plausible,* even though neither of them is the *best* generalization within the context of the tale.

Such a question reflects the rigor of the targeted skill, requiring thought to distinguish the best answer from among the three plausible answer choices.

The following *constructed-response* item, directly related to the same multiple-choice question above, incorporates into one question *all* of the listed concepts, skills, and approximate Bloom's Taxonomy levels. Notice how the criteria on the corresponding scoring guide reflect the "hand-to-glove" fit with the underlined task directions:

- Level 2—PROVIDE (supporting evidence)
- Level 4—DRAW (inferences, conclusions, generalizations)
- Level 5—SUPPORT (inferences, conclusions with text evidence, prior knowledge)

> ***Student Directions:*** Write <u>one or more paragraphs</u> <u>defending your answer choice</u> for the multiple choice question above. <u>State your choice</u> and <u>three examples to</u> <u>support it from the tale</u> *A Bucket of Trouble.* Write a <u>concluding sentence that summarizes or supports</u> your answer choice. Your writing will be scored using the criteria listed on the Constructed-Response Scoring Guide below:

Advanced

Meets all "Goal" criteria *plus*:
- ☐ Includes reasons why selected choice is better than other two choices
- ☐ Includes real-life connection or experience in support of selected choice

Goal

- ☐ States answer choice
- ☐ Supports answer choice with three examples from tale
- ☐ Writes one or more paragraphs
- ☐ Writes concluding sentence that summarizes or supports answer choice

Progressing

Meets 2–3 of the "Goal" criteria

Beginning

Meets fewer than 2 of the "Goal" criteria

Task to be repeated after reteaching

Teacher's Evaluation_____

Comments regarding student's performance:

_____

_____

Step 5: Using the selected-response format, the constructed-response format, the performance-based format, or a *blend* of formats, repeat the same assessment item writing process for the remainder of the questions planned for the end-of-unit post-assessment. Format questions similar to the types of questions students are likely to see on district or school division benchmark assessments, end-of-course assessments, and state or provincial exams. Be sure to include correct *standards* terminology, not simplified terms (e.g., identify, not label; rotation, not turn).

Step 6: *Limit the total number of assessment questions so that student papers can be quickly scored.* General recommendations for the total number of selected- *and* constructed-response questions on the end-of-unit post-assessment for different grade levels are as follows:

- Grades K–1, five or six
- Grades 2–3, eight to ten
- Grades 4–5, ten to twelve
- Grades 6–8, twelve to fifteen
- Grades 9–12, fifteen to twenty-five (maximum)

For assessments using constructed-response and performance-based formats *only*, the total number of items will obviously be fewer. Keep in mind this question when deciding how many items to include: "How many questions do we need to include in order for us to make an *accurate inference* regarding what students understand?"

Step 7: If creating selected-response questions, make a corresponding answer key. If designing constructed-response or performance-based items, create a scoring guide, or rubric, by following the guidelines and examples provided earlier in this chapter.

Step 8: Plan how the students will respond to the unit's Essential Questions with the Big Ideas stated in their own words—either in writing or verbally. The daily focus that Essential Questions give to instructional planning and delivery during the unit carries over to the end-of-unit post-assessment as well. Whereas the selected-response and constructed-response questions are specifically based upon the "unwrapped" Priority Standards for the unit, students' verbal or written responses to the Essential Questions will provide evidence of what the students are likely to remember beyond the "borders" of that one unit of study.

The Start-of-Unit Pre-Assessment

Here are five key benefits to educators that can result from administering a pre-assessment to students at the start of a unit of study:

- Pre-tests (formative assessments) help teachers decide where to aim early instruction.

- Pre-assessments indicate what sorts of skills, knowledge, or attitudes students already have or do not have.

- Pre-assessments reflect "enabling sub-skills" (skills necessary for the unit of study) (Popham, 2003b, p. 10).

- A pre-test/post-test design provides a matching set of "bookend" assessments that are either the same (or alternate forms of the same) assessment.

- "The improvement between the pre-test and post-test constitutes credible evidence of the teacher's instructional success" (Popham, 2003a, p. 51).

Whenever educators begin discussing the hot topic of pre-assessing students at the start of a unit of study, the talk turns lively—and polarizing. The opposing viewpoints seem to converge around these three basic positions: (1) no pre-assessments, (2) aligned pre-assessments, (3) "mirrored" pre-assessments.

Position # 1: No Pre-Assessments

Educators in favor of the first position—no pre-assessments—typically give the following reasons:

- Students want to know if the pre-assessment "is going to count." If it does not, they often will not do their best to demonstrate what they actually know, thereby negating the main reason for giving it in the first place.

- Students experience frustration when they try to respond to the questions but don't know the answers, even though the teacher has carefully explained that the pre-assessment is "only so I can find out what I need to teach you."

- Teachers assume, correctly or not, that the majority of students will be unable to answer any of the questions, since the content upon which the questions are based has not yet been taught—unless the pre-assessment includes a *blend* of students' prior knowledge and skills with concepts and skills yet to be learned.

• Teachers cannot justify the loss of instructional time when the benefits to giving a pre-assessment seem so negligible. They believe that the same time could be much better spent actually teaching students the unit content.

• Teachers conclude that the time it takes to develop, administer, score, and analyze pre-assessment results isn't worth it, citing any and all of the above reasons.

Position # 2: Aligned Pre-Assessments

Educators that favor the second position—aligned pre-assessments—cite these reasons:

• Administering an "aligned" pre-assessment (same concepts and skills as end-of-unit post-assessment, but with fewer questions) will provide teachers with a good starting point for determining what students currently know and can do prior to actual instruction.

• Aligned pre-assessments are shorter in length than the post-assessments, taking less time to administer and score, while still providing important diagnostic information relative to students' current understanding of the unit's "unwrapped" Priority Standards.

• Analyzing the student results from an aligned pre-assessment may actually save instructional time *if* students demonstrate that they already know some of the "unwrapped" concepts and skills. Conversely, if students have little or no understanding of the concepts and skills, a shorter, aligned assessment will provide that same diagnostic information more quickly. Two supporting arguments worth considering: In math, if a student cannot correctly solve one or two regrouping problems, why give that student *five* regrouping problems? In science, if a student cannot identify and explain *one* phase of the moon, why expect that student to identify and explain *all* phases of the moon?

• Teachers can differentiate instruction for any students demonstrating proficiency on the pre-assessment (either aligned or "mirrored") by enriching and extending their understanding relative to the "unwrapped" Priority Standards and supporting standards in focus. As a result, these students will not have to sit through instruction of concepts that they already know and skills they can already demonstrate, but instead will receive learning experiences and related instruction that are individualized for their specific learning needs.

Position # 3: "Mirrored" Pre-Assessments

Educators that support the third position—"mirrored" pre-assessments—offer these reasons:

- Administering a "mirrored" pre-assessment (exact same number and type of questions as on the post-assessment) will provide teachers with a true "apples-to-apples" comparison of what students have learned from the beginning to the end of a unit of study.

- "Mirrored" pre-assessments are likely to provide more statistical reliability of the growth in student learning when grade-alike and course-alike teachers analyze student results during the Data Team meetings that follow the scoring of the pre- and post-assessments.

- "Mirrored" pre-test results (when shared with students at the start of the unit) enable the students to be an active part of the assessment process by setting personal goals for learning based on the same tool used for measuring growth from start to finish.

Keeping always in mind the true purpose of assessment—to pinpoint student learning needs in order to inform instructional decision making—consider this question: "Will an *aligned* pre-assessment with fewer questions provide educators with sufficient information to begin instruction, or would a "mirrored" pre-assessment provide a more comprehensive diagnostic that would better inform subsequent instructional decisions?"

Although I can certainly understand the reasons cited above for *not* administering pre-assessments, the majority of educators agree that there needs to be a "starting point" data set to indicate what students know and can do with regard to the content of a new unit of study about to commence. Otherwise, there is no accurate way for individual educators or instructional Data Team members to accurately measure *growth* in student learning from the beginning to the end of a unit. Also, many educators are sharing pre-assessment data with their students to involve them in setting their own personal goals for improvement that will be measured by results on the end-of-unit post-assessment.

For these reasons, I am advocating *matching* pre- and post-assessments that "bookend" each unit of study. Whether these matching assessments should be *aligned* or *mirrored* is a decision that needs to be made locally. However, I strongly suggest that educators who will be implementing these units in their own instructional programs have an active voice in making this decision. Doing so will greatly minimize the typical polarization of opinions that occurs whenever the topic of pre-assessment arises.

The During-Unit Progress-Monitoring Checks

Whereas educators hold differing viewpoints with regard to pre-assessments, they all seem to be in general agreement about the value of regularly using progress-monitoring checks. Sometimes referred to as assessment "dipsticks," progress-monitoring checks are short, frequent, informal, nongraded assessments that help educators accurately infer student understanding. When *intentionally aligned to the end-of-unit post-assessment*, such mini-assessments help educators decide what instructional changes they need to make in order to help individual students better learn the "unwrapped" concepts and skills that will be more formally assessed at the end of the unit.

Learning Progressions, Revisited

In Chapter 8, I introduced the idea of curriculum designers thinking about "learning progressions" as they prepare pacing calendars for grade-specific and course-specific units of study in a particular content area. It is equally important to revisit this concept as it relates to progress-monitoring checks.

In *Transformative Assessment* (2008), W. James Popham devotes an entire chapter to the topic of learning progressions. The information is so relevant and important for curriculum designers who author the units of study, and for educators who implement those units, that I consider his chapter a "must-read."*

Popham defines a *learning progression* as being composed of the "step-by-step building blocks students are presumed to need in order to successfully attain a more distant, designated instructional outcome. The more 'distant' instructional outcome, known as the *target curricular aim*, is typically a skill ... and usually a significant skill at that—the kind of learning outcome requiring a number of lessons for students to achieve it" (p. 24). These building blocks are ultimately arranged in "an instructionally defensible sequence" (p. 47).

---

*Popham also recommends the "reader-friendly" analysis of learning progressions by Margaret Heritage (2007).

Popham then makes explicit the vital connection between learning progressions and formative assessment:

- Learning progressions are "the backdrop against which teachers and students can determine *when to collect . . .* evidence regarding students' current status. They provide a framework that helps teachers identify *appropriate adjustment-decision points* as well as the kinds of en route assessment evidence they need" (emphasis added, p. 27).

- Formative assessment "is not the occasional administration of classroom tests; it's an integral dimension of ongoing instruction whereby teachers and students adjust what they're doing" (p. 29). Teachers should assess students "before proceeding to the next building block in the [learning] progression, the mastery of which is believed to be dependent on mastery of its predecessors" (p. 30).

In other words, educators should administer progress-monitoring checks *in tandem with* each "chunk" of critical instruction related to the "unwrapped" Priority Standards taught throughout the unit. They can then use those assessment results to make accurate inferences and adjust instruction accordingly for individual students, small groups, and/or the entire class. Due to the *frequency* of these informal checks for understanding, they need to be short and quick.

Dylan Wiliam and his writing colleagues, Siobhan Leahy, Christine Lyon, and Marnie Thompson (Leahy et al., 2005), refer to these quick checks for understanding as "hinge-point" questions: "Teachers can also use questions to check on student understanding before continuing the lesson. We call this a 'hinge point' in the lesson because the lesson can go in different directions depending on student responses. By explicitly integrating these hinge points into instruction, teachers can make their teaching more responsive to their students' needs in real time" (p. 22).

To engage *all* students in responding to these progress-monitoring checks, the authors offer examples of ways educators can do so: providing students with individual dry-erase boards so they can write and hold up their answers simultaneously; giving each student a set of four cards labeled A, B, C, and D, and asking a question in the multiple-choice format (p. 22); and one high school algebra teacher's inventive use of green and red "traffic light" cards that each student uses to signal personal understanding, with green meaning "understand" and red meaning "don't understand" (p. 23).

Students also benefit greatly from these formative "assessments *as* learning." By responding to a teacher's short, frequent checks for understanding and then getting immediate verbal or written feedback from the teacher that confirms a correct answer or clarifies an incorrect answer, a student can better reflect upon what he or she already knows and still needs to learn.

Educators are at liberty to create and use whatever kinds of quick, informal progress-monitoring checks they believe will help them to achieve this purpose. Different examples include: "thumbs up/thumbs down" student responses to a teacher's orally checking for understanding during a lesson; start-of-class warm-up problems or questions; end-of-class quick discussions about the lesson's connection to the Essential Questions; "exit slips" with individual student responses to a lesson summary question—the possibilities are unlimited.

Here is how one middle school educator in West Haven, Connecticut, used a progress-monitoring check to see how her students were coming along with their understanding of the unit's Essential Questions. Near the end of the class period, she distributed colored Post-It Note squares to each student. She asked the students to write what they thought the Big Idea was for each of the unit's Essential Questions. Then she asked the students to share their individual responses with the other students in their cooperative groups, encouraging them to add any additional information they heard from their group members to their own individual Post-It notes. When finished, the students signed their names on their notes and posted them on the appropriate chart papers displaying the Essential Questions as they exited the class.

The educator said that by the time two or three classes had posted their responses, the hundreds of colorful squares created quite a visual display. Yet the power in the practice became evident when she saw the visible evidence of her students' learning, evidence that she was able to use in the days that followed to further clarify and deepen her students' understanding of the unit's Big Ideas.

Reader's Assignment

Create the end-of-unit *post*-assessment and then the matching pre-assessment for the curricular unit of study you are designing. Follow this recommended ten-step summary for doing so:

1. Decide which of the three major assessment formats (selected-response, constructed-response, and/or performance-based) to use.

2. Reference the graphic organizer for the specific "unwrapped" Priority Standards concepts and skills students need to know and be able to do by the end of the unit. Base all of the assessment questions on those concepts and skills, making sure that *all* of them are sufficiently represented in the questions.

3. Practice writing an assessment question—in any of the three major formats—to closely match one of the skills and its corresponding level of Bloom's Taxonomy.

4. For selected-response questions, make all of the distracters *plausible* and reflect common student errors and misconceptions.

5. Repeat the same assessment item writing process for the remainder of the questions planned. Format the questions so they are similar to the types of questions students are likely to see on district or school division benchmark assessments, end-of-course assessments, and state or provincial tests. Remember to use correct standards terminology (the actually wording of the "unwrapped" concepts and skills), and not simplified terms.

6. Referencing the suggested guidelines provided earlier in the chapter for the number of questions to ask at the different grade levels, decide how many total assessment items to include so that (a) the assessments can be *quickly* scored, and (b) educators can make an *accurate inference* regarding student understanding.

7. For selected-response questions, make a corresponding answer key. For constructed-response or performance-based items, create a scoring guide, or rubric.

8. Plan how the students will respond to the unit's Essential Questions with Big Ideas stated in their own words.

9. Discuss the issue of pre-assessments with curriculum designers and educators. Decide whether the pre-assessment will be "aligned" or "mirrored" and create the unit's pre-assessment accordingly.

10. Provide suggestions or examples of different progress-monitoring checks educators can use while delivering the unit of study.

CHAPTER 13
Plan Engaging Learning Experiences

With the foundational standards and assessment components in place for a given unit of study, curriculum designers can now turn their attention to creating the *means* for students to comprehend the unit's "unwrapped" concepts, skills, and Big Ideas—the engaging learning experiences.

I have intentionally chosen the phrase "engaging learning experiences" as opposed to the more traditional "lessons and activities." *Engaging* is synonymous with interesting and compelling. *Experiences* produce personal insights that are deeper and longer lasting than explanations. For students, a rigorous curriculum ought to be both engaging and experiential. It needs to provide them with powerful learning opportunities intentionally designed to motivate, challenge, and support them in making important "aha's" and connections on their own.

This does not mean that every single learning activity within a unit of study must be one dazzling learning experience after another. Certain instructional lessons and activities may not necessarily be "dazzling," but are definitely necessary in terms of developing students' understanding. These include the specific lessons and learning activities suggested or prescribed in textbooks, programs, workbooks, articles, handbooks, and other published resource materials, along with the tasks and materials educators develop on their own to augment these instructional resources.

However, to transform curriculum from the conventional series of routine lessons and activities into a dynamic, interactive set of learning experiences, educators need a new paradigm. Rather than describing the customary types of learning activities educators are already quite familiar with, this chapter will focus on how to envision and create that new paradigm.

A New Curriculum Paradigm

A rigorous, 21st-century curriculum ought to provide students with a dynamic *blend* of customary learning activities *and* authentic and engaging learning experiences. Such engaging experiences ought to reflect these key attributes:

- Authentic (genuine, valid, real)
- Relevant to life situations and contexts
- Interdisciplinary (as distinguished from "thematic")
- Use embedded informational technologies
- Highly motivational, not routine
- Mentally stimulating, thought-provoking
- Incorporate the full spectrum of thinking-skill rigor, especially: reasoning, application, analysis, synthesis, creativity, self-assessment, and reflection
- Include both collaborative and individual work

Actually, such attributes are not at all new in educational curriculum and pedagogy. Many veteran educators have incorporated them into their instruction and assessment practices throughout their careers. However, there has been a noticeable decline in such engaging learning experiences for students over the past decade owing to the intense pressures educators face to "cover" the standards and prepare students for high-stakes tests. It is now time to revive these attributes and incorporate them into the regular curriculum.

In her 1997 landmark work *The Right to Learn,* Linda Darling-Hammond wrote, "Authentic performance is critical to the development of competence. Thus, meaningful performances in real-world contexts need to become both the stuff of the curriculum and the focus of assessment events" (p. 115). In her November 2009 Webinar addressing the topic of international standards and assessments, Darling-Hammond emphasized the use of authentic performance as a powerful means for students to demonstrate on a deep level what they know and can do. Connecting her long-standing endorsement of authentic performance to the educational reform initiatives taking place throughout the world, she cited the following commonalities in all of these initiatives:

- Emphasize expectations for higher-order skills along with rich content that represents core concepts and modes of inquiry.
- Teach less, learn more: Focus the curriculum on standards that are fewer, higher, and deeper to allow more time to apply ideas in depth.
- Increase emphasis on project work and tasks requiring research, analysis, application, self-assessment, and production.
- Expand assessment of these intellectual skills, including the use of performance tasks on tests and in the classroom.
- Develop assessments *of, as,* and *for* learning.

• Arm teachers with learning progressions and greater capacity to use a wide range of assessment tools to analyze and support learning.

Authentic Performance Assessment

There is one comprehensive instruction, learning, curriculum, and assessment model that embodies all these attributes and commonalities. That model is authentic performance assessment, and the reason I regard this particular model as *comprehensive* is that it serves multiple purposes simultaneously.

In terms of *instruction*, it enables educators to teach the Priority Standards and supporting standards through inquiry and problem solving within the context of the performance task they are about to assign to their students. Instruction becomes highly relevant when tied to a specific purpose. When educators use performance assessment as part of their unit instruction and delivery, they are able to "watch students solve problems and infer reasoning proficiency, observe and evaluate skills as they are being performed, and assess the attributes of created products" (Stiggins, 2005).

In terms of *learning*, students have the opportunity to engage in incremental learning experiences—learning progressions—that are designed to help them make their own connections to the standards in focus while developing both conceptual understanding (concepts) and procedural understanding (skills). Performance tasks often "scaffold" from one task to the next in terms of the cognitive demand they place on students, building from foundational concepts and skills to the more rigorous skills of application, synthesis, evaluation, and creativity. Other times they require students to exercise the full range of thinking skills within one task alone. In doing so, students have the opportunity to demonstrate more than just one isolated procedural skill.

In terms of *curriculum*, performance tasks provide the "what" educators will use to give their students truly engaging learning experiences pertinent to the "unwrapped" concepts and skills within any given unit of study. Performance tasks incorporate project-based learning and inquiry-based learning, two powerful learning approaches often absent from more traditional curricula. These active modes of learning do much to promote student discovery of the Big Ideas, the end learning goals of each unit of study.

Last, in terms of *assessment*, performance tasks provide multiple benefits, to educators and to students. Performance tasks provide educators with a "window" into student understanding, giving them the formative diagnostic data they need to monitor and adjust instruction for different students. For students, performance tasks enable them to construct their own understanding of the standards in focus through active participation, not just passive listening and seeing, as they exercise the full range of thinking skills. Aided by task-specific scoring guides that give explicit criteria for producing a quality product or performance, students are able to continually self-assess and reflect upon what they are learning—genuine assessment *as* learning.

The *Making Standards Work* Performance Assessment Model

No mention of performance assessment can be made without citing the contributions of Douglas Reeves. His *Making Standards Work* (1996–2004) performance assessment model reconceptualized the culminating project or performance for a unit of study that has been a staple of American classrooms for years. Rather than having students wait until the *end* of a unit to apply the concepts and skills they had been learning to one big project or major performance event, Reeves presented an alternative approach. He defined "performance assessment" as a *collection* of several related standards-based performance tasks, distributed throughout a unit of study, that progressively develop and reveal student understanding of the standards. The intent of using several performance tasks is not to *replace* the end-of-unit project. Rather it is to increase student understanding of the targeted standards of a unit by providing students with several "mini-culminating events" to complete along the way. Interdisciplinary by design, these three to five performance tasks also help students make connections beyond a single topic of study to other subject matter areas.

For example, during a four-week unit of study, every few days a teacher assigns students a different performance task with an accompanying scoring guide to coincide with that particular "chunk" of the unit. The teacher provides related lessons, materials, and other instructional resources as needed. Students engage in each task, individually and/or collaboratively, producing a corresponding work product or performance that is then evaluated using the scoring guide for that task. Never just randomly selected "fun learning activities," performance tasks are instead deliberately chosen to align with the particular "unwrapped" Priority Standards and supporting standards for that unit.

In my early years of guiding educators through the various steps of the *Making Standards Work* performance assessment model, I began incorporating the additional components—"unwrapped" concepts and skills, Big Ideas, and Essential Questions—into the original model, to reveal the specificity of the Priority Standards and supporting standards upon which the performance tasks were based. Figure 13.1, originally designed by my colleague Lisa Almeida and Diana Greene, Deputy Superintendent of Marion County Schools, Florida, illustrates the intentional connections between *all* of the key standards-based components of an effective performance assessment, including the engaging scenario that is described in the next section.

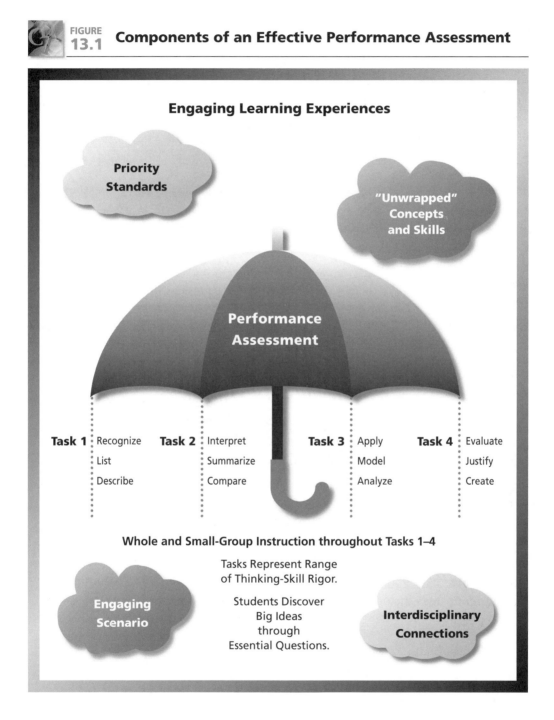

FIGURE 13.1 Components of an Effective Performance Assessment

Figure 13.2 illustrates the connections between the performance tasks and the pre- and post-assessments that "bookend" the unit of study. Note how the informal, progress-monitoring checks take place throughout the unit as the students are moving through the performance tasks and receiving related teacher instruction.

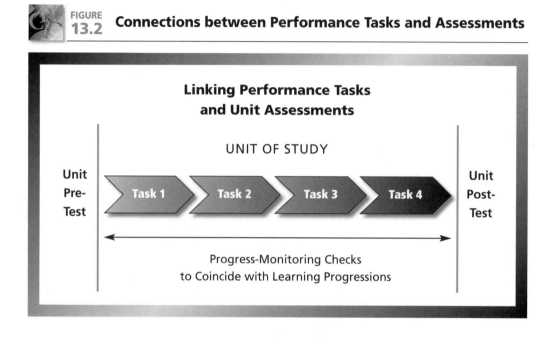

FIGURE 13.2 **Connections between Performance Tasks and Assessments**

Linking Performance Tasks and Unit Assessments

UNIT OF STUDY

Unit Pre-Test | Task 1 | Task 2 | Task 3 | Task 4 | Unit Post-Test

Progress-Monitoring Checks
to Coincide with Learning Progressions

Engaging Scenarios

What better way to introduce an engaging learning experience to students than to present them with a purpose-setting context specifically designed to motivate them? Many educators remember Madeline Hunter's first step in the lesson-design process—the anticipatory set. Its purpose was to "hook" and engage students in the lesson about to commence. Douglas Reeves created a similar device for educators to use when introducing a performance assessment to students—the engaging scenario.

Jay McTighe and John Brown (2005), referencing the backward-design process described in *Understanding by Design* (Wiggins and McTighe, 1998), recommend that authentic tasks include features represented by the acronym "GRASPS":

- A real-world *Goal*
- A meaningful *Role* for the student
- Authentic (or simulated) real-world *Audience(s)*
- A contextualized *Situation* that involves real-world application
- Student-generated culminating *Products and Performances*
- Consensus-driven performance *Standards* (criteria) for judging success

McTighe and Brown write: "Performance tasks having these features provide meaningful learning targets for learners, worthy performance goals for teaching, and the kind of evidence needed to assess true understanding" (p. 239).

Figures 13.3–13.9 are representative samples of engaging scenarios that apply these design features as a way of motivating students to engage in the corresponding performance tasks. These scenarios and performance task synopses were shared by educators in performance assessment workshops I have facilitated. I have included the school system source, if known. Some scenarios are imaginary, others more realistic. For this reason, educators who created these scenarios used the term "challenge," rather than "real-world goal." Yet consider how these tasks—all of which are interdisciplinary—are sure to promote students' critical and creative thinking, their communication, collaboration, and problem-solving skills, and the other attributes associated with authentic performance that are so necessary to use daily in the *real world*.

FIGURE 13.3 **Engaging Scenario: Grade 7 Social Studies Unit: Africa (Anaheim, California)**

Anthropology Today is interested in printing an article on the different members of medieval society in West Africa (situation). The magazine has chosen you (role) as their senior reporter to travel to sub-Saharan west Africa to interview various people who live and work in the region, specifically: the royalty, villagers, and traders. You are to live with the people of the region without the aid of modern conveniences to learn as much as you can about the diverse groups and the geography of the region (challenge). While there, you will meet with representatives of the west African society and interview them in a round-table discussion group format. The readers of *Anthropology Today* (audience) will be able to read a firsthand account of your experience (product).

Task 1: Draw a geographic map of the region (vegetation, landforms, Niger River).

Task 2: Prepare a question-and-answer transcript to be used during the interviews.

Task 3: Write an article to submit to the editors including the information gained during the interviews. (Other students will play the role of the representatives and be prepared in advance with relevant information needed for the interviews.)

Task 4: Edit, revise, and polish the article as a final submission to the editors.

Task 5: Write the transcript for a brief oral report that summarizes your article. Present the oral report and article to the editors (teachers).

FIGURE 13.4 **Engaging Scenario: Kindergarten Science Unit: Plants (Sharonville, Ohio)**

Imagine you are a scientist working with George Washington Carver (situation). You will perform tasks and experiments to discover information about plants and how they grow (challenge). As a scientist (student role) you will need to follow directions and record your observations. You will be sharing your findings with other students and your parents (audience).

Task 1: Learn about George Washington Carver and then follow a recipe to make peanut butter.

Task 2: Find out what plants need to survive and then plant seeds.

Task 3: Sort seeds by their attributes and learn about the edible parts of plants.

Task 4: Learn the difference between deciduous and evergreen plants. Draw pictures and write about how these plants look throughout the four seasons to include in a class book.

 FIGURE 13.5 **Engaging Scenario: Grade 3 Music and Social Studies Unit (Englewood, Colorado)**

You are a world-famous musician who will be putting on a concert in Mexico next month (role and situation). Your manager has quit and now you have to plan the entire concert on your own (challenge). Using a variety of reading comprehension skills and materials, you will complete several tasks to show your audience that you understand the country of Mexico and its culture (products) so as to make your concert a success!

Task 1: Research a Mexican musician and create a two-paragraph biography of that person.

Task 2: Use an atlas to choose your concert city in Mexico and create a map that shows where your concert will take place. Write two detailed paragraphs about the city.

Task 3: Order travel brochures that give information about the city you chose and plan out a schedule for the days you will be there.

Task 4: Read restaurant reviews and choose a restaurant to attend after your concert. Estimate dinner costs for your entire crew and staff (the class) and present your budget.

FIGURE 13.6 **Engaging Scenario: Grade 4 Math Unit: Data, Statistics, and Probability (Dayton, Ohio)**

Would you like to be the next Phil Jackson? The NBA and WNBA have announced a contest to find a student protégé that wants to learn how to become a professional basketball coach (situation). To be selected, you (role) must build your own basketball team from a lottery draft pick and then coach your "virtual" team as they attempt to win a World Championship (challenge). You will then calculate the worth of your team and create a sales pitch for it (product) to present to the contest panel of judges (audience).

Task 1: From the data provided by the teacher, collect two or three sets of data on basketball players from the NBA and WNBA. Create a table to assist in ranking your choice of draft-day preferences.

Task 2: Create a Venn diagram and two other graphs of your choice (line plot, picture graph, line graph, or bar graph) to represent the data for your team players. Data should include field goals, free throws, assists, rebounds, and three-point shots. Identify your team through your choice of team color, team name, and a mascot.

Task 3: Play a virtual game between two teams based on game statistics provided by your teacher. Determine the winning team based on the game statistics.

Task 4: Formulate a written plan to improve your team if one of your two best players is involved in a season-ending accident. (Teacher will randomly draw players for injury.) Play another virtual game, without the injured player, and determine the winner based on game statistics.

Task 5: After playing several games, use range, mean, median, and mode to declare a World Champion Team.

Task 6: Evaluate the worth of your team and create a sales pitch that includes justification for the appraisal value.

FIGURE 13.7 **Engaging Scenario: Grade 8 Science Unit: Matter and Energy (Wayne Township, Indianapolis, Indiana)**

You are a talented reporter who works for a media giant that owns the local newspaper and television stations (situation). As you come into work, there is a breaking news story. A scientist has created a brand new substance that is indestructible, strong as steel, lighter than plastic, and biodegradable. THIS IS HUGE!

The managing editor (audience) rushes up to you in a panic. The anchorperson is sick, the editorial cartoonist is missing, and the science editor is on vacation. You (role) have to save the day! You must find the best way to inform the public by creating the newscast and the editorial cartoon strip (products). Unfortunately, you don't know an atom from a hole in the ground, let alone anything about matter or energy. How can you find out (challenge)?

Task 1: Draw a model of an atom.

Task 2: Compare and contrast an atom of one element to another.

Task 3: Design or create a model or drawing that illustrates the transformation of energy into different forms.

Task 4: Create a category for a *Jeopardy!* game based on the periodic table.

Task 5: Write a newscast in which you address each of our Essential Questions included in your task directions; prepare a list of criteria for your newsroom manager to assess your work. Or, draw an editorial cartoon strip that illustrates each of our Essential Questions; prepare a list of criteria for your managing editor to assess your work.

FIGURE 13.8 **Engaging Scenario: Grade 7 Algebra Unit: Linear Equations (Oakwood School District, Dayton, Ohio)**

It is your dream to own your own car. However, you soon discover that the kind of car you really want will cost at least $20,000 to $30,000 (situation) so you're hoping that maybe you can find a good used car that costs $5,000. You (role) want to convince your parents (audience) that you are responsible enough to own your own car when you turn sixteen. In order to convince them (challenge), you are willing to do the necessary research and planning to prepare a mathematically persuasive case (product) that you will be able to save enough money during the next four years to pay for half of the car. You hope that if your presentation is convincing enough, they may agree to help by paying for the rest of the car!

Task 1: Use the Internet to research the cost of a car based on parameters discussed in class. Document the resources you used.

Task 2: Develop a linear equation based on your predicted monthly payment, total cost of car, and down payment.

Task 3: Create a table, graph, and equation to display your research.

Task 4: Using the research collected in Task 3, develop a persuasive presentation to convince your parents that you can save enough money in the next four years to pay for half of your car.

FIGURE 13.9 Engaging Scenario: High School Chemistry Unit

It has been recently hypothesized that tomatoes may contain chemicals that are antioxidants. Oxidants are believed to play an important role in the aging of cells. Pharmaceutical as well as cosmetic companies are buying up large quantities of tomatoes in an effort to extract these compounds from the juice of the tomatoes in order to test that hypothesis (situation). Deciding to jump on the bandwagon, you (role) went out and purchased seeds for various strains of tomatoes. In order to command the most money for your crop, you must convince the companies that your tomatoes will yield the highest percentage of juice (challenge) by creating a sales presentation (product) to the pharmaceutical or cosmetic company (audience) convincing them to buy your tomatoes.

Task 1: Working in cooperative groups of three or four students, brainstorm together to identify a current scientific problem. Discuss how your group will research this problem and submit a written response.

Task 2: Conduct a survey on a topic of your choice. Construct a data table and display your data as a graph.

Task 3: Using a variety of tomatoes, hypothesize the percentage of water in the tomatoes, and design and conduct an experiment to test your hypothesis.

Task 4: Using results from Task 3, make a sales presentation to the pharmaceutical or cosmetic company convincing them to buy your tomatoes. Your presentation should include a visual or audio component, such as a brochure, poster, radio ad, PowerPoint presentation, TV commercial, etc.

Linking "Unwrapped" Concepts and Skills to Engaging Learning Experiences

Keep in mind when designing these types of powerful learning experiences for students the strong and intentional connections that must be made explicit between the following elements:

- The "unwrapped" concepts
- The "unwrapped" skills and corresponding levels of rigor
- The performance task requirements

A simple way to do this is to reference the graphic organizer section of the unit planning organizer while creating the performance tasks. Figure 13.10 shows a fifth-grade science unit, "The Living Environment," that illustrates these connections.

FIGURE
13.10   **Connections Between Skills/Concepts and Tasks**

Task Number	Skill and Related Concepts	Bloom Levels of Skills	Task Synopsis— Details Provided with Each Task	Bloom Levels of Tasks
1	DESCRIBE (how life depends on sun; needs of single-cell organisms)	2	Create a fan-fold booklet that describes how plants and animals rely on the sun and the needs of single-cell organisms.	1–6
2	OBSERVE (composition of single-cell organisms)	1	Observe and explain the cell parts by creating a cartoon or diorama.	1, 2, 6
3	OBSERVE (characteristics of fungi and animals); COMPARE/ CONTRAST (characteristics)	1 2	Observe the characteristics of fungi and animals; compare and contrast them by completing a graphic organizer.	1, 2
4	EXPLAIN (distinctions between organisms)	2	Create a written summary to explain your graphic organizer.	1–6
5	ALL OF THE ABOVE	1–2	Create a PowerPoint or oral presentation that describes the interdependence of plant and animal life.	4, 5, 6

Notice that none of the tasks in Figure 13.10 are limited only to the identified Bloom's Taxonomy levels of the skills. In Tasks 1 and 4, students will surely use all levels of the thinking-skill spectrum, as indicated in the far-right column. The "unwrapped" skill for Task 2 only expects students to *observe* the composition of single-cell organisms. However, the task directions extend mental rigor beyond mere observation—students will also need to *explain* the different cell parts by *creating* a cartoon or diorama. Even though the culminating Task 5 is likely to involve the lower-level cognitive processes (levels 1–3), the dominant skills students will need to demonstrate in order to fulfill the task requirements are the higher-level ones (4–6): analysis, synthesis, evaluation, and creation.

Enrichment and Extension Activities for All Students

One easy way to begin blending the use of performance assessment tasks with the more traditional learning assignments is to incorporate what educators often regard as "enrichment" or "extension" activities into the regular unit of study that all students will experience.

In this example of a fourth-grade social studies unit on Native Americans created in West Haven, Connecticut, the following activities are listed in the "Enrichment/Extension" column on the unit planning organizer.

- Make a booklet explaining how and why the Native Americans played certain games. Include pictures. Share with class.
- Make a diorama showing how a group of Native Americans lived.
- Research a Native American legend. Act out or read aloud to class.
- In small groups, create a PowerPoint presentation on a group of Native Americans (housing, clothing, food, cultures, traditions, government, economy).
- Present to class using Smart Board.
- Participate in a culminating field trip to Mashantucket Pequot Museum, located at Foxwoods in Mashantucket, CT.

Each of these activities would make wonderful performance tasks that *all* students would benefit from experiencing, not just those who received enrichment or extension activities beyond the regular curriculum for that unit. In Figure 13.11, notice how closely the particular "unwrapped" standards elements for this unit of study match the enrichment/extension activities listed above.

In planning engaging learning experiences, curriculum designers can brainstorm the kinds of activities they might typically create as enrichment and extension activities and turn those into performance assessment tasks to use with *all* students during the unit of study. Another source of possible ideas for performance assessments matched to the targeted standards of the unit is the "interdisciplinary connections" column of the unit planning organizer. When curriculum designers think about how to apply the unit's concepts and skills to other content areas, great ideas for performance tasks can emerge.

Standards and Creativity

Two words rarely used in the same sentence by educators today are standards and creativity. Yet reestablishing an intentional connection between the two will invigorate teaching and learning.

FIGURE
13.11 **"Unwrapped" Standards—Native American Unit of Study**

Concepts (Need to Know)	Skills (Able to Do)	Bloom's Taxonomy Level
• Cultures and traditions of Native Americans • How environment affected their lives • Impact of exploration and colonization on both native peoples and the colonies	IDENTIFY (cultures, traditions)	1, 2, 4
	COMPARE/CONTRAST (cultures, traditions)	2
	*ASSESS (value or importance of Native American cultures, traditions)	5
	ANALYZE (relationships)	4
	EXPLAIN (how exploration/ colonization affected Native Americans and colonies)	2, 4, 5
	*SUMMARIZE (findings)	2, 4, 5
	*indicates additional skill not in targeted standards; added by curriculum designers to increase rigor	

Randi Weingarten, President of the American Federation of Teachers, illustrates how standards *combined with* individual teacher creativity and expertise can accomplish a vision of excellence for student learning:

> "Just as different pianists can look at the same music and bring to it unique interpretations and flourishes, various teachers working from a common standard should be able to do the same" (Isaacson, 2009, p. 36).

The constant is the standard; the variation is in the *creative teaching* of that standard.

During my 24 years as an elementary and secondary classroom educator, my best years were those in which I regularly used performance tasks as the mainstay of a unit of study. Performance tasks allowed me to feel more like a creative professional, one not dependent upon the restrictive and usually unimaginative textbook. They became the perfect vehicles for me to be inventive in the *ways* I imparted the standards. Regardless of the content area, performance tasks allowed me to genuinely engage my students in highly interactive learning experiences. Rather than being the "sage on the stage," I was able to do what I enjoyed more—being the "guide on the side." My teaching had relevance, and I regularly got to see what every teacher regards as any year's brightest classroom moments—the sudden increase of light in students' faces when they experience an "aha" moment of personal understanding.

Throughout those times when I was using performance tasks, I looked upon every new day in the classroom, not with exhaustion, but rather with exhilaration, because I knew the *students* were going to embrace, rather than resist, what I had planned for them to do. The dramatic upsurge in student motivation and involvement produced, not coincidentally, another prized benefit—a marked decrease in student discipline issues. From personal experience, I *know* that performance tasks are the classroom remedy for student boredom and disengagement.

In my work with educators across North America, I have seen a diminishment of that zest for teaching. So often, teachers tell me they feel like their classrooms have become "test-prep factories." They lament the loss of the "teachable moment" and the days when teaching and learning used to be fun. They certainly do not regard standards and creativity as being mutually compatible. But this is where Priority Standards can reveal an unexpected advantage.

Because greater instruction and assessment time must be allocated to teaching and assessing the Priority Standards than the supporting standards, this gives educators more time to do so *creatively*. It encourages them to spend more time planning engaging learning experiences that will really help their students understand the "unwrapped" concepts and apply the "unwrapped" skills of the Priority Standards at the various levels of thinking rigor. The result will be students who understand that the process of learning always takes mental effort and stamina, but inevitably results in a greater ability and confidence to think and reason independently. What better way to engage students in their own learning and have fun in the process?

Research Support

There is abundant research to support the assertion that meaningful performance assessment tasks, even though requiring more class time to administer, actually improve results in student learning.

One of the best sources for broad evidence regarding the value of educators regularly using performance assessment can be found in Linda Darling-Hammond's book *The Right to Learn* (1997), which provides multiple citations associating effective performance assessment with higher scores on standardized tests.

Robert Marzano reports, "Levels of student performance improve when instruction focuses on: active learning, real-world contexts, higher-level thinking skills, extended writing, and demonstration" (Marzano, 2007).

For educators that make performance assessment an integral part of their unit planning, the most persuasive support they can add to the body of published research is their own firsthand evidence of increased student learning, heightened levels of student engagement, and dramatic improvement of overall student work quality. Performance tasks help students make sense of what they are learning, think independently, work collaboratively, make connections to other areas of study, and persevere—skills they are sure to need in the life that awaits them after high school.

The Issue of Resources

One issue that is important to address in connection with the design of engaging learning experiences is that of available resources and materials. Even though educators historically rely on published texts and other instructional resources to teach their curricula, performance assessments cannot depend on having access to specific resources (i.e., full class sets of books, "manipulatives," program materials, or the latest technology hardware). Certainly these materials help, but creative planning can circumvent the problems created by an overreliance on such physical and technological supports.

When designing engaging learning experiences, be creative! Think outside the box, as did the educators who created the engaging scenarios and performance task examples shown earlier in this chapter. Challenge yourself to plan performance tasks that do not depend on particular resources. Call upon one of the most extra-ordinary resources educators should have access to on a daily basis—the library media specialists.

In this digital age of learning, where technology plays such a huge role in our daily lives, library media specialists can work closely with educators to help them find relevant digital media and related Web links for whatever unit of study they are planning. Library media specialists know their library or media center like the proverbial "back of their hand" and can locate specific print and audiovisual resources and materials that will greatly help students to learn the particular "unwrapped" concepts, skills, and Big Ideas in a unit of study.

These educators are waiting to open their worlds of wonder to students and teachers alike. Tap their expertise. Share with them your pacing calendars for the year, and let them help you find what you need to bring your engaging learning activities to life.

Reader's Assignment

Design engaging learning experiences for each unit of study, following this recommended sequence of steps:

1. Refer to the "unwrapped" skills, related concepts, and levels of Bloom's Taxonomy on the graphic organizer for a particular unit of study.

2. Review Figures 13.10 and 13.11, which illustrate the connections between the "unwrapped" skills, Bloom levels, and performance tasks. Brainstorm three to five possible performance tasks that would encompass and "go beyond" the skills and matching levels of rigor on the graphic organizer.

3. Write a synopsis for each of those tasks. Keeping "learning progressions" in mind, list the tasks in the sequence that students will complete them.

4. Beginning with the first task synopsis, draft the *full details* of what students will do to complete that task. Use the following example as a guide:

   Here is a synopsis accompanied by the full details of a seventh-grade social studies performance task. The details reveal the full range of thinking-skill rigor required of students to successfully complete the task.

   Synopsis: Create a list of vital statistics for countries in Africa, Asia, and the southwest Pacific in table form.

   Full Details: Produce or provide a complete list of the vital statistics of the countries in Africa, Asia, and the southwest Pacific. Your list should consist of the current demographics of populations, statistics related to population growth, major cities, landforms, government, economy, leaders, bodies of water, currency, popular attractions, prime natural resources, and the most abundant product. Present your information in a data table form. Include in a separate list or paragraph the reasons why the rates of population growth and life expectancy vary among these countries.

5. Make interdisciplinary connections between the performance task and other content areas. Identify the specific Priority Standards from those other content areas, and list them either on the unit planning organizer or in the accompanying information for the educator. Identify the 21st-century learning skills students will exercise as they participate in the performance task.

6. Create a scoring guide with specific criteria that match "hand-to-glove" the task requirements, following the guidelines presented in the previous chapter.

7. Repeat the same process for the remaining tasks. Include as much detail as necessary in detailing each task so that educators and students will know exactly what is required in the product or performance.

8. Create the engaging scenario to introduce the performance assessment tasks to the students. Remember to include the five key elements of effective scenarios: situation, challenge, student role, intended audience, and product or performance. It's important to mention that the engaging scenario can be created *at any point* during the process of designing the performance tasks. However, educators usually find that it makes more sense to write the scenario *after* they have created the tasks and are considering how best to introduce them to students. Record any ideas for creating the engaging scenario that come to mind as you design the tasks.

9. Review and revise all of the performance task directions, engaging scenario, and scoring guides until they are complete and ready to use as written.

10. Decide the other types of learning activities to also include throughout the unit, either before or after the performance tasks. Remember to directly align these other learning activities to the unit's "unwrapped" concepts, skills, thinking skill levels, and Big Ideas.

CHAPTER 14

Recommend Effective Instruction, Differentiation, Intervention, Special Education, and English Language Learner Strategies

The era of a "one-size-fits-all" instructional delivery approach to an entire class of students is gone. To meet the diverse learning needs of today's students in every grade, course, and content area, educators *must* understand and know when to use specialized instructional strategies and techniques. Only by diagnosing individual student learning needs and matching those needs with the most appropriate instructional strategies can educators accomplish the desired end result: student attainment of the "unwrapped" concepts, skills, and Big Ideas for each unit of study.

The unit planning organizer allocates one or more specific sections to instructional strategies (i.e., research-based, intervention, differentiation, etc.). The strategies curriculum designers intentionally select and list on the unit planner are those they recommend educators use when teaching their students the standards and learning activities for that unit.

For example, under the category of *research-based effective teaching strategies*, designers may list "similarities and differences," "summarizing and note taking," and so on. Under the category of *interventions*, designers may list "grouping of students with similar learning needs and levels," "more frequent progress monitoring," and so on. They may discuss whether or not to provide on the unit planning organizer a detailed listing of *differentiation* strategies, strategies for *English Language Learners*, and suggestions for meeting the learning needs of *special education students*, but then decide that there are just too many different types of strategies to include them all.

Conversely, curriculum designers may realize *they* need to know more about these strategies themselves before being able to offer reliable recommendations to educators about which ones to use. For this reason, it may prove necessary for curriculum *supervisors* to have available all of this related information when designers reach this stage of the curriculum design process.

Because there has been so much written in educational literature about the various types of instructional strategies and methods, to have ready access to all of this information will likely require the gathering of numerous books and articles. It may also necessitate asking instructional specialists for specific advice and recommendations. However, being able to confidently recommend instructional strategies is something that curriculum supervisors and designers should do to assist educators in the effective implementation of the curricular units of study. Without such recommendations, educators who have not yet received professional development related to the proper understanding and use of these highly specialized strategies may not know how to make these important determinations on their own.

My primary goal for this chapter is to present curriculum supervisors and designers with a fairly detailed compilation of these many different kinds of strategies so they can (1) easily reference them during the next steps of the unit-design process, and (2) decide how they might effectively share this information with educators. In addition, this comprehensive reference will assist instructional Data Team members in completing the important fourth and fifth steps of the Data Teams process: *identifying specific strategies* to use with different subgroups of students and *determining results indicators* that provide evidence of the effectiveness of the targeted strategies.

To this end, I have organized the specific types of instructional strategies presented here into six broad categories. This collection should serve as a good starting point for locating more detailed information, as needed. The six categories are:

- 21st-century learning skills
- Research-based effective teaching strategies
- Differentiation strategies (additional supports to use with *all* students, plus enrichment strategies)
- Intervention strategies (Tiers 1, 2, and 3)
- Strategies for special education students
- Strategies for English Language Learners

Before presenting the strategies associated with each of these categories to educators, I wish to offer a word of caution: set the stage by acknowledging up front that many of these strategies, some of which are described in technical terms, may seem to be new and unfamiliar. Explain that the terminology simply "puts a name to" many of the different strategies educators have been using for years. Clarify each term as it is introduced, and determine whether or not educators are familiar with it. Provide more detailed explanations and examples for those terms and strategies that educators identify as being unfamiliar. Share this information over multiple sessions if there are many terms requiring explanation and/or demonstration.

21ST-CENTURY LEARNING SKILLS

Incorporating 21st-century learning skills into the design of rigorous curricula is essential for providing students with the opportunity to exercise a variety of skills that are arguably indispensable to life in today's world society. There has been a surge of recently published books and articles related to 21st-century learning skills and their place in 21st-century classrooms, yet this category may be one that educators are least familiar with. My purpose here is to provide a representative sampling of those skills, several of which appear more than once. Curriculum designers are encouraged to add any others they think important to include when recommending such skills to educators.

In Chapter 1, I cited the seven pairs of 21st-century "survival" skills Tony Wagner (2008) believes students today need to "master [in order] to thrive in the new world of work: (1) critical thinking and problem solving; (2) collaboration and leadership; (3) agility and adaptability; (4) initiative and entrepreneurialism; (5) effective oral and written communication; (6) accessing and analyzing information; and (7) curiosity and imagination" (pp. 21–22).

In the previous chapter, I presented the following attributes of high-quality, engaging learning experiences that students are likely to encounter while working on authentic performance tasks. These attributes reflect quality, relevancy, technology, motivation, depth of thought, rigor, collaboration, work ethic, life skills, effective interpersonal communication, and more—all of them necessary "ingredients" for schools to incorporate into rigorous curricula that help prepare students for future life:

- Authentic (genuine, valid, real)

- Relevant to life situations and contexts

- Interdisciplinary (as distinguished from "thematic")

- Use embedded informational technologies

- Highly motivational, not routine

- Mentally stimulating, thought-provoking

- Incorporate the full spectrum of thinking-skill rigor, especially: reasoning, application, analysis, synthesis, creativity, self-assessment, and reflection

- Include both collaborative and individual work

Connie Kamm (2009) identifies the following 21st-century skills as being essential for students to have in the digital age: teamwork, innovation, creativity, problem solving, flexibility, adaptability, and a commitment to continuous learning (Kamm, 2009).

Andy Hargreaves and Dennis Shirley (2009) see the need for schools to help students acquire personal traits that go hand-in-hand with essential life skills. They write: "Twenty-first century schools must also embrace deeper virtues and values such as courage, compassion, service, sacrifice, long-term commitment, and perseverance" (p. 85).

RESEARCH-BASED EFFECTIVE TEACHING STRATEGIES

Instructional strategies can be defined as the specific actions educators take to help students achieve specific learning targets. In other words, strategies are the methods or techniques teachers use to increase student understanding. During one's own teaching experience, every educator discovers certain instructional strategies or techniques that work well. These experience-based techniques should not be abandoned. But to also know and understand how to apply *research-based* effective teaching strategies adds greatly to their instructional expertise.

For educators today, this is perhaps more important than anything else they do to advance student learning, an assertion that is research-supported by Stephen White (2005): "We now know that teaching practices are even more powerful than content preparation" (p. 78).

The most widely known and respected collection of research-based teaching strategies is presented in the classic volume *Classroom Instruction That Works: Research-Based Strategies for Increasing Student Achievement* (2001), by Robert Marzano, Debra Pickering, and Jane Pollock. These nine strategies, distilled by the authors from decades of research studies, are as follows:

- Identifying similarities and differences
- Summarizing and note taking
- Reinforcing effort and providing recognition
- Homework and practice
- Nonlinguistic representations
- Cooperative learning
- Setting objectives and providing feedback
- Generating and testing hypotheses
- Cues, questions, and advance organizers

The companion volume, *A Handbook for Classroom Instruction That Works* (2001), provides numerous examples of how to use these broad strategies in multiple classroom applications.

In 2007, Robert Marzano updated the original strategies in a new publication, *The Art and Science of Teaching: A Comprehensive Framework for Effective Instruction*. He emphasized the equal importance of educators knowing the latest research on effective instruction *and* understanding students' learning strengths and weaknesses. He proposed that educators look through a "lens" of ten questions when designing instruction.

I have categorized Marzano's questions according to those that directly relate to instructional strategies (the first five) and those that focus on the conditions needed for those strategies to work (the last five).

Instructional Strategies:

1. What will *I* do to establish and communicate learning goals, track student progress, and celebrate success?

2. What will *I* do to help students effectively interact with new knowledge?

3. What will *I* do to help students practice and deepen their understanding of new knowledge?

4. What will *I* do to help students generate and test hypotheses about new knowledge?

5. What will *I* do to engage students?

Conditions That Support Strategies:

1. What will *I* do to establish or maintain classroom rules and procedures?

2. What will *I* do to recognize and acknowledge adherence and lack of adherence to classroom rules and procedures?

3. What will *I* do to maintain effective relationships with students?

4. What will *I* do to communicate high expectations to students?

5. What will *I* do to develop effective lessons organized into a cohesive unit?

The Importance of Nonfiction Writing

Supported by his own and others' research, Douglas Reeves has long advocated the inclusion of a powerful strategy not explicitly stated in any of these lists, but certainly implied: nonfiction writing. Note taking, as an example, is one effective nonfiction writing strategy that educators in any content area can use effectively. In one research study, 90 percent or more of the teachers who implemented effective note-taking strategies (such as Cornell notes) in science classes saw 79 percent of the students score at the proficient and advanced levels on the state assessments. When 10 percent or fewer of the educators implemented the strategies, only 25 percent of the students scored at proficient and advanced levels (Reeves, 2008, p. 14).

Interdisciplinary nonfiction writing, often known as "writing across the curriculum," helps students make larger connections that result in the discovery of broader Big Ideas. The performance assessment model, described in the previous chapter, incorporates nonfiction writing into the design of a majority of its performance tasks.

Angela Peery's *Writing Matters in Every Classroom* (2009b) is an excellent guide educators can use for helping students "write to learn" across the content areas. In it, she writes: "The link between writing and achievement is compelling, and the need for writing instruction is unquestionable. A 2007 meta-analysis of almost six-hundred studies (Graham and Perin) concluded that writing is essential for adolescents. Students without adequate writing skills suffer disadvantages in multiple subjects in school and later in the job market" (p. 19).

Peery also authored The Leadership and Learning Center's seminar and handbook, "Power Strategies for Effective Teaching" (2009a). In her work, she presents three categories of research-based strategies accompanied by examples for each, summarized here:

Category 1: Activate Knowledge

- Personalized learning goals
- Advance organizers
- Anticipation guides
- Teacher- and student-generated comparisons

Category 2: Engage the Learner

- Powerful questioning
- Concept attainment
- Teacher- and student-generated nonlinguistic images
- Collaborative learning
- Individual contracts
- Inquiry projects

Category 3: Strengthen Literacy Across the Curriculum

- Cornell notes
- Socratic seminars
- Interacting with text
- Argumentation

One of the most comprehensive syntheses of research-based practices affecting student achievement ever to be published is John Hattie's *Visible Learning: A Synthesis of over 800 Meta-Analyses Relating to Achievement* (2009). In recommending instructional strategies to educators, curriculum supervisors and designers will benefit greatly by having access to this important resource. Hattie reports that the "aspects of teaching associated with student learning include:

- Paying deliberate attention to learning intentions and success criteria
- Setting challenging tasks
- Providing multiple opportunities for deliberate practice
- Knowing when both the teacher and the student are successful in attaining these goals
- Understanding the critical role of teaching appropriate learning strategies
- Planning and talking about teaching
- Ensuring that the teacher constantly seeks feedback information as to the success of his or her teaching" (p. 36)

Hattie provides a wealth of *specific* instructional strategies and their effect-size impact on student learning in his Chapter 10, "The Contributions from Teaching Approaches—Part II." These include three types of implementations: those that emphasize an *individual's* teaching strategies, those that emphasize *school-wide* teaching strategies, and those using *technologies*.

DIFFERENTIATION STRATEGIES

Because the diversity of individual student learning needs in almost any classroom today is so great, educators must understand and know how to use a variety of instructional approaches. Differentiation strategies are those additional supports that educators use during all high-quality lessons to modify or adjust instruction for students who need a different approach in order to understand.

Differentiation strategies can be used with students learning the standards-based concepts and skills in focus as well as with proficient and advanced students who need enrichment experiences that go beyond those learning targets. The published recommendations aimed at meeting the learning needs of *all* students through differentiated instruction are extensive.

Carol Ann Tomlinson defines differentiation as "the practice of adjusting the curriculum, teaching strategies, and classroom environment to meet the needs of all students" (2001). Her seminal work, *The Differentiated Classroom: Responding to the Needs of All Learners* (1999), provides a solid foundation of principles curriculum designers can reference when recommending to educators different ways they can deliver planned learning experiences to their students.

Tomlinson posits that educators can differentiate "content, process, and product according to a student's readiness, interests, and learning profile, through a range of instructional and management strategies, such as [partial list]:

- Multiple intelligences
- Jigsaw
- Varying organizers
- Varied texts and supplementary materials
- Tiered lessons and products
- Learning contracts
- Small-group instruction
- Group investigation
- Varied questioning strategies
- Varied homework
- Compacting" (1999, p. 15)

In an *Education Update* interview in March 2010, Tomlinson says: "Differentiation doesn't ask teachers to begin by individualizing instruction. In other words, it doesn't call for teachers to create twenty tasks for twenty students who will come to class tomorrow. It asks teachers to look for *patterns of need*" (emphasis added, Varlas, 2010) and to "address varied student needs thoughtfully and smoothly by:

- using formative assessment to see patterns in student need;
- planning for instruction with those patterns in mind; and
- guiding a classroom where, some of the time, more than one thing is taking place" (Varlas, 2010, p. 3).

In her extensively researched and *educator-friendly* article written for a secondary audience but equally applicable to elementary teachers, Diana Lawrence-

Brown asserts: "With suitable supports, including differentiated instruction, students ranging from gifted to those with significant disabilities can receive an appropriate education in general education classrooms" (2004, p. 34).

Lawrence-Brown suggests that differentiation of high-quality lessons should focus on providing students with "Additional supports" (pp. 40–45) that include:

- "Assistive technology" (e.g., "taped books, screen reading programs, software to support written expression, simulation software to illustrate science and social studies concepts, math media that illustrate real-life applications, instructional software equipped with speech capability, reducing interference from reading difficulties") (p. 40)

- Finding of answers in provided texts rather than by random guessing

- Support resources (manipulatives, visual aids, charts, outlines, picture cues, and audiotaped books and instructions) (p. 41)

- Personal assistance from adults and peers

- Emphasis on the most important concepts and skills (i.e., "unwrapped" Priority Standards)

- Clear expectations and examples

- Systematic breakdown of specific strategies, skills, and concepts (i.e., step-by-step explanation of what students are to do)

- Specific connections to prior knowledge and experiences

- Gradual release of direct assistance so students can perform independently

Lawrence-Brown also suggests using the following strategies to meet the differentiated learning needs of **highly capable students** through what she terms an "enriched curriculum" (pp. 46–47):

- More challenging and creative work above and beyond grade-level standards

- Cooperative grouping with assigned roles

- Lessons that emphasize multiple intelligences

- Authentic performance tasks

- Pursuit of related independent study involving higher-level concepts and skills

Sylvia G. Lewis and Kelly Batts (2005) describe differentiation strategies for general education elementary classrooms that can prove equally effective with general secondary classes. These include, but are not limited to, the following:

- Flexible grouping
- Individual student contracts
- Adjusting level of rigor in questions
- Independent study of student-selected projects
- "Compacting" (streamlining or modifying basic content to provide students with tiered assignments)
- "Tiered" assignments (learning tasks designed at different levels of complexity according to students' readiness levels) (pp. 28-29)

Scott J. Nozik, Principal of Dr. Thomas S. O'Connell Elementary School in East Hartford, Connecticut, shared with me, during one of my visits to his school district, a valuable school-based reading program perfectly tailored for differentiation: the Benchmark Education Study. In his article, "Why Differentiating Instruction Should Be at the Top of Your School Improvement Plan" (2009), published by the National Association of Elementary School Principals, Scott describes the program:

"This year, our third and fourth grades were afforded the opportunity to participate in a research study partnership with Benchmark Education Co., a publisher of fiction and nonfiction standards-aligned texts. The Benchmark materials are *leveled books* that directly address the key concepts in our science and social studies curriculum. The 'Big Idea' is the same in each book, but readability levels can vary by more than 1.5 years, paving the way for both proficient and advanced readers to be taught at their instructional levels. There are additional books that provide students with special needs, English Language Learners, or students reading below basic levels, with an opportunity to read and comprehend science and social studies topics at their levels.

"Content vocabulary terms are explicitly taught in all groups, and expanded to challenge students who are reading above grade level" (Nozik, 2009).

Another highly recommended resource for differentiation strategies and related classroom examples is *Differentiating Instruction in the Regular Classroom: How to Reach and Teach All Learners, Grades 3–12,* by Diane Heacox (2002).

INTERVENTION STRATEGIES

Linda Gregg, author of The Leadership and Learning Center's seminar and handbook "Power Strategies for Response to Intervention" (2010), provides a succinct definition written by Candace Cortiella of the widely used process known as Response to Intervention (RTI). The second paragraph of the passage highlights two of RTI's most noteworthy benefits:

"Response to Intervention is a multi-step approach to providing services and interventions to students who struggle with learning at increasing levels of intensity. The progress students make at each stage of intervention is closely monitored. Results of this monitoring are used to make decisions about the need for further research-based instruction and/or intervention in general education, special education, or both.

"The RTI process has the potential to limit the academic failure that any student experiences and to increase the accuracy of special education evaluations. It could also reduce the number of children mistakenly identified as having learning disabilities, when their learning problems are actually due to cultural differences or lack of adequate instruction" (Cortiella, 2006).

Response to Intervention identifies students in need of additional instructional support through a universal screening process. Represented graphically as a pyramid, RTI is based on a three-tiered intervention model: (1) universal, (2) targeted, and (3) intensive. The largest portion of the pyramid is Tier 1 and includes approximately eighty percent of all students—*when and if* the core instructional programs are strong and achieving their intended purpose. Near the top of the pyramid is the relatively smaller section of Tier 2 that represents approximately fifteen percent of the remaining students. At the top is the even smaller Tier 3 tip that represents the remaining five percent of students.

These numbers reflect an approximate 80/20 distribution of percentages in the RTI model. Whenever the Tier 2 section of the pyramid begins to swell to twenty, thirty, or even forty percent or more of the student population, this presents a real challenge for educators. Tier 2 targeted intervention strategies were not designed for use with large numbers of students. A lopsided distribution of percentages to this degree is a clear indication that the *quality* of core instructional programs is in great need of improvement.

Universal interventions are the high-quality, research-based instructional strategies and differentiation that general education teachers use with *all* students. *Targeted* interventions are specialized, scientific, research-based interventions provided to those students who do not respond to Tier 1 interventions. *Intensive* interventions are individualized, responsive interventions given to students who have not responded to Tier 1 and Tier 2 interventions. Each tier provides more intensive instruction and social/behavioral supports than the preceding one. However, the duration and frequency of the interventions vary based on the needs of individual students. Fidelity to and documentation of the implementation of core practices and interventions are crucial.

Specific intervention strategies help accelerate the growth of students who need additional instruction support. The following list of key interventions associated with each of the three tiers is from Linda Gregg's seminar handbook "Power Strategies for Response to Intervention" (2010). For further information specific to the strategies associated with each tier, refer to respected publications on the subject.

Tier 1 (Universal) strategies for all students include, but are not limited to:

- Differentiated instruction (content, process, product)
- Additional instructional time
- Change of environment
- Assistive technology
- Graphic organizers
- Preteach/reteach
- Change pace
- Repetition
- Systematic, sequential instruction
- Modified curriculum
- Manipulatives
- Collaborative learning activities
- Direct/explicit instruction
- "Chunking" (presenting information to students in smaller "chunks")
- Addressing learning modalities (e.g., visual, auditory, kinesthetic, tactile, smell, taste)
- Accommodating learning-style preferences
- Providing additional guided practice
- Research-based effective teaching strategies (see related category)
- Cueing and signaling
- Appropriate questioning and response skills

Tier 2 (Targeted) strategies provide highly individualized assistance to students *in addition to the Tier 1 strategies* that *all* students receive. Tier 2 strategies should *supplement* the instruction of the teacher by providing additional resources to help struggling students. Tier 2 strategies include, but are not limited to:

- Evaluation of Tier 1 interventions

- Increased intervention frequency and intensity, and increased duration of instruction
- Matching of specific strategy to specific skill and changing as needed
- Inclusion of social worker, reading specialist/coach, math specialist/coach
- Double-dosing of instruction
- Before- or after-school tutorial program
- Adult or student mentor
- Computer-assisted instruction or device
- Study skills class
- Study buddy
- Social skills class
- Parent conference
- Alteration of class schedule (if possible)
- Homework hotline
- Video instruction
- Accelerated courses
- Computerized (content) programs
- Advance organizers
- Cross-class courses
- Conducting a task analysis
- Enhanced tutorials
- More rigorous curriculum

Tier 3 (Intensive) strategies should *supplement* the Tier 2 intervention strategies with further resources used by the teacher to help struggling students. Tier 3 strategies include, but are not limited to:

- Evaluation of effectiveness of Tier 1 and Tier 2 interventions
- Increased intervention frequency, intensity, and duration
- Intensive, core, adult support
- Intensive learning plan
- Individual behavior plan (assessment, contract, reinforcement, and modeling)

- Inclusion of occupational therapist, speech and language pathologist, paraprofessional, school psychologist, social workers
- Modification of cooperative group
- Individualized intervention
- Triple-dosing of instruction
- Increased opportunities to use learning-style preferences
- Evaluation of teaching style
- Increased use of sensory modalities
- Individual differentiated content, process, and/or product
- Evaluation and modification of learning environment
- Development of a focus support program (FSP), individual- or small-group pull-out, or resource program for intensive incremental skills

The National Center on Response to Intervention database can also provide invaluable information specific to each U.S. state at *www.state.rti4success.org/index.php* and *www.state.rti4success.org/index.php?option=com_chart*.

STRATEGIES FOR SPECIAL EDUCATION STUDENTS

The U.S. federal government requires special education students to have equal access to the general curriculum. "Special education means *specially designed instruction*. Specially designed instruction (SDI) means adapting, as appropriate to the needs of an eligible child under this part, the content, methodology, or delivery of instruction—(i) To address the unique needs of the child that result from the child's disability; and (ii) To ensure access of the child to the general curriculum, so that the child can meet the educational standards within the jurisdiction of the public agency that apply to all children" (Federal Register, Vol. 71, No. 156).

Linda Gregg shared with me during a conversation a synopsis of Specially Designed Instruction:

> "Specially designed instruction (SDI) for students eligible for special education service begins with the individual assessment of the student. The Individualized Education Program (IEP) team (which includes the student's parent) works together to analyze the results of the assessment. Careful analysis typically will reveal the strengths, challenges, and root causes of the learning or behavior issues. Specific goals are then set for the student. Next, specially

RECOMMEND EFFECTIVE INSTRUCTION, DIFFERENTIATION, INTERVENTION,
SPECIAL EDUCATION, AND ENGLISH LANGUAGE LEARNER STRATEGIES

193

designed instruction is planned to help provide the student with *access to the general education curriculum and to help meet the goals of the IEP.*"

I include the following information for curriculum designers to consider as they think about the appropriate types of instructional strategies to suggest general educators use when customizing or specially designing instruction for their special education students.

Common Misconceptions

Unlike the other categories of instructional strategies (research-based, differentiation, intervention, English Language Learner), there are no specifically designated "SDI strategies." SDI is, instead, a *customized instructional approach based on a student's particular disability identified on the IEP.* Special educators take into account the specific learning needs of a student and then select from a wide variety of instructional strategies (differentiation, intervention, English Language Learner, etc.) those that are most appropriate for the student. They then modify those strategies accordingly.

It is not uncommon for general educators to equate strategies for special education students with Tier 3 interventions, perhaps because Tier 3 interventions include more intensive instruction. Special education students "populate" all three sections of the RTI pyramid. Some may receive Tier 3 interventions during reading instruction but only require Tier 1 interventions in math. Again, the specific disability determines the instructional strategies used and how they are modified. For example, a special education teacher may select a Tier 3 strategy for a particular student and then break the related task down into smaller "chunks" and/or allow the student more time to complete it than a general education student might receive.

Because federal requirements state that special education students must have access to the general curriculum, they must therefore be present in the classroom to receive interventions from highly qualified general education teachers. If special education students are "pulled out" of the classroom to receive instructional support, they may inadvertently be deprived of that access to the general curriculum. One way to ensure that special education students do not miss out on this access is for special educators to "push in" and provide additional doses of instruction *related to the same content* being presented by the general education teacher. This may include using a different strategy and technique or simply giving the student an opportunity to see, hear, and apply the information again.

General education teachers want to learn better ways to meet the needs of their students who have been identified for special education. Working together with special education teachers in inclusive classroom settings is a great way for them to learn how to create specially designed instruction for the students they share. Just as grade-level or course-specific pacing calendars help library media specialists stay informed about what different classes of students are learning and when, pacing calendars can also assist special educators by helping them better prepare their students for the work taking place, or about to take place, in the general education classroom.

In addition to recommending particular instruction, differentiation, or intervention strategies to general educators, special educators can also suggest certain technology and resource materials and how to modify or adapt them for individual students in special education. Although it may prove challenging to schedule collaborative planning time for general and special educators, the resulting benefits to special education students can be significant. The following list of strategies will be useful for such planning.

Suggestions for Creating Specially Designed Instruction

Linda Gregg prepared the following list of suggested strategies that general educators and special educators can collaboratively refer to when creating specially designed instruction for special education students:

Accommodations as per IEP

(Standard of performance and/or core content of the work *are not changed*)

- Additional time
- Nonlinguistic representations via computer
- Technology (high, medium, or low); Alpha Smart; word-recognition software; text readers
- Small-group collaboration

Modifications as per IEP

(Content, instruction, and/or performance *are changed*)

- Menu of products
- Match process to learning style
- Modify quantity of work
- Dictation
- Computer graphics

- Comparison matrix
- Extended time
- Scaffold information
- Differentiate the content, process or product
- Change in pace
- Accessible texts

Cognitive Strategies Designed for Individual Students

(Delivery of direct instruction designed to meet specific disability)

- Explicit direct instruction to address the area of disability
- Modeling and demonstration
- Visual, auditory, tactical, and/or kinesthetic instruction
- Advance organizers (with instruction)
- Mnemonics or memory strategies
- Frequent and short assessments
- Task analysis with student checklist (demonstrated)

Behavioral Strategies Designed for Individual Students

- Consistent reward system
- Explicit feedback on acceptable and nonacceptable behavior
- Use of tangible and nontangible incentives/rewards
- Avoidance of distracting stimuli
- Time for student to break away from task

Note: Several of the Tier 1, 2, and 3 Response to Intervention (RTI) and English Language Learner (ELL) strategies may also be appropriate for students eligible for or identified as special education.

STRATEGIES FOR ENGLISH LANGUAGE LEARNERS

Just as special education students are legally assured access to the general curriculum, the U.S. federal government safeguards English Language Learners in the same way.

Addressing the instructional needs of English Language Learners as they move through the five established levels of language acquisition (beginning, early intermediate, intermediate, early advanced, and advanced) and helping those students access both content and language through Sheltered Instruction (SI) or

Specially Designed Academic Instruction in English (SDAIE) methods are essential to providing all students with the federally required equal access to core instruction.

Curriculum supervisors and designers can suggest to general educators helpful strategies to use with students while they are learning English. Many of the same differentiation and intervention strategies that prove effective with English speakers are also applicable to English learners, whether they are designated as an English as a Second Language (ESL), English Language Development (ELD), or English as a New Language (ENL) learner.

Bonnie Bishop, author of The Leadership and Learning Center's seminar and handbook "Accelerating Academic Achievement for English Language Learners" (2010), drawing from her ongoing work with the Buena Park School District in Buena Park, California, recommends several strategies for educators to use when instructing their English Language Learners:

- Daily, explicit, and systematic ELD/ESL/ENL curriculum instruction

- Flexible grouping

- Cooperative learning groups

- Questioning strategies appropriate to student's level of language acquisition

- Active participation and interactive learning experiences

- Differentiated instruction

She also offers Sheltered Instruction strategies appropriate to make content comprehensible:

- Simplification of the input (verbal or written instructions)

- Scaffolding of information

- Total Physical Response (students respond with body movement to show comprehension)

- Connections to primary language and cultures

- Sufficient "think time"

- Sufficient practice and reinforcement activities

- Ongoing comprehension checks (both oral and written)

- Use of contextual clues

- Frequent checks for understanding

- Learning that is student-centered and content-driven

- Accessing of student's prior knowledge; building background knowledge

- Use of realia, visuals, graphic organizers
- Addressing listening, speaking, reading, and writing skills throughout instruction

A great benefit to educators planning specific ELL and Sheltered Instruction strategies to meet the learning needs of their English Language Learners would be to provide them with a detailed listing of the strategies specific to *each of the five language acquisition levels.* In this way, they can more effectively determine the strategies most appropriate for use based on their students' current language levels.

Prepare a Comprehensive List of Strategies

To sum up, the dual purpose of educators learning and effectively utilizing a wide range of research-based instructional strategies is to improve student achievement and to increase student success. The various 21st-century learning skills, research-based, differentiation, intervention, specially designed instruction, and ELL instructional strategies presented in this chapter are necessary "tools of the trade" that every educator needs to apply daily in order to accomplish the continuously challenging, yet immensely rewarding, job of teaching students.

Reader's Assignment

Prepare a comprehensive list of the various instructional strategies, organized by category, that were presented in this chapter. This instructional resource can be shared with educators within your own school system. Add any other related strategies for each category that you prefer to include. In the next chapter, you will use this list to provide the necessary *details* for each unit of study.

CHAPTER 15

Detail the Unit Planning Organizer

"Unwrapping" the targeted Priority Standards, writing Big Ideas and Essential Questions, creating the pre- and post-assessments, and planning engaging learning experiences for a unit of study produce very specific items to include on or with the unit planning organizer. These elements often need no further detail or clarification; they stand alone, self-explanatory and complete. However, other components of the unit—the various learning activities, the pacing and sequencing of instruction, the different types of teaching strategies—can lack that same degree of specificity. These additional details can be included either on the unit organizer *or in an accompanying document* so that educators can refer to a comprehensive unit planner while they write their weekly lesson plans and design their daily lessons.

All of the recommended elements to include on or with the unit planning organizer are shown here, grouped according to specific or general wording:

Specifically Worded Elements:

- Name of unit of study
- Unit type(s): topical, skills-based, and/or thematic
- Pacing guidelines (number of weeks for the unit)
- Priority Standards and supporting standards
- Correlations to standardized assessments
- "Unwrapped" concepts
- "Unwrapped" skills with associated levels of thinking-skill rigor
- Big Ideas and Essential Questions
- Unit assessments (pre- and post-, and ideas for progress-monitoring checks)
- Assessment answer keys and scoring guides
- Engaging learning experiences (authentic performance tasks with all related components)
- Vocabulary pertinent to the unit (from "unwrapped" Priority Standards, supporting standards, and other unit-specific terms)

Generally Worded Elements:

- Learning activities using text or program
- Instructional pacing and sequencing guidelines for all learning experiences and related instruction
- Research-based instructional strategies applicable to entire unit
- 21st-century learning skills applicable to entire unit
- Strategies for differentiation, intervention, specially designed instruction (SDI), and English Language Learners
- Suggested resources and materials, physical and/or technology-based
- Ideas for enrichment and extension activities
- General listing of interdisciplinary connections

It is important to remember that the full authorship of the curricular units of study is a collaborative process that takes place between the curriculum design teams and the educators who will actually implement the units in their own instructional programs, the majority of whom have not likely been part of the design process. Those educators who serve on the design teams, and also teach students every day, have a dual responsibility: they create the unit planning organizer *and* must later detail it for use in their own classrooms.

For example, when preparing to implement the units of study, all educators will need to determine the *sequence* for delivering the learning activities and experiences, taking into account the logical progression in which to present the "unwrapped" concepts and skills to students. They will have to decide the *specifics* of any generally worded instructional strategies and then match those strategies to the different learning activities and to the various learning needs of all their students. They may choose to do this prior to implementing the unit or as part of their ongoing weekly and daily lesson planning, but either way, it will need to be done.

The most effective way to support the designer-educators and their teaching colleagues in adding the needed details to the units is to provide them with regular opportunities for collaborative planning time throughout the school year. Doing so will help to ensure that the units are completed as thoughtfully as needed. Such ongoing collaborative planning has been a vital key to the success of curriculum redesign efforts in West Haven, Connecticut.

Promoting Collaborative Authorship of the Curricular Units

The West Haven curriculum design teams—made up of classroom and program educators—provided only *general* suggestions for instructional strategies, resources, enrichment and extension activities, and interdisciplinary connections on the unit planning organizer for each unit of study. They left the adding of specific details until later, when they would prepare to implement each unit of study.

District leaders and curriculum supervisors always intended the units to be *co-created* by the designer-educators and their teaching colleagues. For this shared authorship to be successful, they knew they needed to provide collaborative planning time during the contract day for educators to review the units and add the specifics needed for classroom and program use. In the following commentaries, the four curriculum supervisors explain how this took place in their respective content areas. They also discuss how they dealt with issues related to the use of materials and resources, selection of specific instructional strategies, and the daily planning of lessons.

Raffaela Fronc said: "For science in the elementary schools, we have adopted the FOSS program as a tool for curriculum implementation. The kits from the FOSS program provide lesson plans for teachers to use. At the secondary level, teachers plan together during their collaboration times and will often share lessons with each other and conduct the same lab activities and projects. Daily lesson plans are not provided, so most of the ninth- and tenth-grade teams share lessons and assessments on a daily basis. Planning is left to the creativity of the teachers."

Mark Consorte said: "In social studies, the curriculum team provided the following components to the unit planning organizers: the Priority Standards; the "unwrapped" concepts, skills and corresponding Bloom's levels; unit vocabulary word walls; suggested learning activities; recommended research-based instructional strategies; and the common formative pre- and post-assessments for each unit of study. The curriculum team members, all of whom are classroom teachers, felt strongly that the details and day-to-day lesson plans should be left to each teacher to create. In this way, they would be able to maximize their individual teaching strengths and points of emphasis while helping all of their students arrive at the same end destination. As one of our high school teachers, Chris Pelatowski, eloquently explained to the West Haven Board of Education: 'There are many ways to get to New York City from West Haven (I-95 South, the Merritt Parkway, by train, by boat, by helicopter). How one gets there is up to the one who organizes the trip.'"

Amy Jo (A.J.) Palermo said: "The math curriculum writers left the details of creating the day-to-day lessons and learning activities to the classroom teachers. In the elementary units, we listed the lessons and math resources provided in the two commercial programs we are using. The specific units within one of these programs, in particular, provides detailed lessons for each math topic as well as a variety of useful resources (i.e., vocabulary cards, trade books, center activities, daily spiral review, problem of the day, etc.) that teachers can utilize as needed. Elementary teachers have begun sharing lessons, ideas, and math Web sites with the district's math coaches and with me, and we are doing our best to distribute these ideas and resources district-wide.

"The middle school and high school math teachers create their own day-to-day plans based primarily on the math textbook, but, of course, we are trying to encourage teachers to move away from their reliance on the text and incorporate more small group and hands-on activities. Doing so will help math 'come alive' and make the content more accessible for *all* students. Now that we have regularly scheduled collaboration time at the secondary level, math teachers have time to meet and plan out the lessons that will accompany the units of study. They love having this time to share ideas and resources.

"Related to this point, it is important for school systems undertaking the redesign of their curriculum to know that this type of teacher collaboration, although necessary, *does not work* without building and central office leadership being directly involved through understanding the process themselves, recognizing the scope of the project, attending meetings, supporting teachers being out of their classrooms, and so on."

Ann Valanzuolo said: "In English language arts at the elementary level, we provided more materials to the teachers than appear on the unit planning organizer. These materials encompass a variety of published and district-created materials that teachers have received over the past eight or more years. Along with the unit organizer, this year we provided new sample state test questions to accompany each story. In addition, for each unit we provided supplementary poems with corresponding questions. The core materials come from our commercial reading program that also includes daily lessons. Our previous reading comprehension binder, written a few years ago, provides a weekly plan and a reading strategy to focus on for the week. So even though only the unit planning organizers with all the required components are posted on the district Web site, elementary teachers do have quite a number of other resources to guide their teaching.

"At the middle school level, the unit planner serves as the guide, but we didn't provide daily lesson plans, so as to intentionally allow for teacher autonomy and creativity. We did suggest materials (stories, novels, nonfiction), but teachers can use different (approved) ones if they choose. The literature anthology and grammar book do include lessons, questions, and other activities, and we have teacher guides for the commonly taught novels. But it is up to the teachers how much they avail themselves of these resources. Knowing they are accountable for results on the unit-based common formative assessments when those assessments are analyzed in Data Team meetings ensures that the teachers are focusing their instruction on the "unwrapped" Priority Standards for that unit.

"At the high school, the rationale for not providing daily lesson plans is similar to that for the middle schools. However, because the teachers do receive collaborative planning time three days per week, in at least some of the grades, the teachers are able to develop daily lessons together. This is not to say that every day's lesson is the same for each teacher in the grade, but many of the teachers are finding it more productive to develop their lessons together."

West Haven's cooperative authorship of the curricular units is corroborated by the research, as reported here by John Hattie:

"The common themes of what makes various strategies successful are … in particular, teachers talking with other teachers about teaching and planning, deliberate attention to learning intentions and success criteria, and a constant effort to ensure teachers are seeking feedback information as to the success of their teaching on their students. This can be enabled when teachers critically reflect on their own teaching using classroom-based evidence, and it can be maximized when teachers are in a safe and caring environment among colleagues and talking about their teaching" (2009, p. 36).

West Haven Units Online

West Haven's initial units of study in the four Cohort 1 content areas of English language arts, math, science, and social studies were developed during the first year of curriculum redesign efforts. Curriculum writers in the Cohort 2 content areas of visual and performing arts, health and physical education, library media technology, career and business education, and prekindergarten are currently designing their units of study also. The Cohort 1 units of study are posted on the district Web site so that all members of the West Haven education community can view them. Cohort 2 units are being added as they are completed. The unit assessments are secured and will not be posted.

Since the entire school system is in the "construction phase" of comprehensive curriculum redesign, the current units of study are true works in progress. West Haven educators continue to revise and improve them through collaborative discussions both during and after the implementation of the units in their instructional programs. At present, the majority of units list program- or textbook-based lessons, activities, and resources under the column heading of "instructional planning." As the educators continue the revision and refinement process, they plan to include more details and suggestions related to the student learning activities, specific research-based instructional strategies, assisting students in need of intervention, and specialized strategies for special education students and English Language Learners. In doing so, they are creating a body of rigorous curricula that will serve their district educators and students for years to come.

At the time of this writing, West Haven's units of study are accessible by the general public. To view the "work-in-progress" drafts, please visit their school district Web site at *www.whschools.org*. Click on the home page link, "District," and then on the sidebar link "Curriculum." Scroll down to the heading, "Curricula." There you will see the specific units of study organized by content area and grade level. Click on any unit name to open and view the full unit planning organizer.

Adding Pacing and Sequencing Details

A comprehensive unit planning organizer needs to include all of the specific and general elements listed at the beginning of this chapter—*plus* other important details that the curriculum designers may or may not have included initially. The first three of these details focus on pacing and sequencing:

- Suggested number of days or class periods necessary for the different learning activities and experiences so that educators can correctly pace the unit

- Suggested "learning progressions" sequence for presenting the various learning activities and performance tasks planned

- Suggested sequence for teaching the "unwrapped" concepts and skills matched to the various learning activities and engaging learning experiences

Although they may not all *think* they are, educators are actually quite adept at time-management skills. They have to be; there is so much to plan, schedule, and carry out every day that educators must be able to maximize nearly every minute of their available instruction and planning time.

Sequencing and pacing textbook- or program-based learning activities and related instruction is something that educators do well, because they do it so often. Pacing *performance tasks* (engaging learning experiences) to coincide closely with a predetermined number of class periods or lessons can prove trickier. Yet to stay reasonably within the allocated time frame for a unit and administer the end-of-unit post-assessment to students on the date planned, it is necessary to do this.

In my own classroom experience, I found that too often I exceeded the amount of time I had planned to spend on different performance tasks. The reason was actually quite a good one—students were highly engaged in their learning and in producing quality products. But there was a more academic explanation for the fact that certain tasks took longer than others: my students were acquiring concepts and skills that simply required different amounts of time to learn and apply.

Hattie (2009) refers to this as *surface vs. deep* learning intentions: "The amount of time allocated should not be the same for all learning intentions, but should vary depending on whether [students] are developing concepts, skills, or knowledge—*concepts* or *deeper learning* are likely to need more time than, say, the acquisition of knowledge or surface information" (p. 163).

Performance tasks, an essential component in this design model of *rigorous* curricula, promote this kind of "deeper learning" and therefore require more time to implement. This is also true for certain "learning progression" building blocks within those tasks; some just require more time than others for students to thoroughly understand them. However, educators need to remember that because performance tasks and related learning progressions are based *primarily* on the "unwrapped" Priority Standards, the additional time students sometimes need to complete them is justifiable. Plan accordingly, while still being mindful of staying within the recommended time frame. Be flexible within the structure.

An important aspect of detailing each unit of study is to "ballpark" the number of days or instructional periods that classroom educators will need to (1) successfully teach the "unwrapped" concepts and skills, (2) have the students complete the related learning activities and experiences, and (3) keep reasonably within the time parameters listed on the curriculum pacing calendar.

Adding Instructional Strategy Details

In the previous chapter, I presented six broad categories of instructional strategies along with specific examples of each category, and recommended that curriculum designers prepare a comprehensive document listing all of these categories and related strategies. Referring now to that compilation of strategies, design teams can add the remaining details needed to complete each unit planning organizer. Again, these six categories of strategies are:

- 21st-century learning skills matched to each learning activity and performance task

- Research-based teaching strategies matched to the "unwrapped" Priority Standards and student learning experiences

- Differentiation strategies to use when presenting high-quality lessons to all students and the strategies for enriching competent and excelling students

- Intervention strategies (universal Tier 1 strategies for all students; Tier 2 and Tier 3 interventions for at-risk students)

- Specially designed instruction (SDI) prepared for special education students based upon their identified learning disability or disabilities

- Second language acquisition strategies (including Sheltered Instruction) to use with English Language Learners according to their current language levels (beginning, early intermediate, intermediate, early advanced, and advanced)

The inclusion of these various types of instructional strategies is an important part of what makes a curricular unit of study *rigorous*. Educators, planning individually and collaboratively, need to professionally determine (1) which of these strategies are the most appropriate for use with each of the learning activities and experiences and (2) which strategies will best meet the particular learning needs of their own students.

A Detailed Accompaniment to the Unit Planning Organizer

Because so many West Haven units have been developed using the original unit planning organizer, it would be counterproductive to change the unit organizer this far into implementation. I discussed with Assistant Superintendent Anne Druzolowski and her curriculum supervisors the most efficient way we might assist West Haven educators in adding the necessary details to the unit planners. I shared with them my prototype for a *second* template that could easily and effectively be used in conjunction with the original unit planning organizer. They thought the idea of an accompanying document made sense.

At my request, they completed a detailed second template representing the various types of instructional strategies and included several specific suggestions for *how to use* each of the instructional strategies listed. This supplemental document will *accompany,* not replace, the original unit planning organizer everyone in the school system is accustomed to using. In the fall of 2010, curriculum supervisors will ask educators to field-test this detailed unit accompaniment to evaluate its effectiveness as they continue implementing and revising the units of study in their own classrooms and instructional programs.

To illustrate how this supplemental document will work in tandem with the unit planning organizer, Figure 15.1 shows a sample original unit planning organizer created by members of the West Haven science curriculum design team.

FIGURE 15.1 **West Haven Unit Planning Organizer—Grade 2 Science**

Subject: Science

Grade: 2

Unit: Pebbles, Sand, and Silt

Pacing: November–January

Essential Question(s):

1. Does soil just contain little rocks? How do you know?
2. Can we tell if the soil on the beach and the soil in the desert are the same?
3. How does soil help us survive?

Big Idea(s):

1. Different soils have air, water, living things, and plant remains.
2. Properties of soil are color, texture, and loam.
3. Soil keeps plants, animals, and humans alive.

Connecticut State Standards (includes West Haven's Priority GLEs in bold, and Supporting Standards:

Priority Standards or GLEs	Supporting Standards
2.3.2—Classify soils by properties such as color, particle size (sand, silt, or clay), or amount of organic material (loam).	2.3.1—Use senses and simple tools (e.g., sieve and beakers) to separate soil into components such as rock fragments, water, air, and plant remains.
2.3.3—Explain the importance of soil to plants, animals, and people.	
2.3.4—Evaluate the quality of different soils in terms of observable presences of air, water, living things, and plant remains.	2.3.5—Conduct a fair test to investigate how different soil types affect plant growth and write conclusions supported by evidence.

FIGURE 15.1 **West Haven Unit Planning Organizer—Grade 2 Science** *(continued)*

"Unwrapped" Concepts and Skills, and Bloom's Taxonomy Levels (BL):

Concepts (Need to Know)	Skills (Able to Do)	BL
Components of soil • Rock fragments • Water • Air • Organic material	Observe/Analyze (soil components)	4
Separate soil to identify sand, silt, clay, particles.	Classify (properties)	2
Name particles by • Color • Size • Texture • Loam	Explain/Evaluate (importance of soil)	2
Soil Importance to • Plants • Animals • People		
Soil affects plant growth		

Shown in Figure 15.2 is the first section of the supplemental document, detailed by Science Supervisor Raffaela Fronc. It contains the Essential Questions and Big Ideas (listed again for emphasis) along with the details regarding the "learning progressions," instructional pacing, and sequencing of learning activities. The "unwrapped" concepts, skills, and Bloom's Taxonomy levels for the entire unit now directly match each specific learning activity.

FIGURE
15.2

West Haven Unit Planning Organizer
ACCOMPANYING DETAILS—Grade 2 Science

Subject: Science   **Grade:** 2

Unit Topic: Pebbles, Sand, and Silt

Essential Question:
Does soil just contain little rocks? How do you know?

Big Idea:
Different soils have air, water, living things, and plant remains.

Essential Question:
How can we tell if the soil on the beach and the soil in the desert are the same?

Big Idea:
Properties of soil are color, texture, and loam.

Essential Question:
How does soil help us survive?

Big Idea:
Soil keeps plants, animals, and humans alive.

Weeks Planned for Unit: 6-8	"Learning Progressions" Instructional Sequence	"Unwrapped" Concepts Specific to Each Learning Activity	"Unwrapped" Skills Specific to Each Learning Activity	Bloom's Taxonomy Level
Pacing: 2 weeks	2.3.2- FOSS Pebbles, Sand, & Silt; Investigation 2, Part 1: River Rock.	Components of soil • Rock Fragments • Water • Air • Organic Material	Observe and analyze (soil components)	4
Pacing: 1 week	2.3.3—FOSS Pebbles, Sand, & Silt; Investigation 2, Part 2: River Rock by Size.	Soil importance to • Plants • Animals • People	Explain and evaluate (importance of soil)	2
Pacing: 1 week	2.3.1—FOSS Pebbles, Sand, & Silt; Investigation 2, Part 3: Sand & Silt.	Separate soil to identify sand, silt, clay, particles		4
Pacing: 2 weeks	2.3.4—FOSS Pebbles, Sand, & Silt; Investigation 3, Part 1: Rocks in use.	Name particles by • Color • Size • Texture • Loam	Classify (properties)	2
Pacing: 1 week	2.3.5—FOSS Pebbles, Sand, & Silt; Investigation 4, Part 2: Soil search.	Soil affects plant growth		5

Detailing Made Simpler

The remaining sections of the additional template list all of the different types of instructional strategies by categories—research-based, differentiation, intervention, special education, and English Language Learner (21st-century learning skills have yet to be added). Particularly helpful for educators will be the provided suggestions for how to *use* each of the strategies.

Next to each strategy and suggestions for its use is a blank column to record the specific learning activity or experience to which the strategy will be applied. Certain categories of strategies (interventions, special education, and English Language Learner) also include a blank column for listing the *names of students* who will receive instruction through those specialized strategies.

The master document prepared by curriculum supervisors Raffaela Fronc, Ann Valanzuolo, and A.J. Palermo, shown in Figure 15.3, can be duplicated again and again to use with *all* unit planning organizers, thus saving educators time and effort required to create the specific details for each separate unit.

FIGURE 15.3 **Instructional Strategies Master Document**

RESEARCH-BASED EFFECTIVE TEACHING STRATEGIES

	Strategy	Suggestions for How to Use Strategy	Applied to Specific Learning Activity or Experience
1	Identifying Similarities and Differences	• Assign in-class and homework tasks related to the knowledge/skills: — Comparison and classification — Metaphors and analogies	
2	Summarizing and Note Taking	• When engaged in activities related to the knowledge/skills, ask the students to: — Generate verbal summaries — Generate written summary — Take notes — Revise notes, correcting errors and adding information	
3	Reinforcing Effort and Providing Recognition	• Recognize and celebrate students' progress toward learning goals/objectives • Recognize and reinforce the importance of student's effort(s)	
4	Homework and Practice	• Assign homework for the students to practice skills taught • Provide specific feedback on all assigned homework	
5	Nonlinguistic Representations	• When engaged in activities related to the knowledge/skills, ask the students to: — Generate mental images representing content — Draw pictures or pictographs representing content — Construct graphic organizers representing content — Act, draw, and "talk it out"/role-play — Make physical models of the content — Make revisions to their mental images, pictures, photographs, graphic organizers, and physical models	

FIGURE
15.3 **Instructional Strategies Master Document**
(continued)

RESEARCH-BASED EFFECTIVE TEACHING STRATEGIES

	Strategy	Suggestions for How to Use Strategy	Applied to Specific Learning Activity or Experience
6	Cooperative Learning	• Place the students into cooperative and/or flexible ability groups when appropriate • Model and apply peer questioning	
7	Setting Objectives and Providing Feedback	• Set specific learning goals for the students: — Ask the students to set their own learning goal(s) — Provide feedback to the students on learning goal(s) — Ask students to keep track of their progress on learning goals — Provide the students with summative feedback — Ask the students to assess themselves	
8	Generating and Testing Hypotheses	• Engage the students in projects that involve generating and testing hypotheses: — Problem-solving tasks — Decision-making tasks — Investigation tasks — Experimental inquiry tasks — Systems analysis tasks	
9	Cues, Questions, and Advance Organizers	• Prior to presenting new content: — Ask questions that help the students recall what they might already know about the content — Help the students make direct links to what they have previously studied — Provide ways for the students to organize or think about the content	
10	Nonfiction Writing	• Use engaging text for students to practice interdisciplinary nonfiction writing	

FIGURE
15.3 **Instructional Strategies Master Document**
(continued)

DIFFERENTIATION STRATEGIES
(Represented here as Tier 1 Universals for ALL Students Plus Enrichment Strategies)

	Strategy	Suggestions for How to Use Strategy	Applied to Specific Learning Activity or Experience
1	Multiple intelligences	• Provide support resources (manipulatives, visual aids, charts, outlines, picture cues, audiotape books, and instructions) • Vary assessment type (i.e., performance task, open response, multiple-choice, etc.)	
2	Graphic organizers	• KWL chart (what do we already know, what do we want to find out, what did we learn) • Sequencing • Venn diagram • Compare and contrast • Word and number webs	
3	Flexible grouping	• Jigsaw • Group investigation • Small-group instruction	
4	Individual student contracts	• Gradual release of direct assistance so students can perform independently	
5	Adjusting level of rigor in questions	• Finding of answers in provided texts rather than by random guessing • Varied questioning strategies	

FIGURE
15.3 **Instructional Strategies Master Document**
(continued)

DIFFERENTIATION STRATEGIES
(Represented here as <u>Tier 1</u> Universals for ALL Students Plus Enrichment Strategies)

	Strategy	Suggestions for How to Use Strategy	Applied to Specific Learning Activity or Experience
6	Independent study of student-selected projects	• Using scoring guides (rubrics) to guide development of a student-selected independent project	
7	Compacting (streamlining or modifying basic content to provide students with tiered assignments)	• Clear emphasis on the most important concepts and skills (i.e., "unwrapped" Priority Standards)	
8	Tiered assignments (designed at different levels of complexity according to students' readiness levels)	• Varied texts and supplementary materials • Varied homework • Assignment "menu" (choices)	
9	Connect new concepts to prior learning	• KWL, use real world ideas, topics and contexts that are appropriate and engaging	
10	Other		

FIGURE
15.3 **Instructional Strategies Master Document**
(continued)

INTERVENTION STRATEGIES

Tier 2 (Targeted) interventions include, but are not limited to:

	Tier 2 Strategy	Suggestions for How to Use Strategy	Student Names	Applied to Specific Learning Activity or Experience
1	Smaller grouping of students (may include individual student)	• Tutor • Title I pull-out/push-in • Resource teacher • Aide • Guided reading groups • Needs-based groups • Interventionists		
2	Instruction highly focused on specific skills and/or learning strategies	• Explicit instruction • Teach common misconceptions before errors occur • Additional 20 to 40 minutes of instruction		
3	Frequent monitoring and assessment of progress and social development	• Monthly data points, progress-monitoring checks to monitor learning and adjust instruction accordingly		
4	Matching of specific strategy to specific skill need and changing as needed	• Adapt ways of presenting task to address a variety of learning modalities		
5	Repetition	• Copy material or write it again • Rehearse things mentally or aloud • Repeat information to be recalled • Recite steps in a procedure, facts, lists, labels, or rules		

FIGURE
15.3 **Instructional Strategies Master Document**
(continued)

INTERVENTION STRATEGIES

Tier 2 (Targeted) interventions include, but are not limited to:

	Tier 2 Strategy	Suggestions for How to Use Strategy	Student Names	Applied to Specific Learning Activity or Experience
6	"Chunking" of information/time into smaller segments	• Break instructional duration into smaller chunks of time • Break instructional content into smaller chunks		
7	Providing more (or less) time	• Adjust the length of time for instruction, assignments, assessments, and projects according to student need		
8	Use of technology	• Smart Board • Calculators • Computer • Overhead projector • CDs • Student response clickers • Videos • Web sites		
9	Other			

FIGURE
15.3 **Instructional Strategies Master Document**
(continued)

INTERVENTION STRATEGIES

Tier 3 (Intensive) strategies include all of Tiers 1 and 2 PLUS:

	Tier 3 Strategy	Suggestions for How to Use Strategy	Student Names	Applied to Specific Learning Activity or Experience
1	Smaller teacher-student ratio and one-on-one instruction	• Tutor • Title I pull-out/push-in • Resource teacher • Aide • Guided reading groups • Needs-based groups • Interventionists		
2	More intensive supplemental interventions	• Supplemental resources • Individualized intervention • Increase in duration and intensity		
3	Longer duration of instruction	• Adjust pacing calendar to include more reteaching of key concepts/skills		

4	Detailed attention to the social environment	• Minimize distractions in environment:
		  — Close shades
		  — Close door
		  — Move seat
		  — Clear desk
		  — Put pencils away
		  — Put tennis balls on legs of chairs
		  — Provide study corral		

5	More frequent progress monitoring	• Daily/weekly data points; daily progress-monitoring checks to monitor learning and adjust instruction accordingly		
6	Other			

FIGURE
15.3 **Instructional Strategies Master Document**
(continued)

SPECIALLY DESIGNED INSTRUCTION

The general and special educators create specially designed instruction for each special education student according to specific disabilities indicated on the student's IEP (Individualized Education Program). These may include any differentiation and intervention strategies along with specific accommodations and modifications to content.

COGNITIVE Strategies:

	Strategy	Suggestions for How to Use Strategy	Student Names	Applied to Specific Learning Activity or Experience
1	Follow instructions from IEP	• Plan collaboration time with special education and/or resource teacher		
2	Repetition	• Copy material or write it again • Rehearse things mentally or aloud • Repeat information to be recalled • Recite steps in a procedure, facts, lists, labels, or rules		
3	Simplify the input (verbal or written instructions)	• Use lower-level reading books • Rephrase, reword, and simplify		
4	Scaffolding	• Simplify the task to make it more manageable for the student, then provide structure to get to the next level/stage		
5	Total Physical Response (TPR)	• Students respond with body movement to show comprehension		
6	Extended wait time	• Provide uninterrupted periods of time for students to consider what their personal response will be		
7	Teaching one concept at a time and allowing sufficient processing time	• Pace: ensure mastery of strategy by introducing concepts in chunks • Focus on both the process and content of learning		

FIGURE
15.3 **Instructional Strategies Master Document**
(continued)

SPECIALLY DESIGNED INSTRUCTION

COGNITIVE Strategies:

	Strategy	Suggestions for How to Use Strategy	Student Names	Applied to Specific Learning Activity or Experience
8	Home school communication	• Share instruction methods with family for home practice of skills • Letters home or newsletters • Family Nights		
9	Categorize	• Picture or word webs • Multiple-meaning words		
10	Use drawings, photographs, and common objects	• Use word and number webs, reference charts, common objects		
11	Use of technology	• Assistive Technology • Writing with symbol program • Special education Web sites • Slant board Tracker • Smart Board • Calculators • Computer • Overhead projector • CDs • Videos • Web sites • Student response clickers		
12	Use sensory feedback techniques	• Raised line paper • Tactile letter cards		
13	Clear and explicit expectations	• Scoring guides (teacher and student generated) • Systematic breakdown of specific strategies, skills and concepts (i.e. step-by-step explanation of what students are to do)		
14	Other			

FIGURE 15.3 **Instructional Strategies Master Document** *(continued)*

SPECIALLY DESIGNED INSTRUCTION

BEHAVIORAL Strategies:

	Strategy	Suggestions for How to Use Strategy	Student Names	Applied to Specific Learning Activity or Experience
1	Consistent reward system	Decide with student in advance; make reward relevant and motivational to student		
2	Provide explicit feedback on acceptable and non-acceptable behavior	• Use examples • Make students part of deciding rules/logical consequences		
3	Use tangible and non-tangible incentives/rewards	• Free time • Sticker charts • Sit with a friend • Homework pass • Class helper • Choice of assignment • Positive note or call home • Class reward		
4	Avoid distracting stimuli	• Close shades • Close door • Move seat • Clear desk • Put pencils away • Put tennis balls on legs of chairs • Provide study corral		
5	Provide time for children to break away from task	• Give physical outlet to children, stand and stretch		
6	Other			

FIGURE
15.3 **Instructional Strategies Master Document** *(continued)*

STRATEGIES FOR ENGLISH LANGUAGE LEARNERS

Use the Differentiation and Tiered strategies *in addition* to the following:

	Strategy	Suggestions for How to Use Strategy	Student Names and Current Language Levels	Applied to Specific Learning Activity or Experience
1	Simplify the input (verbal or written instructions)	• Lower-level reading books • Rephrase, reword, simplify		
2	Scaffolding of information	• Simplify the task to make it more manageable for the child, then provide structure to get to the next level/stage		
3	Total Physical Response (TPR)	• Students respond with body movement to show comprehension		
4	Connections to primary language and cultures	• Students bring information/objects from home • Reflect diversity in classroom		
5	Sufficient "think time"	• Provide uninterrupted periods of time to process information and reflect on what is being said		
6	Sufficient practice and reinforcement activities	• Provide daily practice of critical skills/concepts (i.e., Daily Math Review template or Daily Oral Language)		
7	Ongoing comprehension checks (both oral and written)	• Running records • Questions • Retelling of story • Summarizing of story • Story frames		

FIGURE
15.3 **Instructional Strategies Master Document**
(continued)

STRATEGIES FOR ENGLISH LANGUAGE LEARNERS

	Strategy	Suggestions for How to Use Strategy	Student Names and Current Language Levels	Applied to Specific Learning Activity or Experience
8	Use of contextual clues	• Bits of information from text that allow students to decide the meanings of unknown words (i.e., antonyms, synonyms)		
9	Frequent checks for under-standing	• Have students restate directions, provide opportunities for them to ask their own questions		
10	Learning that is student-centered and content-driven	• Help students discover their own learning styles and teach them how to set achievable goals and develop study skills		
11	Access student's prior knowledge; build background knowledge	• Connect concept to students' lives/interests • Increase the variety and depth of out-of-class experiences • Provide "virtual experiences" • Provide direct vocabulary instruction		
12	Use drawings, photographs, and common objects	• Use number webs and reference charts (display in classroom)		
13	Categorize	• Picture or word webs • Multiple-meaning words • Classification games		
14	Addressing listening, speaking, reading, and writing skills throughout instruction	• Provide varied opportunities to practice all four of these methods of communication each day in all content areas		

FIGURE
15.3 **Instructional Strategies Master Document**
(continued)

STRATEGIES FOR ENGLISH LANGUAGE LEARNERS

	Strategy	Suggestions for How to Use Strategy	Student Names and Current Language Levels	Applied to Specific Learning Activity or Experience
15	Repetition	• Copy material or write it again • Rehearse things mentally or aloud • Repeat information to be recalled • Recite steps in a procedure, facts, lists, labels, or rules		
16	Home school communi- cation	• Share instruction methods with family for home practice of skills • Letters home/newsletters • Family Nights		
17	Other			

One Template or Two

Admittedly, this second template is *long*. Yet remember its essential purpose—to provide educators with a comprehensive unit planning tool for detailing a *rigorous* curricular unit of study. Once again, form has to follow function.

In the event that curriculum teams have not yet finalized their unit organizer *or* developed many of their units of study, they may want to consider revising their template to include all of these needed details before proceeding any further. They will then have no need for a supplemental template. Everything will be provided in one all-inclusive unit planning organizer. However, the result may be less user-friendly than the two templates shown in the West Haven example.

Remember that when curriculum design teams first brainstormed the elements and components to include on the unit planning organizer, most likely they did not anticipate the eventual need for this level of detail. Even if they had, the idea of including so many types of specialized instructional strategies might have seemed—

in the beginning—too unwieldy and complicated to include on one all-encompassing template.

My recommendation is that curriculum teams start with a more simplified unit planning organizer and then add a second template for the details when they arrive at this stage of the process. However, there are other factors to consider before making such a decision.

Adding the Details—Who Does What and How Much?

West Haven's regularly scheduled "production days" and in-school collaborative planning work sessions have enabled the designer-educator teams to continue developing and refining the units and providing additional details as needed.

However, this approach may not be feasible for other school systems that are not yet able to provide such extensive collaborative planning time. In such instances, it may be necessary for the *curriculum designers* to provide as many specific details as possible on the unit planning organizers.

In considering how best to complete the units of study so they are ready to be implemented, a conversation needs to take place between school system leaders, curriculum supervisors, and the design team members in order to answer two important questions:

- How much additional detail do *we* include on the unit planning organizer and in any accompanying documents?
- How much detail do we leave for the *educators* to provide?

Here are a few pros and cons to consider with regard to both positions that will hopefully assist you in making your final decision.

Detailing by the Educators

The *benefits* of leaving the details for the educators to decide:

- Respects educators as professionals capable of completing the planning on their own
- Promotes a genuine "shared ownership" of curricular units between designers and educators who were not part of the initial unit creation
- Provides a solid framework with built-in flexibility
- Encourages professional creativity and customization
- Allows educators to bring their unique strengths to the unit

- Promotes collaborative planning
- Encourages sharing of lessons, activities, and instructional tips

The *potential drawbacks* of *not* providing specific unit details:

- Causes uncertainty about whether units will be completed as intended
- Leaves too much for educators to do during their limited planning time
- Assumes that the "unwrapped" concepts, skills, and corresponding Bloom's Taxonomy levels will be specifically matched to each learning activity and experience
- Presupposes that educators have the background knowledge of the various types of specialized instructional strategies to know *how* to supply these details
- Lacks specificity with regard to pacing of the unit on a week-to-week basis
- Creates possible inability to complete the unit on time as per the pacing calendar

West Haven's decision to delegate the unit detailing to the educators was a necessity for them, due to the fact that their curriculum designers had to create an extensive number of curricular units for multiple grade levels, courses, and content areas, while *simultaneously carrying on their teaching responsibilities.* Under such demanding circumstances, providing so much detail is far too time consuming for designer-educators to be able to accomplish on their own. Instead, creating a second template for detailing the units that the designers-educators collaboratively complete as they prepare to implement each unit of study is likely to preserve all of the benefits and avert all of the drawbacks listed above.

There is another important reason that West Haven's coauthored approach to curriculum redesign is worth considering. Because implementing this rigorous curriculum model is almost guaranteed to require a change in the way many educators view standards, teaching, and assessment practices, it is important that the educators who did not create the initial unit planning organizers have some degree of ownership in the process. This will enable them to better understand the importance of all of the elements included on both the unit planning organizer and the detailed accompaniment and how to implement these elements effectively.

Shifting long-set paradigms is never easy, and the most effective way of helping people change habitual ways of thinking is by enabling them to act or experience their way into new beliefs. In this context, such shifts in understanding and the resulting "buy-in" can best be accomplished through the collaborative *completion* of the new curricular units.

Detailing by the Designers

If, on the other hand, curriculum designers decide to add this level of detail to the unit organizers, each unit of study will be sure to contain the desired specificity.

The *benefits* of providing fully detailed units to educators:

- Prevents busy teachers from having to identify and supply what is missing

- Ensures the delivery of a quality, rigorous curriculum, complete and ready to use

- Provides more defined parameters for implementing units within pacing calendar time frames

- Shows the "unwrapped" concepts, skills, and corresponding Bloom's Taxonomy levels specifically matched to each learning activity and experience

- Includes the various types of instructional strategies that classroom educators can reference when planning their weekly and daily lesson plans

- Offers *new* educators a detailed set of units to follow and *experienced* educators a valuable resource that they can still personalize

The *potential drawbacks* to this approach:

- May be overly ambitious and unrealistic for design teams to accomplish within available time and scheduling parameters

- Overly prescriptive details may be misinterpreted by educators as micromanaging instruction—their domain of responsibility

- May jeopardize the goal of a shared-ownership curriculum

- May elicit a "you-have-got-to-be-kidding" reaction in educators when they see the unit planning organizer and extensive supplemental details document for the first time

Keep in mind that the educators who are not part of the curriculum writing teams will not understand the makeup of the units as well as those educators who initially created them. As a result, they will understandably have a greater "learning curve" and will need additional support from those who *did* serve on the teams. To expect them to supply the additional details at the desired level of quality and rigor may be unrealistic.

As mentioned in the previous chapter, knowing how to select and apply the highly specialized types of instructional strategies (research-based, differentiation, intervention, special education, English Language Learner), along with 21st-century learning skills, may prove difficult for certain educators who have not had prior professional development in learning how to use all of these strategies. Here is where resident special educators can be of great help to general education teachers in planning specially designed instruction for special education students. Similarly, "in-house" ELL instructors can help general education teachers understand and use specific strategies that align with English Language Learners' current levels of language acquisition. Intervention specialists can provide job-embedded professional development to assist general educators in learning how to appropriately apply the tiered intervention strategies.

Curriculum supervisors and designers will need to clearly explain the rationale for including so many details when they first present the units to colleagues. The good news is that when educators are intentionally provided with a comprehensive set of curricular units that are "ready to use," they can spend their valuable and limited planning time on deciding how best to *implement the unit components through the weekly plan and the related daily lessons* rather than on working out the specific details of what any general suggestions or strategies might mean in terms of actual day-to-day use.

Create the Second Template

Curriculum designers can reference the following three documents to create their own version of the supplemental template entitled, "Details to Accompany the Unit Planning Organizer":

- The list of specific instructional strategies prepared in response to the Reader's Assignment at the conclusion of Chapter 14

- The accompanying details document used in West Haven (Figure 15.3)

- The list in Figure 15.4 of specific guidelines for adding unit details

This second template will assist whoever details the units—the educators, the curriculum designers, or a combination of both.

FIGURE
15.4
Specific Guidelines for Adding Unit Details

Specific Guidelines for Adding Unit Details

- Propose a "learning progressions" sequence for delivering all of the *engaging learning activities and experiences,* along with the approximate number of weeks necessary to complete them, so as to keep on pace for the allocated amount of time scheduled for the unit.

- Suggest a "learning progressions" sequence for teaching the *"unwrapped" concepts and skills.*

- Specify particular *21st-century learning skills* for the different student learning activities and experiences.

- Specify particular *research-based instructional strategies* for the different student learning activities and experiences.

- Make specific suggestions for *differentiating instruction* relative to those tasks and activities that include additional supports to use with *all* students and specific strategies for *enriching* competent and excelling students.

- Offer specific ideas for *intervention strategies* to assist all students (Tier 1) and at-risk students (Tiers 2 and 3) in their efforts to complete the learning tasks and understand the "unwrapped" concepts and skills.

- Recommend that general education teachers reference the provided instructional strategies and consult with special educators to create *specially designed instruction (SDI)* for special education students based upon their identified learning disability or disabilities.

- Suggest *regular and Sheltered Instruction strategies for English Language Learners* based on their level of language acquisition (beginning, early intermediate, intermediate, early advanced, or advanced).

- Include possible *accommodations and modifications* for English Language Learners and special education students specific to each of the learning activities listed on the detailed accompaniment to the unit planning organizer.

Reader's Assignment

1. Discuss and decide with colleagues and school system administrators *who* will provide the needed details for each of the unit planning organizers. In doing so, consider:

   • how the benefits and potential drawbacks presented in this chapter apply to your particular situation;

   • how much "shared ownership" of the units is appropriate based on the culture, needs, and philosophy of the school system;

   • how feasible it is to hire substitutes and release educators during the contract day to complete the work (budget, personnel, location, frequency of work sessions, etc.); and

   • how much professional development in the various types of instructional strategies will most likely be needed for the curriculum designers and/or classroom educators.

2. To make sure that the other fundamental elements and details needed for a rigorous curricular unit are included in the planning documents, decide whether to:

   • *revise the original* unit planning organizer to include all of the added details; *or*

   • *create a second template* to accompany the original unit organizer (recommended).

3. Create the supplemental template entitled, "Details to Accompany the Unit Organizer" as described above for use by those who will do the actual detailing of the units.

CHAPTER 16

Write the Weekly Plan;
Design the Daily Lesson

When the units of study are at last designed, detailed, and ready to implement, educators can start thinking about how they will administer the units in their own classrooms and instructional programs. And the place to record their thinking is on the weekly and daily lesson plan templates.

Unlike the issue of *who* should detail the unit planning organizer, deciding who should write the weekly plan and design the daily lesson is not in question—these are the rightful responsibilities of the classroom educator. Yet there are other issues to consider, and one of them is whether written plans are indeed necessary, especially for veteran educators who know their curriculum inside and out.

The SOP Lesson

Whenever I am talking with educators about lesson plans, I recall a long-ago conversation that took place between a colleague and me one morning before school in the teachers' lounge as we stood next to each other, pulling miscellaneous papers out of our respective mailboxes.

Me: "So, what are you planning for your math lesson today?"

She: "I don't know yet. I guess we'll have to wait and see."

Later in the day, we crossed paths again, and our conversation picked up right where we had left off.

Me: "So how did the math lesson go?"

She: "Actually, great. It turned out to be one of my best ones so far."

Me: "The SOP lesson triumphs again!"

We laughed and parted company. "SOP" was our acronym for "Seat of the Pants," a type of lesson that we both privately admitted to using more often than we would have ever announced at a faculty meeting with our principal present. Both of us were experienced teachers who had been planning thorough, and sometimes not-so-thorough, daily lessons for a long time. We knew what we were doing, but the reality for us, as elementary teachers, was that there simply were not enough hours in the day to detail every single lesson for every single subject every single day. So there was the occasional lesson that required … improvisation.

The Purpose of Lesson Plans

Educators need to see a clear benefit for filling out a daily or weekly lesson planner, or it becomes difficult to justify the time required to do it. This becomes especially true when each page of the planner is divided into minuscule square boxes that provide too little space to write anything of much use.

Many educators admit to seeing the completion of formally written lesson plans as busywork, something required by the administrator for no other *apparent* reason than proof that the educator wrote them. Others believe that having to submit lesson plans is an infringement upon their academic freedom, or that their professionalism is being called into question. In truth, written lesson plans, along with classroom observational visits, benefit administrators by helping them determine (1) the quality of lessons taking place in the classrooms, and (2) the degree to which the learning needs of *all* students are being met. Since both the educator *and* the administrator are accountable for student learning, written lesson plans, along with related discussions, help administrators determine how to support educators in whatever ways needed.

However, detailed written plans—not SOP lesson plans where the teacher just "wings it"—primarily benefit the educators who write them and the students who receive the results of those efforts. Thorough lesson plans focus instruction, enable use of individual teaching strengths, maximize class time, and advance learning for *all* students. Such plans provide educators with solid evidence that their teaching practices are *intentional* rather than accidental.

Writing a detailed plan is also worth doing because it gives the educator *clarity of thought* about what to teach, how to teach it, and which students need a different approach to ensure their learning. Just as "unwrapping" standards gives educators absolute certainty about *what* students need to know and be able to do, writing weekly and daily lesson plans allows educators to carefully think through exactly *how* they intend to make that educational vision happen during the lesson.

This is especially necessary today, when specialized instructional techniques and differentiated learning activities must be part of each and every lesson. There are far too many complex elements to just leave to chance. Every educator knows that the "best laid plans" can go off course in the classroom at any time. Having a definite, written plan prepared in advance makes it much easier for educators to make those inevitable spur-of-the-moment changes without losing their focus.

To keep everything seamlessly connected, the templates for each unit of study need to be clearly linked to one another. The weekly template needs to align with the unit planning organizer templates, and the daily lesson plan template needs to align with the weekly template. To ensure this alignment, these different planners should all share a majority of the same elements.

WRITE THE WEEKLY PLAN

Writing the weekly plan, whether in general terms or exhaustive detail, is a necessary planning step that educators routinely take as they begin thinking about and preparing for each new week of lessons and learning activities. This advance planning provides them with a guide to follow during the busy hours of each day when their minds are intensely focused on the learning needs of their students. In short, weekly lesson plans help educators plan the work, so that they can later work the plan.

The weekly planner shown in Figure 16.1 is the one I developed for this purpose. Notice how it closely aligns to the template for adding details to the unit planning organizer. Even though this template contains more sections than the traditional weekly planning grid, the greater degree of specificity it provides will sharply focus instructional planning. Next to certain types of specialized instructional strategies is a column for recording student names. This will allow educators to match specific strategies to specific students.

A Completed Weekly Planner

In the previous chapter, I presented a West Haven example of how to detail an entire science *unit* using a commercial kit of instructional resources. In this chapter, I show how to detail *one engaging learning experience* (authentic performance task) for a middle school social studies unit, using the weekly planner format in Figure 16.1.

Students will complete four performance tasks during the course of the four-week unit of study—one per week with related lessons and activities. This first performance task is based upon the "unwrapped" concepts and skills from the "unwrapped," unit-assigned Priority Standards in social studies. The task is interdisciplinary and incorporates standards in science and English language arts. The student directions for this task are shown in Figure 16.2. The scoring guide is not provided as part of this example.

FIGURE 16.1 **Weekly Planner**

Subject:			Date:	
Grade:			Time:	
Unit of Study:			Teacher:	

Days Planned: 5	"Learning Progressions" Instructional Sequence	"Unwrapped" Skills, Concepts, and Bloom's Taxonomy Levels Specific to Each Day's Learning Activity	Research-Based Teaching Strategies Specific to Each Day's Learning Activity	21st-Century Skills Specific to Each Day's Learning Activity
Day 1				
Day 2				
Day 3				
Day 4				
Day 5				

Materials/Resources (Physical)	Materials/Resources (Technology-Based)	
Differentiation Strategies (Inclusive for All Students)	**Differentiation Strategies (Enrichment or Extension)**	**Student Names**
Additional supports to use during high-quality lessons:		
Tier 1 Interventions (Universals)		
Strategies to use with all students that are matched to specific learning activities/experiences:		

FIGURE
16.1 **Weekly Planner** *(continued)*

Tier 2 Intervention (Targeted)	Tier 2 students: (individual names listed; strategies matched to individual students)
Tier 3 Intervention (Intensive)	Tier 3 students: (individual names listed; strategies matched to individual students)
Specially Designed Instruction (SDI) as per Student IEP	Special Education students: (individual names listed with suggestions for using strategies, applying accommodations/modifications as needed)
ELL Strategies (including Sheltered Instruction) Matched to Students' Current Language Acquisition Levels	ELL students: (individual student names listed with corresponding language levels; suggestions for applying strategies with individual students)

FIGURE 16.2 Student Directions for Performance Task 1

Engaging Learning Experience
(Authentic Performance Assessment)

Grade 6 Interdisciplinary Social Studies, Science, and Writing
Prehistoric Unit
Pacing Calendar Duration: Four Weeks

Student Directions (Task 1, Full Description):

Research a prehistoric animal of your choosing. Create a poster of information
that includes the following categories:

- Physical attributes (size, shape, weight, body covering, etc.)
- Location and era (when and where it lived)
- Biome and characteristics of habitat
- Dietary category (herbivore, carnivore, omnivore)
- Interesting facts
- Inferences and conclusions about animal's life
- Illustrations

Read the task-specific scoring guide criteria for more detailed information about
how your poster will be evaluated. Refer to the scoring guide often as you
complete your project to self-assess your progress.

Taking into consideration the "surface vs. deeper learning" considerations
presented by Hattie (2009), the "building blocks of learning progressions" explained
by Popham (2008), and my own middle school classroom teaching experience, I
determined the sequence of the five daily lessons and how long each part of the
week-long performance task would most likely take students to complete. Figure
16.3 shows the completed version of the Weekly Lesson Plan Template.

FIGURE 16.3 **Sample Weekly Lesson Plan Template**

Days Planned: 5	"Learning Progressions" Instructional Sequence	"Unwrapped" Skills, Concepts, and Bloom Levels Specific to Each Day's Learning Activity	Research-Based Teaching Strategies Specific to Each Learning Activity	21st-Century Skills Specific to Each Learning Activity
Days 1–2	Form cooperative groups; choose animal; jigsaw task—each member assigned different category; research, gather facts/key information, take notes.	(1) DESCRIBE (topic) (2) SUMMARIZE (facts) (2) INTERPRET (information)	Setting an objective; Cooperative learning (students grouped heterogeneously); Interacting with text; Note taking; Interpreting and summarizing information; Inquiry project	✓ **Check all those that apply to the learning activity:** ☑ Teamwork and Collaboration ☑ Initiative and Leadership ☑ Curiosity and Imagination ☐ Innovation and Creativity ☑ Critical Thinking and Problem Solving ☑ Flexibility and Adaptability ☐ Effective Oral and Written Communication ☑ Accessing and Analyzing Information
Day 3	Use research notes to draft category descriptions.	(4) INFER (from scientific facts) (5) CONCLUDE (from evidence) (3) APPLY (relevant information)	Nonfiction writing process; Summarizing information; Making inference from scientific facts; Drawing conclusion from evidence	✓ **Check all those that apply to the learning activity:** ☑ Teamwork and Collaboration ☑ Initiative and Leadership ☐ Curiosity and Imagination ☑ Innovation and Creativity ☑ Critical Thinking and Problem Solving ☐ Flexibility and Adaptability ☐ Effective Oral and Written Communication ☑ Accessing and Analyzing Information
Day 4	Receive feedback from group members/teacher; revise and edit descriptions.	(4–6) REVISE (expository writing)	Receiving constructive feedback; Reinforcing effort; Revising and editing expository writing	✓ **Check all those that apply to the learning activity:** ☑ Teamwork and Collaboration ☐ Initiative and Leadership ☐ Curiosity and Imagination ☐ Innovation and Creativity ☑ Critical Thinking and Problem Solving ☑ Flexibility and Adaptability ☑ Effective Oral and Written Communication ☑ Accessing and Analyzing Information
Day 5	Create other poster elements (illustrations, title, headings, etc.); plan and organize poster layout; finalize poster.	(4) ORGANIZE* (information) (6) CREATE* (representation of facts) *These two skills will be emphasized throughout Days 3–5	Nonlinguistic representation	✓ **Check all those that apply to the learning activity:** ☑ Teamwork and Collaboration ☑ Initiative and Leadership ☑ Curiosity and Imagination ☑ Innovation and Creativity ☑ Critical Thinking and Problem Solving ☑ Flexibility and Adaptability ☐ Effective Oral and Written Communication ☐ Accessing and Analyzing Information

FIGURE
16.3 **Sample Weekly Lesson Plan Template** *(continued)*

Materials/Resources (Physical)	Materials/Resources (Technology-Based)	
Poster board; markers; index cards; glue sticks; print materials and related Internet links in library/media center	Internet sites to be determined; simulation software to illustrate science and social studies concepts, characteristics, and task-assigned categories of selected prehistoric animal	
Differentiation Strategies (Inclusive for All Students)	**Differentiation Strategies (Enrichment or Extension)**	**Student Names**
Additional supports to use during high-quality lessons: • Multiple intelligences • Jigsaw task responsibilities • Group investigation • Visual aids, charts • Personal assistance from teacher and peers • Step-by-step breakdown of task requirements • Cooperative grouping with assigned roles • Emphasis on most important concepts and skills ("unwrapped" Priority Standards)	• More challenging and creative work above and beyond task requirements (listed on Advanced level of task scoring guide) • Task extension to express multiple intelligences • Pursuit of related independent study involving higher-level concepts and skills (produce clay model or cartoon strip of animal, etc.)	

Tier 1 Interventions (Universals)

Strategies to use with all students that are matched to specific learning activities/experiences:
- Differentiated instruction of content, process, product
- Additional time
- Graphic organizers
- Systematic sequential instruction
- Collaborative learning activities
- Direct/explicit instruction
- "Chunking" of information into smaller bits
- Help with locating related research information
- Support resources (visual aids, charts, picture cues; audio resources; Internet links)

Tier 2 Interventions (Targeted)	Tier 2 students: (individual names listed; strategies matched to individual students)
• Increased intervention frequency, intensity, and duration of instruction • Matching of specific strategy to specific skill and changing as needed • Double-dosing of instruction • Computerized assistance	

FIGURE 16.3 **Sample Weekly Lesson Plan Template** *(continued)*

Tier 3 Interventions (Intensive)	Tier 3 students: (individual names listed; strategies matched to individual students)
• Longer time to complete portions of task • Individually differentiated content, process, and product • Increased intervention frequency, intensity, and duration • Intensive, core, adult support • Intensive learning plan • Individual behavior plan (assessment, contract, reinforcement, and modeling) • Modification of cooperative group • Individualized intervention • Triple-dosing of instruction • Increased opportunities to use learning-style preferences • Increase the use of sensory modalities • Evaluation and modification of learning environment	
Specially Designed Instruction (SDI) as per Student IEP	Special Education students: (individual names listed with suggestions for using strategies, applying accommodations/modifications as needed)
Accommodations as per IEP: • Additional time • Nonlinguistic representations via computer • Technology (high, medium, or low): Alpha Smart, word recognition software, text readers • Small-group collaboration **Modifications as per IEP:** • Menu of products • Matching process to learning style • Modifying quantity of work • Dictation • Computer graphics • Comparison matrix • Extended time • Scaffolding information • Differentiation of content, process, and/or product • Change in pace • Accessible texts	

FIGURE 16.3 **Sample Weekly Lesson Plan Template** *(continued)*

Specially Designed Instruction (SDI) as per Student IEP *(continued)*	
Strategies designed to meet the needs of individual students and specific disability: • Explicit, direct instruction to address area of disability • Modeling and demonstration • Visual, auditory, tactile, or kinesthetic instruction • Advance organizers (with instruction) • Mnemonics or memory strategies • Frequent (short) assessments • Task analysis with student checklist (demonstrated)	
ELL Strategies (including Sheltered Instruction) Matched to Students' Current Language Acquisition Levels	ELL students: (individual student names listed with corresponding language levels; suggestions for applying strategies with individual students)
• Direct instruction and modeling • Questions/strategies related to appropriate level of language acquisition • Assistance from cooperative group members • Regular differentiation strategies • Scaffolding of information • Quick writes/quick draws • Visuals and realia (where applicable) • Connections to primary language (wherever possible) • Ongoing comprehension checks (both oral and written)	

Notice how the research-supported teaching approaches associated with *educator's planning* by Hattie (2009, p. 36), cited in the previous chapter and repeated here, are reflected in the detailed planning of this weeklong task, as indicated parenthetically:

• "Paying deliberate attention to learning intentions and success criteria" (concepts, skills, levels of rigor, task-specific scoring guide)

• "Setting challenging tasks" (includes levels 1–6 in Bloom's thinking-skill hierarchy)

- "Providing multiple opportunities for deliberate practice" (during five days of task)
- "Knowing when both the teacher and the student are successful in attaining these goals" (evidence provided by completion of poster as per directions and scoring guide criteria)
- "Understanding the critical role of teaching appropriate learning strategies" (matching research-based strategies/21st-century skills to "learning progressions" sequence; listing of students by name to receive appropriate strategies—enrichment, intervention, SDI, ELL)
- "Ensuring the teacher constantly seeks feedback information as to the success of his or her teaching" (monitoring of group work as students complete each day's related assignment, providing guidance and corrective instruction as needed)

Figure 16.4 provides a summary of steps for completing the weekly lesson plan template shown in Figure 16.1. These steps are applicable to all types of student learning experiences. Writing weekly plans that include this level of detail will provide the educator with helpful clarity for designing the *daily* lesson plans, the subject of the remainder of this chapter.

DESIGN THE DAILY LESSON

One stumbling block that occurs when designing daily lessons is the difficulty of finding the balance between writing too little and too much detail. To write a thoughtful, comprehensive lesson plan takes time, thought, and energy. Teachers want the lesson plan to be comprehensive, but not take so long to write that they are unable to adequately prepare for the *other* lessons they must teach.

Collaborative planning and writing of daily lessons can be a great help in this regard. Teachers can divide up the workload while sharing ideas with one another. Not only does this result in the exchange of effective ideas for implementing the lesson, it also promotes consistency and quality in the daily plan and reduces needless redundancy. Collaboration makes it possible for educators to "work smarter, not harder" and build a shared confidence in planning a quality lesson that includes all the key elements they know to be necessary.

The intentional alignment between the weekly template and the daily template helps ensure implementation of the weekly plan in daily "installments." For this reason, the format of the daily template may be nearly identical to that of the weekly template shown earlier in Figure 16.1.

FIGURE 16.4   **Guidelines for Writing the Weekly Plan**

Guidelines for Writing the Weekly Plan

- Propose a "learning progressions" sequence for delivering all of the engaging learning activities and experiences, along with the approximate number of lessons or class periods necessary to complete them, so as to keep on pace for the allocated number of weeks scheduled for the unit. Decide how much of the sequence can be done in each class period or lesson.

- Reference the "unwrapped" concepts, skills, and levels of rigor on the unit planning organizer; plan on which days to explicitly teach each of those elements.

- Reference the general list of research-based effective teaching strategies included on the unit planning organizer; plan on which days to explicitly use each of those strategies and with which learning activities and experiences.

- Identify the 21st-century learning skills that students will exercise each day.

- Identify instructional resources and materials needed for the task.

- Reference the details provided with the unit planning organizer. Select differentiation, enrichment, and universal (Tier 1) intervention strategies to use with all students and with individual students, as needed.

- Select intervention strategies (Tier 2 and Tier 3) applicable to identified students at risk.

- Collaborate with special educator to select specific strategies and plan specially designed instruction (SDI) for special education students based on their identified learning disability or disabilities (cognitive and behavioral).

- Select specific ELL strategies (including Sheltered Instruction) appropriate to each student's current language acquisition level.

The *content* of the two templates will also be much the same. For example, the same specialized strategies targeted for use with specific students during the *entire week* will probably be used each day. The chief differences will become evident in the learning tasks, "unwrapped" concepts and skills, lesson-specific research-based teaching strategies, and 21st-century learning skills. All of these are likely to change daily.

Just as the task of writing the weekly plan and designing the daily lesson is rightfully the role of the educator, creation of the weekly and daily lesson plan templates should be left to the individual educator or school faculties to decide. However, curriculum designers can certainly create and share sample templates for them to consider.

Sample Lesson Plan Formats

The schools in Middletown, Connecticut, have latitude in creating their own school-specific lesson plan templates. However, there is general agreement within the district that common elements are important to include on every school's individualized daily lesson plan template. They are listed in Figure 16.5.

Even though lesson plan formats do vary by school and level (elementary, middle, high), the majority of these same *elements* appear on all of them. I selected the following three Middletown lesson planning documents as representative examples: Lawrence School Comprehensive Lesson Plan Template (Figure 16.6); Keigwin Middle School Lesson Plan (Figure 16.7); and Middletown High School Lesson Plan (Figure 16.8).

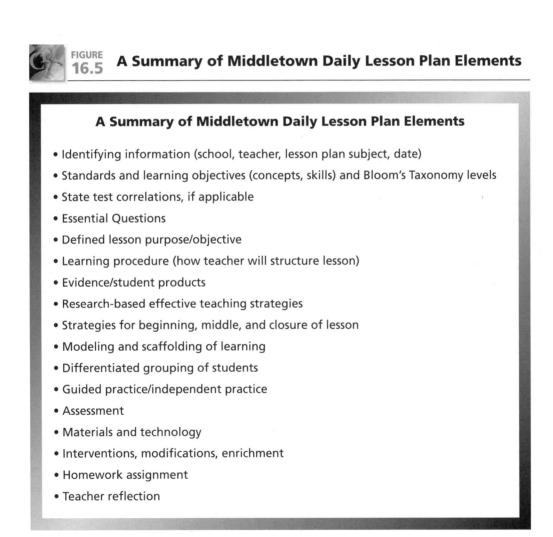

FIGURE 16.5 **A Summary of Middletown Daily Lesson Plan Elements**

A Summary of Middletown Daily Lesson Plan Elements

- Identifying information (school, teacher, lesson plan subject, date)
- Standards and learning objectives (concepts, skills) and Bloom's Taxonomy levels
- State test correlations, if applicable
- Essential Questions
- Defined lesson purpose/objective
- Learning procedure (how teacher will structure lesson)
- Evidence/student products
- Research-based effective teaching strategies
- Strategies for beginning, middle, and closure of lesson
- Modeling and scaffolding of learning
- Differentiated grouping of students
- Guided practice/independent practice
- Assessment
- Materials and technology
- Interventions, modifications, enrichment
- Homework assignment
- Teacher reflection

FIGURE 16.6 Lawrence School Comprehensive Lesson Plan Template

Lesson Plan: Subject:	Teacher(s): Grade:	Date: Time:
Standard(s):		CMT Strand (if applicable):
Essential Question:		
Objective(s):		
Materials:		Technology:
Learning Procedure: Based on the 5 Steps of Gradual Release of Responsibility *1. Define it 2. Model 3. Collaborate 4. Guided Practice 5. Independent Practice*		
Effective Teaching Strategy:	Prior Knowledge/Connections:	Vocabulary:
1. Objective/Purpose (Define it):		
2. Model (5–7 minutes):		
3. Scaffold (Teacher collaboration with students; 2–4 minutes):		
4. Guided Practice: Differentiated Grouping		
Intervention/Below Level:	On Level:	Above Level:
5. Independent Practice		
Intervention/Below Level:	On Level:	Above Level:
Assessment:		Check all that apply: ___ informal ___ formal ___ formative ___ summative
Reflection:		

Middletown educators and school leaders created these nearly two years before the development of this rigorous curriculum design model. Yet notice how many of the recommended elements of the model are included in their templates. As such, they serve as excellent examples of daily lesson plan formats that educators and leaders can refer to as they prepare to design their own.

Gradual Release of Responsibility

Here is a bit of background information relevant to the first of these templates. Lawrence School incorporated the Gradual Release of Responsibility instructional model (Pearson and Gallagher, 1983) into their comprehensive lesson plan template. The sequential stages of this model are: direct and modeled instruction, guided practice, collaborative practice, and independent practice. The concept behind the model is that the educator intentionally transitions from carrying "all the responsibility for performing a task ... to a situation in which the students assume all of the responsibility" (Duke and Pearson, 2002, p. 211). This gradual release can occur within a single lesson or through multiple lessons.

Douglas Fischer reports that specific research studies support the Gradual Release of Responsibility instructional model as an effective means for improving student achievement in writing (Fisher and Frey, 2003), reading comprehension (Lloyd, 2004), and literacy outcomes for English Language Learners (Kong and Pearson, 2003).

The Middle and High School Lesson Planning Template

Kristen Freeman, Assistant Principal at Woodrow Wilson Middle School in Middletown, designed a lesson plan template that was first used at Woodrow Wilson and later revised and adopted by Keigwin Middle School and Middletown High School.

Kristen describes the process she and Tracey Koff, Principal of Keigwin Middle School, followed to create the lesson plan template:

"Tracey has for years been of great help to me in setting and carrying out student achievement goals, especially those related to instruction. We regularly work closely together on instructional matters related to maintaining consistency between our two middle schools. Prior to the start of the school year, Tracey and I met to discuss how to modify our lesson plan template to better support teachers' emphasis on differentiating instruction.

"After our discussion, I began working on the redesign of the middle school template. The primary sources I referenced were *Classroom Instruction That Works*

(Marzano et al., 2001) and the *Art and Science of Teaching* (Marzano, 2007). I also used the materials I received during a Connecticut-sponsored professional development seminar on research-based instructional strategies that included ideas from *A Handbook for Classroom Instruction That Works* (Marzano et al., 2001).

"When I was finished, I sent the template to Tracey for her review. We both agreed that it would be a good model for our two middle schools. Later I shared the template with Bob Fontaine, Principal of Middletown High School, who thought it would also work well for the high school staff."

In *Classroom Instruction That Works* (2001), Robert Marzano, Debra Pickering, and Jane Pollock propose the idea of planning a *unit* that includes three phases: beginning, during, and end. Each phase incorporates specific research-based effective teaching strategies pertinent to that particular phase (p.146). Kristen included this three-phase structure in both the Keigwin Middle School and Middletown High School *daily* lesson plan templates.

These templates are shown in Figures 16.7 and 16.8. The middle school template is blank, to highlight the specific template components. The completed high school template was written by Karey Stingo, Eric Marszalek, Trevor Charles, and Lisa Geary, for a lesson in American studies.

Middletown High School provides an additional document as part of their school-wide lesson plan, a listing of effective teaching strategies for each of the three phases along with specific examples of each strategy (Figure 16.9). This information was also adapted from three of the sources cited earlier: *Classroom Instruction That Works* (Marzano et al., 2001), *The Art and Science of* Teaching (Marzano, 2007), and the Connecticut-sponsored seminar on research-based instructional strategies that included ideas from *A Handbook for Classroom Instruction That Works* (Marzano et al., 2001).

FIGURE 16.7 **Keigwin Middle School Lesson Plan**

Subject: _____ Date: _____

Teacher: _____ Special Educator: _____

Priority Standards:

Essential Questions:

Content—What Will Students Learn?	Effective Teaching Strategies	Rigor—Degree of Difficulty
Conceptual Objectives: (What do students need to know and understand, including *new vocabulary*?) • • • **Skills Objectives:** (What do students need to be able to do?) *See Bloom's Taxonomy* • • • **Procedure:** (How will I structure the lesson?) 1. 2. 3. **Evidence/Products** (What will be collected /measured to determine student mastery/proficiency of objectives?) • • •	**Beginning:** ☐ Establish Objectives/ Engage Learner ☐ Cueing ☐ Learning Environment: Effort/Recognition ☐ Nonfiction Writing ☐ Advance Organizers **Middle:** ☐ Comparing/Contrasting ☐ Classifying ☐ Note Taking ☐ Questioning ☐ Nonlinguistic Representations ☐ Cooperative Learning/Grouping ☐ Practice ☐ Generating and Testing Hypotheses ☐ Direct Instruction **Closure:** ☐ Providing Feedback ☐ Summarizing lesson ☐ Homework **Homework assignment:** **Reflection/Next Steps:**	**Bloom's Taxonomy** ☐ **Create** (design, construct, produce, invent, revise) ☐ **Evaluate** (hypothesize, critique, test, judge, monitor) ☐ **Analyze** (deconstruct, organize, structure, compare) ☐ **Apply** (use, implement) ☐ **Understand** (interpret, summarize, classify, compare) ☐ **Remember** (list, describe, identify, retrieve, name, locate) **Technology needed:** **Interventions/ Modifications:** **Enrichment:**

FIGURE 16.8 Middletown High School Lesson Plan

Teacher Authors: Karey Stingo, Eric Marszalek, Trevor Charles, and Lisa Geary

Dates:

Subject: American studies

Priority Standards: Related to Colonialism in America; *The Scarlet Letter*

Essential Questions: 1. What does it mean to be an American?
2. How has the human desire for freedom impacted America?

Content—What Will Students Learn?	Effective Teaching Strategies	Rigor—Degree of Difficulty
Conceptual Objectives: (What do students need to know and understand, including *new vocabulary*?) • Examine vocabulary words from Unit 3. • Review and list Presidents 17–32. • The reasons for the English colonization of North America as well as how the original 13 English colonies took hold. • Interpret *The Scarlet Letter* for Puritan themes: predestination, divine mission, Puritan work ethic, through author's craft. **Skills Objectives:** (What do students need to do?) *See Bloom's Taxonomy* • Examine the impact that the meeting of three distinct and disparate cultures had on the formation of America and American history during the late 15th and early 16th centuries. • Analyze the economic, social, and political growth of the 13 English colonies and examine how the colonies and Britain began to grow apart. • Compare/Contrast the life and times of Nathaniel Hawthorne to that of the novel. • Analyze theme, character, setting and purpose in chapters 1–8 of *The Scarlet Letter*. **Procedure:** (How will I structure the lesson?) 1. Journal/reflective writings 2. Group activities on assessing characters, themes and symbols in novel 3. Chapter readings and summaries from *Americans* textbook 4. Note taking/questioning 5. See attached for further daily activities **Assessment:** (What will be collected/measured to determine student mastery/proficiency of objectives?) • Writing assignments on the novel as well as chapter summaries • Reflective writing—American Dream; Puritan thought	**Beginning:** ✓ Establish Objectives/ Engage Learner ☐ Cueing ✓ Learning Environment: Effort/Recognition ☐ Nonfiction Writing ☐ Advance Organizers ☐ Other_____ **Middle:** ✓ Comparing/Contrasting ☐ Classifying ✓ Note Taking ✓ Questioning ☐ Nonlinguistic Representations ✓ Cooperative Learning/Grouping ☐ Practice ☐ Generating and Testing Hypotheses ✓ Direct Instruction ☐ Other_____ **Closure:** ✓ Providing Feedback ☐ Summarizing lesson ✓ Homework ✓ Other: Reflective Writing **Homework assignment:** See attached syllabus for week	**Bloom's Taxonomy:** ☐ **Create** (design, construct, produce, invent, revise) ✓ **Evaluate** (hypothesize, critique, test, judge, monitor) ✓ **Analyze** (deconstruct, organize, structure, <u>compare</u>) ☐ **Apply** (use, implement) ✓ **Understand** (<u>interpret</u>, <u>summarize</u>, classifying, <u>comparing</u>) ✓ **Remember** (<u>list</u>, describe, <u>identify</u>, retrieve, name, locate) **Technology needed:** Smartboard/Data Projector/V Brick for *Scarlet Letter* clips **Interventions and Challenge:** How will I modify instruction to meet the needs of students: a. Who are struggling learners? *Follow IEPs and 504 plans* b. Who are easily meeting expectations? *As a Data Team, we will devise writing prompts and various activities accordingly.* **Reflection:** What worked/what did not work?

FIGURE 16.9 Effective Teaching Strategies

Beginning of Learning:

☐ **Establish Objectives/Engage Learner:** State goal in clear language; state what learner is expected to be able to do; sometimes describe product; narrow what students focus on; students are encouraged to personalize teacher goals

☐ **Cueing:** Focus on what is important rather than what is unusual; use explicit cues—direct approach; KNU (know, need to learn, understand); BKWLQ (background, know, want to know, learned, questions); activate prior knowledge

☐ **Learning Environment—Effort/Recognition:** Create hope; respect power; build relationships; express enthusiasm; use rubric for effort and student chart progress; provide recognition

☐ **Nonfiction Writing:** Writing prompts; students reflect on learning to clarify information or misconceptions; students record thoughts in journal frequently; entrance (or exit) slips; RAFT (Role, Audience, Format, Topic)

☐ **Advance Organizers:** Help students use background knowledge to build new knowledge; most useful when information is not well organized; examples: expository advance organizer, narrative advance organizer, skimming, graphic organizers

Middle Stage of Learning:

☐ **Comparing/Contrasting:** Examine information for similarities and differences; focus on important details and characteristics of information; apply tools (Venn, matrix, double-cluster, double bubble)

☐ **Classifying:** Organize information into groups based on categories; done after comparing; apply tools (table, bubble chart, tree map)

☐ **Note Taking:** Notes considered a work in progress; notes are used as study guides; refer to and enhance notes; approaches include outlines, webbing, combination including summary, Cornell, two-column

☐ **Questioning:** Ask questions before a learning experience; use wait time; three levels of questioning that can incorporate content, personal knowledge, and/or real-world connection (relevance)

☐ **Nonlinguistic Representations:** Descriptive pattern organizer; time-sequence pattern; process/cause-effect pattern organizer; episode patterns; generalization/principle pattern; concept pattern; making physical models; creating mental pictures; drawing pictures and pictographs; engaging in kinesthetic activity

(continued)

FIGURE 16.9 Effective Teaching Strategies *(continued)*

☐ **Cooperative Learning/Grouping:** Ability level grouping done sparingly; groups kept small in size (3–4); do not overuse to deny independence; groups can be informal, formal, or base

☐ **Practice:** Guided or independent; must be repeated for maximum benefit; focus practice on complex skills or processes; plan time for students to *conceptualize* understanding of skill or process

☐ **Generating and Testing Hypotheses:** Can be deductive (use general rule to make a prediction, whole to part) or inductive (part to whole, trial and error, drawing conclusions based on observations); used for systems analysis, problem solving, historical investigations, invention, experimental inquiry, decision making

☐ **Direct instruction:** Teacher plans and directly presents lesson to whole class and/or smaller groups of students*

Closure of Learning Time:

☐ **Providing Feedback:** "Corrective" in nature; timely; specific to a criterion; students can effectively provide some of their own feedback

☐ **Summarizing:** Keep, delete, substitute; summary frames

☐ **Homework:** Direct effect on achievement; must have homework policy; parental involvement should be kept to minimum; purpose (*practice* of a familiar concept/skill or *preparation/elaboration*) is identified and clearly articulated to students; should always be commented on (vary feedback); provide time in school to complete homework

---

* John Hattie provides an expanded definition of Direct Instruction in *Visible Learning* (2009), pp. 204–207.

Design Weekly and Daily Lesson Plan Samples

In addition to the lesson plan shown here, curriculum designers can refer to essential elements provided earlier in this chapter when preparing to create sample weekly and daily lesson plan templates to share with educators. The information contained in these two figures, presented earlier, will help promote alignment between the weekly and daily templates:

- Guidelines for Writing the Weekly Plan (Figure 16.4)
- A Summary of Middletown Daily Lesson Plan Elements (Figure 16.5)

A Final Word to Designers

Designing sample weekly and daily lesson plan templates to share with educators is the final "official" step in this model of rigorous curriculum design. I hope you will take the time to acknowledge and celebrate the tremendous accomplishment you have achieved when you reach this point in the process. Your first drafts of rigorous curricular units are the direct result of all the time, effort, thought, and energy you and your design-team colleagues have invested to make this vision a reality.

Think of it: these units of study—especially after they have been implemented, revised, and further improved—will be used by educators in every grade level, course, and content area, to benefit the learning of *all* students for *years* to come. This is a great and lasting contribution you have made to your school system.

Reader's Assignment

1. Discuss and draft a position statement about the recommended use of intentionally aligned weekly and daily lesson plan templates that include an agreed-upon set of essential elements.

2. Review the Guidelines for Writing the Weekly Plan (Figure 16.4) and A Summary of Middletown Daily Lesson Plan Elements (Figure 16.5). Draft a weekly lesson plan template; then draft a daily lesson plan template. Be sure the two templates closely align.

3. Discuss and decide whether or not to recommend an established lesson plan model, such as the Gradual Release of Responsibility or the three-phase model of Marzano, Pickering, and Pollock. Refer to Chapter 10 in Marzano's *The Art and Science of Teaching* (2007) for excellent ideas to consider when planning daily lessons in segments.

4. Plan how you will share the weekly and daily lesson plan templates with educators.

CHAPTER 17

Implement the Unit of Study

When educators are ready to implement one of the completed curricular units of study in their own classroom or instructional program, all they need to do is refer to the pacing calendar for a content area of choice, select a corresponding unit for their grade or course, and refer to the comprehensive information provided on the unit planning organizer and the accompanying document that contains the unit details.

The following sequence of steps for implementing each of the units of study, first introduced in Chapter 4 and expanded here, will assist educators as they guide their students through the various learning experiences, related instruction, and unit assessments.

1. **Introduce the Unit of Study to Students.** Present the unit's Essential Questions to students and explain that they will be exploring and investigating these questions throughout the coming weeks. Let them know they will be able to respond to each of these important questions in their own words by the end of the unit. Share with students the "word wall" of vocabulary terms for the unit: the "unwrapped" concepts from the Priority Standards and other key academic terms or technical language listed on the unit planning organizer.

2. **Administer the Unit Pre-Assessment.** Set the stage by first explaining to students the purpose of a pre-assessment (not for a grade, but to find out what they already know and don't know about the upcoming unit of study so that the teacher can plan instruction accordingly). Then administer the common formative pre-assessment (or individual classroom or program pre-assessment) to the students.

3. **Score and Analyze Student Data.** Score and analyze student pre-assessments individually or with colleagues in grade-level or course-specific instructional Data Teams to diagnose student learning needs. Set a SMART goal representing the desired improvement of student performance to be achieved and demonstrated on the end-of-unit post-assessment.

4. Discuss How to Differentiate Instruction. Refer to the unit planning organizer, the supplemental document that provides the unit details, and the comprehensive instructional strategies resource compiled from the information in Chapter 14. Discuss how to differentiate instruction for specific students based on assessment evidence—including the enrichment of any students who are already proficient prior to unit instruction. Select strategies accordingly. Identify specific Tier 2 and Tier 3 intervention strategies to use with at-risk students and those specific language acquisition strategies (including Sheltered Instruction) to use with English Language Learners. Consult with special educators to create specially designed instruction (SDI) for special education students that is based on students' identified disabilities (cognitive and behavioral). Determine results indicators, the means for determining the effectiveness of the selected instructional strategies. Decide how to monitor the application and effectiveness of those strategies throughout the unit of study.

5. Begin Teaching the Unit. Referring to the first week's lesson plans, begin teaching the "unwrapped" concepts and skills in the predetermined "learning progressions" sequence for specific learning activities and engaging learning experiences (authentic performance tasks). Use the preselected instructional strategies with *all* students, different groups of students, and individual students as planned.

6. Administer Progress-Monitoring Checks. Administer frequent, informal progress-monitoring checks—aligned to the end-of-unit assessment—to coincide with the building-block progression of "unwrapped" concepts and skills. Use the assessment results to make accurate inferences regarding students' current stages of understanding. These informal checks will also assist instructional Data Teams in monitoring the effectiveness of their targeted teaching strategies for the unit.

7. Differentiate Instruction Based on Progress-Monitoring Checks. Modify and adjust instruction for individual students, small groups, and/or the entire class based on the results of the informal checks for understanding.

8. Schedule Mid-Unit Evaluation of Instructional Strategies. Schedule a mid-unit evaluation of the targeted strategies to determine their effectiveness. During this meeting, participating teachers will share effective use of the strategies and may decide to substitute other strategies for any that are not accomplishing their intended purpose. "Singleton" teachers can do this step on their own, but are encouraged to meet with colleagues in horizontal teams (same grade level in one or more schools) or vertical teams (grade spans or the entire department in one or more schools) to conduct this mid-unit evaluation of strategies collaboratively.

9. **Continue Teaching the Unit.** During the remaining weeks of the unit, continue teaching the "unwrapped" concepts and skills in the pre-determined "learning progressions" sequence for specific learning activities and engaging learning experiences (authentic performance tasks). Continue using the targeted instructional strategies with *all* students, different groups of students, and individual students as planned.

10. **Continue Modifying and Adjusting Instruction.** Continue modifying and adjusting instruction as needed for individual students, small groups, and/or the entire class based on evidence derived from ongoing progress-monitoring checks.

11. **Administer End-of-Unit Assessment.** Administer the end-of-unit classroom assessment or common formative/summative post-assessment.

12. **Score and Analyze Student Data.** Score and analyze student data individually or with colleagues in grade-level or course-specific Data Teams. Celebrate successes! Plan how to address the identified learning needs of individual students during the "buffer" week.

13. **Enrich, Remediate, and Intervene.** During a "buffer" week that is scheduled between the unit of study just completed and the next one about to begin, enrich those students who are proficient and advanced. Reteach *differently* those students who are still not proficient by continuing to use Tier 2 and 3 intervention strategies for at-risk students, custom-designed strategies for special education students, and second-language strategies and other appropriate differentiation and intervention strategies for English Language Learners. Reassess all nonproficient students. Use assessment information diagnostically to determine "next steps" for students still not proficient.

14. **Reflect on the Unit.** Take a few minutes to reflect on the successes and challenges of the unit just completed. Write down what worked as planned and what needs to be revised or changed before administering the unit again in the future. Last, refer to the pacing calendar and prepare to repeat the process with the next unit of study.

The Role of Administrators in Organizing the Work

For those given the responsibility of organizing and overseeing the implementation of curriculum redesign efforts in a school system, the prospect of doing so can seem both daring and daunting. Rather than having to "forge a new path without a compass or map," such leaders gratefully welcome guidance, suggestions, and recommendations from those who themselves have already done this work.

Part 4 opens with two powerful chapters—firsthand accounts from system leaders who are directly responsible for overseeing curriculum implementation and sustainability efforts. The book's final chapter presents a compilation of invaluable advice from administrators—superintendents, deputy superintendents, principals, and an assistant principal—who have successfully led standards-based reform efforts in their own school systems. In it they provide research-supported ideas and advice about how other administrators can organize, monitor, and sustain the implementation of curriculum redesign, common formative assessments, and Data Teams. This information will prove extremely helpful to all leaders who are just beginning, or who are already well into, the process of designing and instituting rigorous curricula within an integrated standards-instruction-assessment system.

Reader's Assignment

1. Discuss with colleagues the 14 steps presented in this chapter for effectively implementing the curricular units of study.

2. Identify the steps that educators are already familiar with and using on a regular basis.

3. Identify the steps that educators are either not familiar with or *have not been using* on a regular basis.

4. Decide how and when to provide professional development to educators who are unfamiliar with particular steps (e.g. the "unwrapping" standards process, the Data Teams process).

5. Decide also how to encourage educators to begin using again any "neglected" steps on a more systematic and regular basis. Remind everyone of the big picture connections presented in Chapter 3. To maximize the effectiveness of the rigorous curricular units, they need to be implemented within that *system* of interdependent professional practices.

Organizing, Monitoring, and Sustaining Implementation Efforts

CHAPTER 18

West Haven's Comprehensive Redesign of Pre-K–12 Curricula

Undertaking the redesign of an entire school system's Pre-K–12 curricula requires a mixture of visionary thinking, careful planning, fortitude, perseverance, humor, and flexibility, with a dash of adventure thrown in for good measure.

There are the anticipated challenges: finding enough time, enough money, and enough willing personnel to start and complete the huge amount of work such a project entails. Then there are the other challenges to deal with as the process unfolds: the necessary midcourse corrections, the occasional miscommunications, and the difficulties always inherent in change.

To meet the challenge of getting everyone on board, start with the "big picture" that I presented in Chapter 3. This will do much to show the vital connections between all of the interdependent components. Be sure to emphasize right away that the initiative will take place over several *years*. Then get people involved *to some degree* so they can better understand what it all means.

Getting everyone *equally* involved in the complete authoring of new curricula is not feasible, especially in larger systems. Not only is this a near impossibility logistically, it is unrealistic to think that everyone will be equally interested in doing this kind of in-depth work. Leaders need to decide how best to promote buy-in from educators who are not involved in the initial writing of the curricular units. The best means for accomplishing this is to follow West Haven's shared-ownership approach described in Chapter 15. Asking educators to add details to the units of study and encouraging them to suggest revisions and refinements after implementing them in their own instructional programs will do much to promote widespread understanding and acceptance of the new curricula.

The West Haven Story—From the Beginning

When together they announced West Haven's plan for district improvement, newly appointed Superintendent Neil Cavallaro and Assistant Superintendent Anne Druzolowski clearly stated to their entire education community: "This is a *five-year* plan. It is a *process.*" They urged all staff to improvise, revise, and communicate, saying: "Be willing to accept feedback from everyone. Do not be afraid to make changes along the way. Do not wait until the end of the school year to modify *anything.*"

At my request, Dr. Druzolowski kindly provided the following detailed account of how West Haven organized, implemented, and is sustaining comprehensive district improvement that includes a complete revamping of *all* of their former curricula.

What is singularly impressive about West Haven's systemwide efforts to completely redesign their curricula—while simultaneously enhancing the professional skills of every one of their more than five hundred educators—is the fact that they did all of this in less than a year and a half. They are living proof of what visionary leadership, sharp focus, unwavering commitment, and a lot of hard work by a lot of dedicated professionals can accomplish in a relatively short amount of time.

The "Behind-the-Scenes" Activities That Took Place to Organize and Implement Our Comprehensive District Improvement

By Assistant Superintendent Anne Druzolowski

In January 2009, West Haven's new administrators (superintendent and assistant superintendent) introduced to the Board of Education a five-year professional development action plan that the board subsequently adopted. The five-year plan incorporated all of the research-based components of the Connecticut Accountability for Learning Initiative (CALI):

1. Making Standards Work (prioritizing and "unwrapping" of the K–12 state standards in all subject areas);

2. Common Formative Assessments;

3. Data-Driven Decision Making; and

4. Research-Based Instructional Strategies.

These four core practices are at the center of these many components, as represented in a state-created graphic that we refer to as the "CALI Flower" (Figure 18.1).

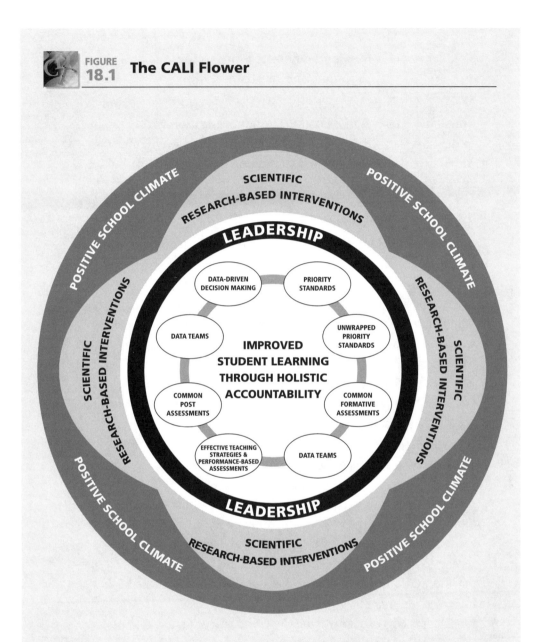

FIGURE 18.1 The CALI Flower

Our intention is to ensure that the CALI practices will all be implemented with fidelity in every school within our system. Here is a brief history of how West Haven began its journey toward achieving this goal:

Making Standards Work (MSW)
Seminar and Implementation

Making Standards Work (MSW) was the first CALI flower component we chose to implement. The administration felt that in order to develop Data Teams and common formative assessments, it was imperative that we all spoke the common language of curriculum across grade levels and content areas. We strongly believed that *all* classroom teachers required a complete understanding of the CALI flower, where MSW fit into the district-wide professional development plan, and the direction we would be taking to focus our instruction.

To that end, *all* of our approximately 550 classroom teachers received professional development in the MSW seminar from Larry Ainsworth of The Leadership and Learning Center throughout that spring. It is important to note that not all curricula were in place at that time. The existing curricula had not been reviewed for several years. The MSW process gave us a common philosophy and vocabulary for prioritizing all of the standards and aligning them to state and national standards as a first necessary step in thoroughly reviewing and updating our curricula.

All school administrators also received the MSW seminar from Larry Ainsworth during a modified professional development session. It was imperative that administrators understood the nature and magnitude of the work being done by the curriculum writing teams. During the numerous professional development sessions for teachers, several of our board members and parents attended a one-day orientation meeting to learn about the five-year school improvement plan.

The process of prioritizing the Connecticut State Content Standards, "unwrapping" those standards, and developing corresponding units of study and pacing guides began immediately after the completion of the MSW professional development sessions for all teachers and administrators. Curriculum revision teams were established in all content areas. These teams were split into two cohorts to facilitate the scheduling of teachers so they could meet during the school day. Cohort 1 teams represented the K–12 content areas of mathematics, English language arts, social studies, and science. Cohort 2 teams represented fine arts, early childhood education, business education, technology education, world languages, physical education, and health education. The Cohort 1 content-area supervisors developed a West Haven unit planning organizer to be used across all content areas and grade levels for the development of the curricular units by the writing teams.

These Cohort 1 content-area supervisors—Ann Valanzuolo (English language arts), Raffaela Fronc (science and English Language Learners), A.J. Palermo (math and professional development), and Mark Consorte (social studies)—communicated continuously with district leadership while overseeing the curriculum design work of their individual writing teams. The supervisors had the latitude to personally select their individual teams and chose two or three teachers from each grade level and content area. English language arts had to choose separate teachers to represent reading and English. English Language Learner, special education, and reading support teachers were distributed throughout the grade-level and content-area teams in order to ensure that all subgroups were well-represented across each of the content areas and to ensure establishment of a knowledge base in each of the content areas.

The goal for any curriculum review and writing process must be consistency. The teams had representation from all district schools, so there would be greater commitment as well as "resident experts" in each building.

Selection of team members in both cohorts was based on the following professional characteristics: belief in the work; experience in teaching; work ethic; commitment to the project; strong interpersonal skills; willingness to take risks; flexibility; and attention to detail. Members could opt out of the project at any time, but we did ask for a full commitment. Some members that started the work had job changes, life changes, or found the work to be too daunting or the scope too broad; therefore, "new blood" was added along the way.

We established several "production days" for individual content-area curriculum teams to design their units of study. A minimum of one production day per content area was held under the guidance and facilitation of Larry Ainsworth. In addition to assisting Larry on those days, the curriculum supervisors and I facilitated the other production days ourselves.

The content-area supervisors are to be commended for the excellent facilitation skills in on-demand troubleshooting and brainstorming that they demonstrated throughout the work sessions with their individual teams. While these skills are a necessary part of any supervisory role, it was an added challenge to carry them out effectively while learning a new process right along with those whom they were supervising.

The review of all our curricula is ongoing. The curricular units will continue to be reviewed *each year* and modifications will continue to be made as necessary. As district leaders, we are continually reviewing the process with the entire district teaching staff and administrators to reassure them that this truly is a *five-year process*.

Common Formative Assessment (CFA) Seminar and Implementation

Cohorts 1 and 2 attended an introductory Common Formative Assessment seminar with Larry Ainsworth after prioritizing and "unwrapping" the standards and assigning them to grade- or course-specific units of study. CFAs and accompanying answer keys and scoring guides—directly aligned to the particular "unwrapped" Priority Standards within each unit—are continuing to be developed and revised by all teams in both cohorts.

In addition to our ongoing production days, Cohort 1 curriculum revision team members were provided with five stipend days during the summer of 2009. During this time, the teams completed the "unwrapping" components of all their units. They also wrote CFAs for one or two of their grade- or course-specific units. Our goal in providing these additional summer work days was to have the units and CFAs ready to implement by the start of the new school year in September 2009. We anticipate the need to also offer the same stipend days to Cohort 2 teams during the summer of 2010. Even though Cohort 1 teams are one year ahead of Cohort 2 teams in the development and revision phase of CFAs, we anticipate that both cohorts will be at the same stage of completion by September 2010.

As with the prioritization and "unwrapping" of the standards, much of the CFA design work has taken place during the scheduled production days and additional days we continue to offer through-out the school year. In both cohorts, entire K–12 subject area teams work together. Occasionally, the teams subdivide into elementary (K–5) and secondary (6–12) configurations. Often they break into smaller grade-span teams (K–2, 3–5, 6–8, 9–12), and occasionally they even work as single grades. This particular organization has greatly reinforced alignment of standards and units of study across grade levels, both horizontally and vertically.

All of the prioritized standards and grade-level expectations (GLEs) and the "unwrapped" standards for specific units of study are posted on the district Web site for all teachers, administrators and parents to view. Because we regard the units as being ongoing works-in-progress, continually open for review and improvement, we emphasize the word "draft" in those postings. The public should be well aware of this. CFAs are secured and not accessible through the Web site.

On August 27, 2009, the opening district-wide professional development day, the Cohort 1 core curriculum revision teams "rolled out" all of the core curricula. The content-area coordinators distributed hard copies of all the units and corresponding CFAs completed to date to all of their respective content-area teachers.

Data-Driven Decision Making (DDDM) and Effective Teaching Strategies (ETS) Seminars and Implementation

Data-Driven Decision Making is another petal of the CALI flower. It is critical that all teachers better understand the purpose of using good data to inform instruction, as well as to adjust and modify curricula. DDDM had been introduced into a very few Title I schools in need of improvement prior to January 2009. At that time, however, it was a school-based approach to student improvement, and was not connected to any district-wide plan. Because of this past practice, two of our schools are ahead of the others in using the DDDM process to inform instruction. However, all of our schools are now receiving professional development in DDDM by regional educational service center staff members, all of whom are certified as trainers by The Leadership and Learning Center. Some Title I schools require additional training to reinforce the information they received prior to January 2009. These schools are also receiving continued support from the regional service centers, as well as from the Connecticut State Department of Education.

The Effective Teaching Strategies seminar is being offered through The Leadership and Learning Center, utilizing a two-stage approach. While attendance is not mandatory at this time, it will be during the next few years. Beginning in the spring of 2009, the high school special educators and the English Language Learner teachers were provided with a two-day ETS session from The Center. Our focus was on those staff members in need of immediate intervention relative to their teaching strategies. Since that time, we have offered five to six additional ETS sessions open to district staff on a first-come, first-served basis.

In combination with attendance at the ETS sessions, all teaching staff members are required to demonstrate to a Center consultant during scheduled classroom visits the *application* of what they have learned in ETS. The principal in each building accompanies the consultant on these classroom visitations and follows up with a written critique of what he or she observed relative to the teacher's use of specific teaching strategies. The critiques include positive recognition for effective use of the strategies along with any recommendations or suggestions for improvement. The intent of providing this level of direct support from a Center consultant is to hold our teaching staff accountable for implementation of all the professional development they are receiving. Our philosophy and position is that it is not enough for teachers to learn the content of a particular research-based practice; they must *apply* the new knowledge in order to improve their students' performance.

Modifications While the "Airplane Is Flying"

It has been necessary to make some changes while the curriculum redesign "airplane" is still under construction, yet already flying. These changes have been made in response to teacher requests and resource needs. Time, as always, is a particularly needed resource at the elementary school level, where collaborative planning and meeting time is nonexistent. Time is also a factor when we examine the amount of content we expect elementary teachers to teach and assess.

Given the fact that all elementary teachers are responsible for teaching all four core content areas, we initially planned that they implement the new curricular units in *all four* areas. Shortly after the administration of the CFAs for the second units of study, we responded to the teachers' feedback and modified our initial plan. A much more realistic expectation, especially in this first full year of implementation, is to focus on only *two* of the four areas: English language arts and science. Full implementation of the social studies and math units of study *at the elementary level* has now been scheduled to begin in year two of our five-year plan.

This modification was clearly necessary. We were expecting elementary teachers to learn an entirely new curriculum framework and approach to instruction and assessment in all four content areas. In addition, there had never been a social studies and math curriculum in place at the elementary level. This was especially problematic in mathematics; all teachers had relied solely on a commercial program as their curriculum for the past ten years. While the majority of elementary teachers were still using this same program, others were being asked to pilot new math resource materials that closely align with our new curricular units. These complementary new resource materials will be in district-wide use in September 2010. Given these reasons, it only made sense to delay implementation of the new math units until that year. We anticipate that teachers will be better able to administer reliable and valuable CFAs under the new schedule.

By delaying the implementation of the new social studies units until year two, we are planning for a better integration of social studies (and science) into the reading and language arts curriculum. Teachers are examining both the quality and quantity of nonfiction reading and writing explicitly being taught in language arts. Rather than teaching social studies and science as separate disciplines, the teachers are taking a more interdisciplinary approach by modifying the language arts curriculum to increase the amount of nonfiction reading and writing using social studies and science content.

Sustainability

Our message to the entire West Haven education community continues to be that this is a long-term, five-year process. We do not anticipate immediate results; rather, we expect progressive growth in our teachers' skills. We foresee that over the next five years, all of the CALI components will continue to be reinforced and supported through our district and school administrators and through our ongoing partnership with The Leadership and Learning Center.

One of the major steps we took to ensure sustainability of the initiative was to hold an in-district CFA certification course conducted by Larry Ainsworth in October 2009. We invited a select group of teachers, department heads, and central office staff that included me and the four Cohort 1 supervisors to receive an in-depth, three-day review of the entire process. As a result, we now have twenty-five certified CFA staff able to serve the school system by giving teachers feedback, guidance, and support with regard to the quality of their unit-based CFAs. District leaders in attendance at the course developed a feedback tool teachers can use to provide CFA-related suggestions for district supervisors and curriculum revision teams to consider.

Our district plan to ensure greater sustainability of our initiative as a whole is to continue certifying additional staff members in as many of the CALI "flower" components as possible.

Lessons Learned—Recommendations from West Haven

In organizing and implementing this comprehensive improvement initiative, we have learned much that will hopefully benefit other school systems that embark upon the curriculum redesign journey. The following list, organized by category, summarizes some of the lessons we learned and the issues we faced while moving through the process:

Visibility of District Leaders:

- Visible leadership is imperative. The content-area supervisors and assistant superintendent were visible throughout *all* of the professional development sessions and production days. The supervisors also visited (early in the year) every elementary school to attend grade-level meetings and discuss the implementation of the new curricula.

- It is important to speak a common language. If everyone speaks the same language—from the superintendent to the board members to the teachers—then everyone begins to understand that this is not just an initiative, but rather an enduring philosophy with no quick fixes.

English Language Arts:

- The English language arts units of study and CFAs in grades K–2 look different from those in grades 3–12, due to the emphasis in early grades on students learning to read. This is important for everyone to know *in advance,* so the primary grade English language arts curriculum writing teams do not try to adhere to the same "look" of the units as those in the upper elementary, middle, and high school grades.

- English language arts curriculum teams at all grade levels set pacing calendar dates to administer the CFAs before all of the units had been created. Often the curriculum writers were developing units "just ahead" of the CFA schedule, and it was difficult to keep up at times. Quality control often *followed,* rather than *preceded,* the distribution of the CFAs for a unit.

Starting the unit design process earlier than we did would have helped.

- For the English language arts pre- and post-CFAs that require reading selections, select "cold reads"—passages that students have not seen before—not those from stories, books, or articles students have already read or used during the unit.

Assessments and Consistency in Scoring:

- For those grade levels and courses implementing their units within the Data Teams structure, it is critical to reach agreement about the scoring of assessments to ensure consistency and common understanding. For example, teachers wanted an agreed-upon level of proficiency, and many conversations were focused on what the "cut score" should be. Clearly delineated levels for the different performance levels on student assessments are now established district-wide and are used consistently by Data Teams for analysis and goal-setting.

- CFAs for the units of study were written by the Cohort 1 and 2 curriculum design teams for district-wide use, rather than by teams of teachers school by school. This approach to assessment creation allows for a greater level of consistency and better quality control.

- Preferences about whether to use "mirrored" or aligned CFAs varied by content area and grade, but overall, we have been leaning more toward using "mirrored" CFAs to determine student progress.

- Teachers are at liberty to develop or customize their own progress-monitoring checks ("dipsticks"), homework, etc., for use during the different units of study. We remind teachers of the importance of aligning these informal checks for understanding to the end-of-unit CFAs.

Instructional Materials and Resources:

- We purchased as permanent resources only those texts that specifically coincided with each of our professional development sessions. Primary sources included *Power*

Standards (Ainsworth, 2003a), *"Unwrapping" the Standards* (Ainsworth, 2003b), *Common Formative Assessments* (Ainsworth and Viegut, 2006), and *Classroom Instruction that Works* (Marzano et al., 2001).

• Whenever possible, use existing resources and materials that are familiar to teachers and students, and purchase only what you truly need or are lacking. Keep a wish list for the purchase of additional materials and supplies in the future. For the elementary math program we are piloting, it was necessary to purchase new resources that supported teachers' use of Essential Questions, Big Ideas, and higher-order questioning skills. Be aware that it may prove a challenging adjustment for some teachers to become comfortable with the new resources.

Standards and Web-Based Resources:

• We provided copies of K–12 state standards and frameworks by content area along with state testing information and district results on the state tests so we could make informed decisions about which standards to prioritize. We also demonstrated for staff how to access particular sections of the state Web site that contain much valuable information for informing curriculum development.

• We provided the Cohort 2 subject areas (business education, computer education, automotive, etc.) with links to national standards for alignment of the curriculum.

Communicating to School Leaders:

• Continually explain to all administrators that it is necessary to have teachers out of the buildings more than usual and that support from administrators is "non-negotiable." This position must be supported by both the superintendent and the assistant superintendent.

• Use your administrative council meetings to get feedback from principals as to how the work is progressing and to keep them in the loop relative to curriculum changes and professional development planning.

- Be sure that the principals conduct classroom "walk-throughs" on a regularly scheduled basis and that they speak honestly about problems and issues. It is mandatory, not optional, for school leaders to be an active part of the process.

Organizing Professional Development Sessions and Production Days:

- Start planning in the summer. Have your professional development days in place so that principals can work in advance to secure substitute teachers. Do not release too many teachers at the same time from the same buildings.

- Plan a comfortable venue in an environment that promotes learning, one where it is easy for people to see and to hear. Invest in some quality audio-visual equipment and provide wireless Internet access, if at all possible. Be sure to provide a good breakfast and lunch!

- Order your books and materials early. Make sure that name-tags, large chart paper, Post-Its, markers, highlighters, etc., are readily available.

The Big Picture:

- Most importantly, keep bringing everyone back to the "big picture" connections between all of the research-based powerful practices, such as those represented on our state's CALI diagram. Keep emphasizing that this is a multiple-year plan; an ongoing *process*. Help people understand that curriculum development is not a separate piece of the school system's improvement plan, but rather the beginning of a long journey to improved student achievement.

Reader's Assignment

1. Referring to the West Haven detailed summary by Assistant Superintendent Anne Druzolowski presented in this chapter, consider how to organize the "launch" of a curriculum redesign initiative in your own school system. Specific elements to keep in mind include the following:

   - "Big picture" vision of the various components and how they all connect
   - Long-term commitment to project
   - Communication to school community
   - Targeted content areas needing curriculum redesign
   - Composition of design teams (system-level administrators, curriculum coordinators, classroom educators)
   - Responsibilities of direct supervisors and team members
   - Time frame for completion of the curricular units
   - Gathering of needed resources (standards, frameworks, existing curricula, etc.)
   - Associated professional development (prioritizing and "unwrapping" standards, common formative assessments, performance tasks and scoring guides, research-based instructional strategies, etc.)
   - Role of school administrators in curriculum development process
   - Procedures for receiving feedback and making midcourse adjustments
   - Specific needs of each targeted content area
   - Authoring of a parent-friendly version of the new curricula to make available to the community
   - Other issues to be decided
   - Other points to consider

2. Determine the broad headings for organizing the project (content areas, selection of personnel, time frames, professional development, needed resources, communication, etc.) and then "assign" each of the above elements to its appropriate heading.

3. Begin drafting detailed plans for implementing each of the organizational headings.

CHAPTER 19

Bristol's Established Process for Curriculum Development and Revision

In 2001, Douglas Reeves and Elle Allison of The Leadership and Learning Center assisted the leaders of Bristol, Connecticut, public schools in developing and implementing a district-wide accountability plan. An accountability task force convened to create a comprehensive, multiyear plan to transform the teaching, learning, and assessment culture of Bristol schools and dramatically improve student performance.

In June 2004, I worked closely with Mike Wasta, Superintendent, Susan Kalt Moreau, Deputy Superintendent, and Denise Carabetta, Director of Teaching and Learning, to implement the standards-based components of that broad initiative. Focusing on the standards and performance assessment modules, I presented the *Making Standards Work* professional development series to all of the Bristol central office and school leadership teams. Over the course of three days, the K–12 leaders and educators learned how to prioritize and "unwrap" the state standards, write Big Ideas and Essential Questions, and create performance tasks with accompanying scoring guides for any content area, grade level, and course.

In the years since that time, Bristol has continued to work diligently to refine their implementation efforts and to sustain with fidelity *all* of the state-recommended "best practices" for improving student achievement. This includes, but is not limited to, common formative and summative assessments, research-based effective teaching strategies, and the heart of their accountability plan—Data Teams.

Bristol's Data Teams are of three types: district, building, and instructional. The *district* Data Team communicates regularly with each of the building (school) Data Teams and looks at student improvement across the district. Each *building* Data Team communicates regularly with all of its *instructional* Data Teams (grade- and course-specific teams of teachers) and looks at student improvement from the perspective of the whole school. Instructional Data Teams focus on student improvement within each particular grade or course level.

All of Bristol's decisions for improving student achievement are based on multiple types of data that their schools and the district collect and analyze regularly. The steady gains in improvement for *all* of their students, as measured by state assessments, have been so significant that other school systems throughout Connecticut and from across the United States continue to send visiting leadership teams to Bristol to see for themselves how this one district has accomplished such a remarkable transformation of their culture in a few short years. "The Bristol Way"—as it has come to be known—today stands as an exemplary model of comprehensive district improvement.

I asked Denise Carabetta if she would be willing to provide a summary of the process Bristol has used to develop, review, and revise their curricula. In particular, I requested that she address the four key areas of focus in this final part of the book: organizing the work, the role of administrators, monitoring progress, and sustaining implementation. In response, Denise generously contributed the following detailed description of Bristol's *established* process for curriculum development and redesign along with related Board of Education-approved policy documents.

The Bristol Curriculum Development Model

By Denise Carabetta, Director of Teaching and Learning

Bristol, Connecticut, is a city of 60,000 inhabitants located in central Connecticut. This is a diverse community, with 8,800 students attending fifteen schools. The school population is 26 percent minority, and we are faced with a steadily increasing poverty rate among our families—the poverty rate has risen from 24 percent in 2000 to 38 percent in 2010. Although facing mounting challenges as we strive to educate an increasingly disadvantaged student population, student achievement across grade levels and within subgroups has improved significantly over the past ten years, with nearly 90 percent of *all* our students proficient on the Connecticut Mastery Test and the Connecticut Academic Performance Test. Our high school students are accepted at top-ranked colleges, our drop-out rate has declined to 3.4 percent, and matched cohort analyses show that students who remain in Bristol schools for two or more years show tremendous academic growth. Our curriculum model is one of the key strategies we have used to improve student achievement.

Organizing the Work

How the important work of curriculum design and review is organized and scheduled determines what gets done. In a large school district such as ours, it is critically important to institute and follow certain protocols. We now have an established process for curriculum development and revision that all staff must follow. The Board of Education has a policy and regulation for curriculum development and revision. All of our work is aligned with the requirements of board policy and regulation, as shown in the documents in Figures 19.1 and 19.2.

Curriculum is developed or revised when: (1) the state standards are updated, (2) an implementation review indicates that changes are needed, or (3) a new course of study is created.

In Bristol, curriculum revision begins with a proposal that is submitted to the Curriculum Planning Council. This council is comprised of teachers and administrators representing various content-area disciplines and grade levels from across the district. The proposal is presented to and discussed by the council members, who then vote to approve or not approve the proposal. Often, recommendations about the curriculum revision process are made by council members.

Proposals to pilot a new course are also presented to the Curriculum Planning Council. If the pilot proposal is approved by the council, timelines for implementation and evaluation are set. At the end of the pilot period, the council decides to accept the pilot for full district implementation, to modify the pilot, or to reject the pilot. Curriculum is developed as a part of the pilot project. Figures 19.3 and 19.4 show the required forms that we use for curriculum revision proposals and pilot proposals.

Upon approval of the proposal by the Curriculum Planning Council, the supervisor of teaching and learning for that particular discipline begins the work. In Bristol, curriculum committees are comprised of the teaching and learning supervisor responsible for that content area and teachers of that discipline who either volunteer or are selected on recommendation of an administrator. In

FIGURE 19.1 **Bristol Board of Education Curriculum Development Policy**

BRISTOL BOARD OF EDUCATION 6140 <u>POLICY</u>

Instruction

Curriculum Design/Development/Revision

Continuous work is required to maintain up-to-date and effective curriculum in a constantly changing world. The Board shall entrust to the Superintendent the primary responsibility for development of district curriculum.

The Board of Education shall establish a school district curriculum committee. This subcommittee of the Board of Education, called the Student Achievement Committee, will review and approve all curricula prior to referral to the full Board of Education for final approval.

Actual curriculum development planning shall be the responsibility of the Director of Teaching and Learning and the administrators responsible for the various curricular areas. The Director of Teaching and Learning and subject-area supervisors shall organize curriculum committees, consisting of teachers and administrators, for development, review, and revision of district curricula. All teachers have professional obligations to the school program which include work on curriculum committees. The Board may also authorize approved curriculum work during the summer months.

All curricula shall be aligned with the Connecticut Curriculum Frameworks as adopted by the Connecticut State Board of Education.

All curriculum development and revision shall be in keeping with the Bristol Board of Education policies and state requirements and regulations. Curriculum development/revision shall be guided by:

1. The Connecticut Curriculum Frameworks and where such frameworks do not exist, by national standards;

2. Needs assessments and information concerning the education of district students;

3. Range of student abilities, aptitudes, and interests;

4. Mobility of district population;

5. Avoidance of discrimination;

6. Reduction of duplication of effort and repetitive curricula among various school levels and coordination of courses of study; and

7. Provisions of negotiated agreements.

(Legal References listed on complete board document)

Policy Adopted: April 5, 1995
Policy Revised: April 2, 2008
Policy Revised   February 3, 2010

FIGURE **Bristol Board of Education**
19.2 **Curriculum Development Regulation**

BRISTOL BOARD OF EDUCATION 6140 <u>REGULATION</u>

Instruction

Curriculum Design/Development/Revision

Curriculum development and revision is an ongoing process. The Board of Education delegates authority for curriculum design/development/revision to the administration. The Student Achievement subcommittee of the Board of Education will review and approve all curricula prior to referral to the full Board of Education for final approval.

Whenever the Connecticut State Board of Education adopts new Connecticut Frameworks for a curriculum area, when a new course needs to be added, or a current curriculum needs to be revised, the formal curriculum development/revision process shall be implemented and a new curriculum shall be produced. The formal curriculum development/revision process is:

1. A proposal is made to the Curriculum Planning Council by the appropriate curriculum supervisor and staff.

2. Upon approval of the proposal for a full curriculum revision or development of curriculum for a new course by the Curriculum Planning Council, a curriculum committee is formed, headed by the appropriate curriculum supervisor, with representation from the appropriate teaching and administrative staff. In cases of minor revisions to an existing curriculum, revisions will originate with the content teachers and content-area supervisor.

3. Each written curriculum shall consist of the title of the curriculum area, the grades or course for which the curriculum is written, a program or course description, prerequisite courses for high school-level curricula, the department philosophy and goals, the Connecticut standards from the Connecticut Framework for the specific curriculum area or the national standards if Connecticut standards do not exist, the Power Standards, Essential Questions and Big Ideas, learning objectives for students, and instructional strategies and assessments.

4. The new or revised curriculum will be presented to the Student Achievement Committee of the Board of Education for a first reading. After review and any needed revision, the Student Achievement Committee will send the new or revised curriculum to the full Board as a second reading and a decision item for vote by the Board of Education.

When curriculum is developed or revised, professional development seminars will be provided to the appropriate administrative and teaching staff.

Regulation Adopted:　April 2, 2008

Regulation revised:　February 3, 2010

FIGURE 19.3   **Bristol Curriculum Revision Proposal**

Bristol Public Schools
Bristol, Connecticut

CPC ACTION: _____
☐ Approved   date
☐ Not Approved

Curriculum Planning Council—Curriculum Revision Proposal

School/Program Submitting Proposal: _____

Department Coordinator: _____

Curriculum or Course: _____

Directions: This form is to be used to request a curricular revision or a significant change to the methodology/materials used for instruction. All of the requirements below must be satisfied prior to submitting this proposal to the Curriculum Planning Council. Completed proposal packages should be forwarded to the Director of Teaching and Learning to be placed on the council's agenda. *This form may be reformatted for your convenience.*

1. Explain the need for this curricular revision as determined by alignment with the Connecticut Frameworks and/or national standards and CMT or CAPT. (*It is not sufficient to say that the curricula are not aligned to the state frameworks, state standards, and/or state tests.*) [Please explain exceptions.]

2 . Explain how the revision of this course/curriculum will assist the district in meeting Tier I Accountability goals.

3. What evaluative tools will be used to measure the successful implementation of this course/curriculum? What specific data sources will be used? How and at what intervals will data be collected? Who will be responsible for data collection and analysis?

4. What is the timeline for this revision? *Try to include as many specifics as possible.*

5. How will this revision impact other courses, grades, or levels?

6. What efforts will be made to integrate technological resources and the CT Technology Standards into this course/curriculum?

7. Whom do you recommend to participate in this work (curriculum writing/materials selection team)?

8. What technical assistance will be needed from the Curriculum Planning Council or Office of Teaching and Learning?

9. What professional development will implementers need (type and time)?

10. What are the specific budgetary implications attached to this proposal? Please include staffing, facilities, materials and any other issues for consideration.

FIGURE 19.4 **Bristol Curriculum Pilot Proposal**

Bristol Public Schools
Bristol, Connecticut

CPC DATE _____
ACTION: ☐ Approved
　　　　　☐ Not Approved
REVIEW
DATES _____

Curriculum Planning Council—Curriculum Pilot Proposal

School/Program Submitting Proposal: _____

Curriculum/Department Coordinator: _____

Administrator Signature:_____

Date:_____

Directions: This form is to be used to request the piloting of a course or a significant change to the methodology/materials used for instruction. All of the requirements below must be satisfied prior to submitting this proposal to the Curriculum Planning Council. Completed proposal packages should be forwarded to the Director of Teaching and Learning to be placed on the council's agenda. *This form may be reformatted for your convenience.*

1. Describe the proposed pilot program/materials/course, including teacher and student selection criteria.

2. Based upon the formal needs-assessment you conducted (attach findings), explain the need for this pilot in your program of studies.

3. Explain how the addition of this course/materials will assist the district in meeting Tier I Accountability goals.

4. Include a brief statement and attach appropriate support materials demonstrating the relationship between the proposed course/methodology/materials and the Connecticut Frameworks and/or national standards, the Bristol Curriculum and the CMT or CAPT. (*It is not sufficient to say that they are aligned.*) [Please explain exceptions.]

5. What evaluative tools will be used to measure the success of this pilot? What specific data sources will be used? How will data be collected? At what intervals will data be collected? Who is responsible for data collection and analysis?

6. What is the timeline for this pilot?

7. How will the addition of this course/materials impact other courses, grades, or levels?

8. What are the specific budgetary implications attached to this proposal? Please include staffing, facilities, materials and any other issues for consideration.

9. How will technological resources be integrated into this pilot?

10. What is the source of this pilot?

11. What technical assistance will be needed from the Curriculum Planning Council or Office of Teaching and Learning?

12. What professional development will implementers need (type and time)?

order to facilitate vertical alignment between the grades, we try to include at least one teacher from another grade level. For example, when revising the grade 8 mathematics curriculum, a grade 9 math teacher will also be included. Committees are intentionally small, usually one administrator and four to six teachers. This allows the work to be done efficiently. Committee members communicate with other teachers while the curriculum work is taking place.

Each June, I meet with all of the content-area supervisors to plan the work calendar for the next school year. Together, we determine dates when each curriculum development and revision committee will convene and when implementation meetings will occur. This pre-planning allows us to manage our budget for curriculum meetings and textbook purchases and to align the work in accordance with curriculum and textbook recommendations that will be made to the Board of Education. Budgets must be developed *a year in advance* in order to secure the funds for summer work and for materials and textbooks.

The curriculum document shown in Figure 19.5 is sent to the Bristol Board of Education for approval. (The document has been "collapsed" for space considerations and to emphasize the specific headings that coincide with the necessary components of this rigorous curriculum design model.)

To make any changes in the Board of Education-approved curriculum document, we must return to the board for approval. Last year, two controversial phrases in our previous curriculum documents created an interesting, and at times stressful, situation for everyone. The two phrases were: "instructional strategies that *may* be used" and "assessments that *may* be used." This intentional wording had been based on our department philosophy that the curriculum committee would specify learner objectives (the *what* of teaching) and then provide a list of *options* for instruction and assessment (the *how* of teaching). We felt that *teachers* needed to determine how to teach and assess based on the needs of their students. The board, however, asked for wording that specified instructional strategies and assessments which all teachers would be *required* to use.

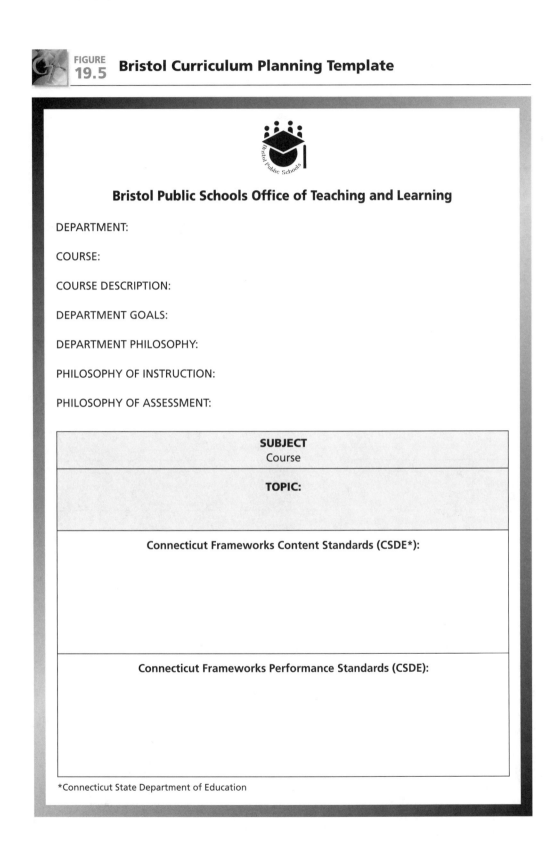

FIGURE 19.5   Bristol Curriculum Planning Template

Bristol Public Schools Office of Teaching and Learning

DEPARTMENT:

COURSE:

COURSE DESCRIPTION:

DEPARTMENT GOALS:

DEPARTMENT PHILOSOPHY:

PHILOSOPHY OF INSTRUCTION:

PHILOSOPHY OF ASSESSMENT:

SUBJECT Course
TOPIC:
Connecticut Frameworks Content Standards (CSDE*):
Connecticut Frameworks Performance Standards (CSDE):

*Connecticut State Department of Education

FIGURE 19.5 **Bristol Curriculum Planning Template** *(continued)*

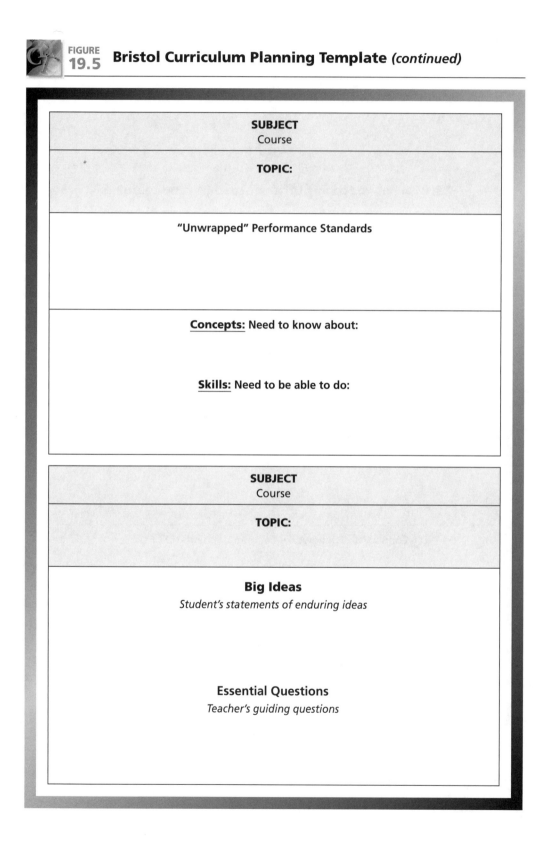

SUBJECT
Course

TOPIC:

"Unwrapped" Performance Standards

Concepts: Need to know about:

Skills: Need to be able to do:

SUBJECT
Course

TOPIC:

Big Ideas
Student's statements of enduring ideas

Essential Questions
Teacher's guiding questions

FIGURE 19.5 **Bristol Curriculum Planning Template** *(continued)*

SUBJECT
Course

TOPIC:

Learning Objectives

The students will be able to:

SUBJECT
Course

TOPIC:

Instructional Strategies

Based on our department philosophy for student learning, science teachers will:

SUBJECT
Course

TOPIC:

Assessment/Common Learning Experiences

Through these assessments/experiences, students will demonstrate mastery of the learning objectives. Teachers will assess and provide feedback to students about the following:

As a result, the teaching and learning supervisors and I added two sections, called the *Philosophy of Instruction* and *the Philosophy of Assessment*, and a change of language that now states:

- **"Instructional Strategies:** Based on our department philosophy for student learning, teachers will: _____." *The instructional strategies which **must** be implemented with **all** students are then listed.*

- **"Assessments/Common Learning Experiences:** Through these assessments/experiences, students will demonstrate mastery of the learning objectives. Teachers will assess and provide feedback to students about the following: _____." *The assessments/common learning experiences which **must** be implemented with **all** students are then listed.*

Even though this policy change was difficult for many to accept at first, everyone is now happy with it, because this revised language does indeed reflect our educational philosophy that *all* students should have access to the *same* quality instruction and assessment opportunities.

As a supplement to the board-approved curriculum document, we also develop an implementation guide. The implementation guide contains all the supplemental information that teachers need, such as text readings, vocabulary, and recommended instructional strategies and assessments that go *beyond* those that are required. Because our Board of Education approves curriculum, we do not give them the detail in the implementation guide, so that we can make changes to the document. Pacing guides are also developed and revised as needed.

Adding New Curricula and Selecting Textbooks

We have found it necessary to add new courses of study to the Bristol curriculum. The process for making these course additions begins with the teaching and learning supervisors creating "backwards planning" maps of courses from grade 12 to grade 6. This reflects our Board of Education mission statement: "To maintain a safe and secure learning environment that provides all students with the necessary knowledge and skills to *successfully complete college, and other post-high school education or training.*" Figures 19.6 and 19.7 show sample course maps.

As a result of this mapping, we realized the need to develop a multiple-year plan for the addition of Advanced Placement courses. We identified the courses to be added, planned the sequence for the addition of courses over three years, and selected teachers to teach each AP course. Those teachers who will be teaching the new AP courses are required to attend in-depth summer training sessions as preparation. During that following school year, the curriculum is written using the College Board and national standards, the syllabus is submitted to the College Board, textbooks are reviewed and

FIGURE 19.6 Bristol Public Schools English Language Arts Curriculum Course Map

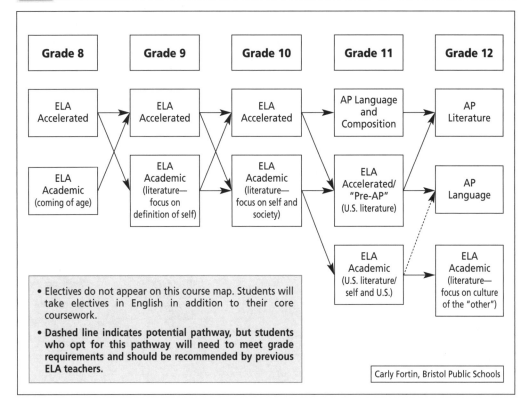

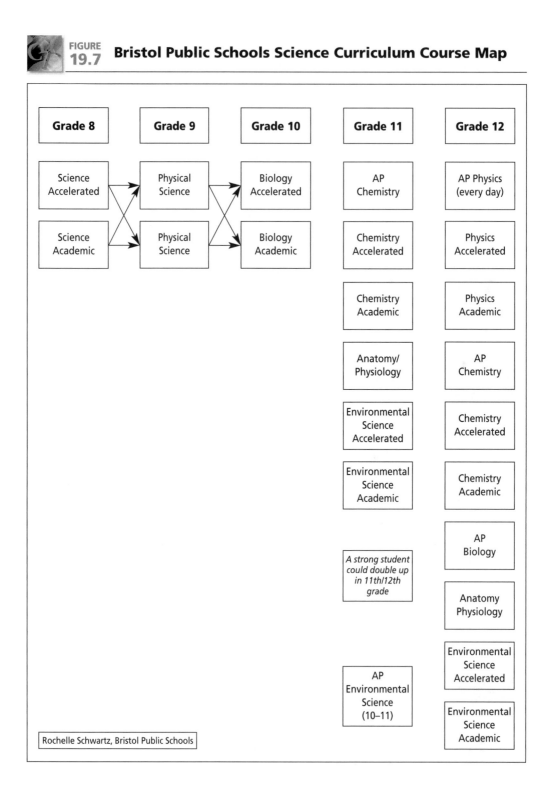

FIGURE 19.7 Bristol Public Schools Science Curriculum Course Map

Grade 8	Grade 9	Grade 10	Grade 11	Grade 12
Science Accelerated	Physical Science	Biology Accelerated	AP Chemistry	AP Physics (every day)
Science Academic	Physical Science	Biology Academic	Chemistry Accelerated	Physics Accelerated
			Chemistry Academic	Physics Academic
			Anatomy/ Physiology	AP Chemistry
			Environmental Science Accelerated	Chemistry Accelerated
			Environmental Science Academic	Chemistry Academic
				AP Biology
			A strong student could double up in 11th/12th grade	Anatomy Physiology
				Environmental Science Accelerated
			AP Environmental Science (10–11)	Environmental Science Academic

Rochelle Schwartz, Bristol Public Schools

selected, and the curriculum and textbooks are presented to the Board of Education for approval. All of this requires careful timing. Funds must be placed in the budget a year in advance for the summer training sessions, the curriculum work, and the purchase of textbooks.

Once any new curriculum is written, the textbook and materials selection process begins. We emphasize to all staff that *a textbook is not the curriculum*. A textbook is to be used as a *resource to support* curriculum implementation.

We require that at least two textbooks be evaluated. The textbook evaluation document in Figure 19.8 is what we use when reviewing new textbooks for possible purchase. Note how all of the criteria require *evidence* that the textbook does indeed meet the specific criteria for selection. Note also that the first two criteria, requiring close alignment with the state frameworks and Bristol curriculum objectives, are *doubly weighted* for importance. Even though completing such a thorough evaluation of potential textbooks is a time-consuming task, it is a necessary step to ensuring that our textbooks *support* our standards-based teaching, learning, and assessment focus.

Once we complete the textbook evaluation process, our recommendations are presented to the Board of Education for approval. Later, the alignment of the board-approved textbook to the Bristol curriculum is then written into the curriculum implementation guide.

During the development of the budget each year, the middle school curriculum coordinators and high school department heads meet with the content-area supervisor and identify items to be placed in the budget as *essential* or *supplemental* for implementation of the curriculum. The elementary supervisor does this for the elementary schools. This leads to consistency and uniformity across the district and makes it possible for each teacher to have the essential materials needed to implement the curriculum.

During the budget review process, I review the schools' budgets with assistance from the supervisors. Together, we monitor and question related budget items. When budgets need to be reduced,

FIGURE 19.8 **Bristol Textbook Evaluation Template**

Bristol Public Schools
TEXTBOOK EVALUATION

Text Title: _____

Authors: _____

Publisher:_____ Copyright Date:_____

Readability Rating: _____ Course/Grade: _____

Text Reviewer: _____

Circle the appropriate responses. **Provide specific examples/evidence for each item.**

double weighting	1. Matches CT Frameworks *EVIDENCE:*	(1) weak	(2) adequate	(3) strong
double weighting	2. Correlates to Bristol Curriculum Objectives *EVIDENCE:*	(1) weak	(2) adequate	(3) strong
	3. Provides multiple opportunities to achieve the concepts and skills in the Bristol Power Standards *EVIDENCE:*	(1) weak	(2) adequate	(3) strong
	4. Aligns with previous and next grade/course curriculum *EVIDENCE:*	(1) weak	(2) adequate	(3) strong
	5. Presents content accurately *EVIDENCE:*	(1) weak	(2) adequate	(3) strong
	6. Allows students to construct their own meaning *EVIDENCE:*	(1) weak	(2) adequate	(3) strong
	7. Provides in-depth information *EVIDENCE:*	(1) weak	(2) adequate	(3) strong
	8. Promotes higher-order thinking *EVIDENCE:*	(1) weak	(2) adequate	(3) strong

FIGURE
19.8 **Bristol Textbook Evaluation Template** *(continued)*

9. Includes authentic activities aimed at building students' understanding **EVIDENCE:**	(1) weak	(2) adequate	(3) strong
10. Addresses skills identified in the curriculum **EVIDENCE:**	(1) weak	(2) adequate	(3) strong
11. Supports authentic, performance-based assessments **EVIDENCE:**	(1) weak	(2) adequate	(3) strong
12. Utilizes a variety of modalities to meet the needs of a diverse group of learners **EVIDENCE:**	(1) weak	(2) adequate	(3) strong
13. Integrates technological resources **EVIDENCE:**	(1) weak	(2) adequate	(3) strong
14. Facilitates differentiated instruction for students with varying abilities, interests and learning styles **EVIDENCE:**	(1) weak	(2) adequate	(3) strong
15. Provides content that is accessible to a variety of reading levels **EVIDENCE:**	(1) weak	(2) adequate	(3) strong
16. Provides an appreciation for diversity **EVIDENCE:**	(1) weak	(2) adequate	(3) strong
TOTALS:	_____	_____	_____

Overall rating: _____   (out of 54)

every effort is made to keep the *essential* curriculum materials in the budget.

The Role of Administrators in Curriculum Design

Administrators play a key role in the development and revision of curriculum. They facilitate discussions among the committee members, keep everyone continually focused on the work, and find any resources needed. Ideally, there is a teaching and learning supervisor for each content area who takes the lead in curriculum development and revision. In large school districts, this is usually the case. However, in small districts with fewer administrators, often a principal will lead a curriculum committee.

Content of the curriculum, that is, learner outcomes, instructional strategies, and assessments, must be consistent in curriculum documents across all disciplines and align with Board of Education policy. Such consistency is critically important so that all students receive the same high level of instruction across all grades and subject areas. Ensuring this consistency through regular communication and collaboration is the responsibility of the director of teaching and learning, the teaching and learning supervisors, and any other administrators working on curriculum. They must also make sure that teachers understand the required elements of the curriculum. To be able to do this, administrators must have a thorough and deep understanding of curriculum design.

Another key responsibility of the administrator is to make curriculum and related resources easily available and usable for teachers. If teachers cannot find something or only have parts of a document or kit, those curricular resources are not going to be used effectively. To help with this, we have set up an internal Web site so that all staff can access the entire set of curriculum documents, implementation guides, and pacing guides. Even though it has been a challenge to regularly manage and keep abreast of this amount of information, it has proven very beneficial to do so.

Administrative monthly cabinet meetings are effective for communicating curricular changes to administrators. When a curriculum is written and approved for use in our classrooms, all building administrators and special education administrators need to be knowledgeable of it. To facilitate this, an overview of the new curriculum is presented to administrators at our monthly cabinet meetings. Observation guides, incorporating the Big Ideas, Essential Questions, state standards, major concepts, assessments, and key vocabulary, are developed for administrators to use during classroom observations to help them determine if a teacher is "on target" with curriculum implementation and the corresponding pacing guide. Teaching and learning supervisors also provide a brief summary of what administrators should be looking for with regard to the curriculum as they visit classrooms.

Monitoring Implementation Efforts

When a curriculum is written, it represents the collective best thinking of the teachers and administrators regarding what to teach, how to teach, and how student learning will be assessed. Through curriculum development and revision, teachers improve their content knowledge and pedagogy. However, the reality of implementation is usually different from what was originally planned. It is through *monitoring* of the implementation of a curriculum that we discover the revisions which need to be made.

As I stated earlier, I believe that what is monitored gets done. Bristol's approach has long been to monitor implementation constantly, as we have been doing for years in our instructional Data Teams that meet at least twice a month to talk about instruction. Through these teams, teachers identify, implement, and evaluate effective instructional practices that will meet the learning needs of all our students.

However, monitoring the implementation of curriculum is challenging, especially given the size of our school system. To accomplish this, we are currently using a monitoring approach developed by three of our teaching and learning supervisors: Carly Fortin, Dominique Fox, and Rochelle Schwartz.

When a curriculum is developed or revised, it is critically

important that teachers become familiar and comfortable with it. Often, we prepare an overview for use when presenting the new curriculum to teachers. We strive to always include special education staff in these overviews. Special educators need to know the general curriculum so they can assist their students as they progress through it. By having supervisors hold regular meetings with the teachers, who are implementing the new or revised curriculum, and providing ongoing coaching from instructional coaches, implementation issues are found and problems solved.

One approach we have used quite successfully is to provide an opportunity for teachers to meet with the curriculum supervisor by arranging substitutes to release teams throughout the school day. During these meetings, the teams discuss implementation of the curriculum, share model lessons, effective learning activities, and informal assessments, discuss the concepts with which students are struggling, brainstorm new approaches, and design lessons together to teach difficult concepts.

Another effective approach we have used is to schedule longer, half-day sessions for teacher teams to meet and discuss curriculum implementation issues. We record suggested curriculum changes and share this information across the district to keep everyone informed and to allow for further discussion and input. All recommended revisions are then presented to the Board of Education for approval.

Still another strategy we use is to have our literacy and mathematics coaches provide ongoing support to classroom teachers while they are implementing the curriculum. Coaches work with teachers on a regular basis to resolve issues they may have concerning the implementation of a curriculum, including those related to specific instructional strategies, content, or the use of varied resources.

Sustainability Suggestions

For professional practices to be sustained, they must become part of the regular work and routine of the entire staff. This becomes particularly challenging when teachers and administrators retire and new staff members are hired to replace them. Established systems for record-keeping procedures and other types of documentation must be in place and followed. We have established procedures for organizing and maintaining accurate documents and discarding old curricula. Records of Board of Education-approved curricula are maintained electronically and in paper form. Textbook adoption records, including the author, title, edition, publisher, and copies purchased must also be maintained.

One way we have promoted the sustainability of our practices is through the orientation of new teachers and administrators to the curriculum. New teachers participate in an "induction academy" for one to two weeks in August prior to the start of school. The purpose of this academy is to orient new staff to curriculum implementation and instructional practices. Each summer, the teaching and learning supervisors meet with new teachers to explain the Bristol curriculum and our use of common formative and summative assessments and instructional Data Teams. During this time we also provide support to any teachers who are transferring to different grade levels or courses to make sure these teachers understand what is, for them, a new curriculum.

For any curriculum to be implemented as it was intended, it needs to be continually *in use*. Curriculum documents should not be "sitting unused" in a notebook on a shelf. But how do leaders keep everyone's attention focused on curriculum implementation and revision? There are several ways:

- Establish pacing guides which are to be followed by all staff.

- Create and use summative assessments tied directly to the curriculum and pacing guide at the middle and high school levels.

- Focus the work of instructional Data Teams on student learning and using effective instructional practices to help students learn the concepts and skills in the curriculum.

- Observe instruction in classrooms to monitor implementation of the curriculum.

- Meet regularly with teachers to discuss curriculum implementation and needed revisions/adjustments to the curriculum.

- Assist teachers with learning the content and pedagogical knowledge needed for students to learn. This can be accomplished most effectively through an instructional coaching model.

- Revisit and revise the curriculum *every year.*

- Link budget requests for books and supplies to curriculum objectives and instructional strategies.

In Bristol, we firmly believe that we must hold ourselves accountable for student learning, that it is *our* responsibility to make sure that students are learning. Each of us has a role to play in our students' achievements. The way we strive to do this is by developing rigorous curricula, by ensuring that the curricula are well implemented, and by establishing procedures and processes for the development, revision, monitoring, and sustaining of curricula as administrative and teaching staff change.

Reader's Assignment

1. Referring to Bristol's established model for developing and revising curricula, discuss with colleagues the points of particular relevance to your own school system.

2. Key points from Bristol's established process to discuss:
    - Development of a system-wide accountability plan
    - Circumstances necessitating curriculum design and redesign
    - Establishing a curriculum council and process for selecting members
    - Composition of design teams (system level administrators, curriculum coordinators, classroom educators)
    - Responsibilities of administrators, content area supervisors, and team members

- Providing professional development related to curriculum revision
- Drafting a step-by-step process for developing and revising curricula
- Procedures for receiving feedback and making midcourse adjustments
- Involvement of the school system's governing board
- Development of a curriculum implementation guide
- Process for selecting textbooks that directly support curriculum objectives
- Coordination of curricular resource needs with budgetary priorities and procedures
- Ideas for sustaining the work
- Other points to consider

3. Look for the similarities between West Haven's approach to curriculum redesign and that of Bristol's established process so as to more clearly identify the important steps to replicate when organizing, implementing, monitoring, and sustaining the work in your own school system.

4. Further clarify, add to, or revise the organizational plan you began drafting at the end of the previous chapter.

CHAPTER 20
Advice to Administrators from Administrators

For the successful implementation, monitoring, and sustainability of each new professional practice in school systems, administrators at every level who are in any way associated with that practice must be in full knowledge and support of it. To demonstrate full knowledge and support, several essential criteria are necessary:

- Complete understanding of the process through direct, personal experience
- Creative scheduling of time to enable educators to collaboratively revise and improve their units of study
- Facilitation of the process in whatever ways are needed so the work can progress
- Regular monitoring of the practice while educators are implementing it
- Intentional long-term planning to make the practice an integral part of the school system's culture

Over the last decade, the school systems that I have seen make the most progress in improving student achievement are those in which the administrative leaders—from the superintendent to the assistant principal—have been actively involved in the implementation of the initiative. By "actively involved," I mean the leaders have personally:

- attended the related professional development sessions;
- taken a full "hands-on, minds-on" approach to learning the new practices;
- worked side-by-side with educators to create related work products;
- actively listened and asked questions of the presenter and of educators; and
- collaboratively planned with leaders at *all* levels (central office, school, classroom) how best to implement the new practice.

I remember well the words of one superintendent whom I privately thanked for attending all three days of professional development sessions that I had conducted for his instructional personnel and administrators. He politely said to me in reply,

"Where else would I be? How can I possibly expect my staff to implement something that I haven't experienced and evaluated myself?" *That* is the kind of administrator who understands the critical importance of professional development—for leaders *as well as* educators—and who models that understanding by personal example.

One of the most frequent requests I receive from leaders is this: "How have other administrators you've worked with implemented these powerful practices to improve student achievement? What advice can you give us as we begin?" In this final chapter of the book, leaders who have personally organized, implemented, monitored, and sustained the work of curriculum design and related powerful practices to improve student achievement share through firsthand narratives their valuable experience.

Advice Generously Offered

In the fall of 2009, I began asking several administrators, from school systems across the United States in which I have presented professional development, for practical advice and guidance they might offer to other administrators beginning the implementation of new initiatives in their own educational settings. Reflecting months and years of personal experience, the administrators' responses I received are worth their proverbial "weight in gold."

Even though much of the advice pertains specifically to the effective implementation, monitoring, and sustainability of common formative assessments and instructional Data Teams, the advice is applicable to all "best practices," including that of rigorous curriculum design.

Because administrators naturally view the implementation of any new initiative from the vantage point of their own individual roles and responsibilities, I have organized this advice as being specific first to *system-level* administrators and then to *school-level* administrators. However, collectively, the counsel is applicable to *all* administrators, as evidenced by how similar and recurring it is from one administrator to the next, regardless of the individual's position.

SYSTEM-LEVEL ADMINISTRATORS
Superintendent

John Van Pelt is the Superintendent of Lake Villa School District 41 in Lake Villa, Illinois. He has personally led his school system in the organization and implementation of best practices related to standards, assessments, and data-driven decision making for years. With regard to curriculum design, Dr. Van Pelt presents here his "must dos" as they relate to the role of administrators, monitoring implementation efforts, and sustaining implementation:

Role of Administrators

- Principals and other instructional leaders need to receive ongoing professional development in curriculum, instruction, and assessment.
- Curriculum design must be aligned with the work of collaborative teams, common formative assessments, monitoring, and reporting.

Monitoring Implementation Efforts

- Principals and other instructional leaders need to receive ongoing professional development in walk-though classroom observations along with effective follow-up and reflective conversations.
- Administrators and other instructional leaders are the ones to determine:
  - if professional development supporting curriculum implementation is actually changing classroom practices; and
  - if the written curriculum design is being taught (implemented) with fidelity.
- District office administrators and principals need to meet regularly with collaborative teams to discuss curriculum implementation, assessment results, and student interventions.
- Grade-level common formative assessment or benchmark assessment results must be reported during the school year in reading, writing, and math. High school *common* end-of-course assessment results need to also be reported.

Sustaining Implementation

- District-level leadership needs to:
  - create and maintain a comprehensive accountability framework for all school improvement and professional development initiatives;
  - provide the focus and direction for curriculum, instruction, and assessment; and
  - make available the time, resources, and ongoing support necessary for building the capacity of all staff to be proficient in curriculum, instruction, and assessment.
- District-level *and* building-level leaders need to:
  - identify instructional strategies and student interventions that have the greatest impact on student learning and achievement;

> — cultivate a "results orientation"; and
>
> — regularly celebrate "early wins," successes, student progress, and staff accomplishments.

- Administrator, teacher, and staff evaluations, incentives, and recognition must be aligned with school improvement initiatives.

Superintendent

Mike Wasta is the former Superintendent of Bristol, Connecticut, who personally initiated, directed, and oversaw, during his five-year tenure as Superintendent, all of the implementation and sustainability practices of Bristol's comprehensive district improvement model.

Here are his top five "must do" actions:

1. **Develop as broad a consensus as possible** about the benefits of and need to *simultaneously* implement *both* practices: common formative assessments (CFAs) and Data Teams. This is the most frequently skipped step. People just want to get going and they don't take the time to build understanding and support *across and within* stakeholder groups. Then, as things get difficult and the "glow" around the new initiative begins to diminish, *and* people start to realize that they actually may have to change the way they work, support vanishes and another initiative is heaped on the "discard" pile. Senior leadership needs to have the support of the policymakers and political establishment as well as the professional people who will actually be implementing the work. Sooner or later, there will be a tough decision about resources—the kind of decision only these people can make. Without *understanding of* and *support for* these powerful practices, they can "pull the rug out" in a second.

2. **Create a small group at the top** that will monitor the implementation. There will be continuous and numerous unanticipated issues that arise, some of which need to be resolved quickly. A nimble, powerful group that can get things done will be crucial. This will have to be in place for a long, long time.

3. **Go deep, not broad.** If you are focusing on these two practices (CFAs and Data Teams), you really *can't be doing anything else* of a major comprehensive nature for at least a couple of years. This requires a sustained and focused effort if it is to be done effectively.

4. **Admit mistakes.** The best laid plans will go awry. "Oops" memos to all staff are OK!

5. **Nobody can do the work for you.** Everyone involved in the process has to figure things out for themselves. This is sometimes painful and slow. There are *no shortcuts.* As Richard Elmore says, "The work is the work." From the top down, everyone has to do their part. If the superintendent never attends the related professional development sessions, that speaks volumes to the staff regarding his or her commitment to the work.

Dr. Wasta concludes his advice by saying: "Outside organizations and individuals can only advise leaders on how to do things and offer the benefit of their experience, but that cannot replace all of the stakeholders *making the process their own* by thinking about it, trying things, evaluating efforts, regrouping, stepping back when necessary, moving forward, etc. In my experience, places that fail do so because they think that all that is needed are a few workshops, and then everyone will automatically get it and make it happen. No way."

Deputy Superintendent

Susan Kalt Moreau, Deputy Superintendent of Bristol, Connecticut, began the full-scale implementation of these same best practices with Dr. Wasta. Now finishing Bristol's tenth year of implementation, Dr. Moreau and Denise Carabetta, Director of Teaching and Learning, continue together to lead and sustain the work district-wide. Her advice:

1. **Be the most knowledgeable person** on your staff, so that staff members know:
   a. *you* get it;
   b. you want *them* to get it; and
   c. you can *help them* to get it.

2. **Follow through**—visit the teacher teams while they are working and help solve problems and answer questions. *Know where you need to be.*

3. **Don't "fly" other initiatives in and out.** This is what you are expecting teachers to be focused on *right now.*

4. *Celebrate Successes!* This is hugely important to keep the "wind in the sails" all along the way. Small wins keep everyone moving ahead with energy and optimism.

5. **Stay the course.** Change doesn't happen instantaneously.

To illustrate, back in 2001 we set proficiency benchmarks at 90 percent—lofty goals for us at that time, especially given the fact that 12 percent of our students required special education. However, we met those benchmarks over time, and last year we increased the high school CAPT (Connecticut Academic Performance Test) benchmarks to 91 percent and 92 percent in reading and writing, respectively. Recently our District Data Team met, and we raised mathematics also to 91 percent.

For the CMT benchmarks (Connecticut Mastery Test, grades 3–8), we raised mathematics grade 7 to 92 percent and Grade 8 to 91 percent. In grade 7, we also raised our reading proficiency target to 91 percent.

It is because we first held to the belief and expectation that *all* students can learn, and then put that belief into action by raising our benchmark targets to *also include special education students* meeting proficiency, that we have been able to exceed 90 percent for *all* students.

Know that these practices *do* work when you have a District Accountability Plan as the foundation, and couple that plan with uniform curriculum, pacing guides, common assessments (formative and summative) in alignment with state tests to monitor progress, ***and** people who love to see students succeed*!

Executive Director

Cathy Lassiter is the Executive Director of Middle Schools in Norfolk, Virginia. Dr. Lassiter supervises nine middle schools serving 8,000 students. She writes:

Here is my short-list of advice of what we have found that school leaders *must* provide their faculties with in order to facilitate the deeper implementation of common formative assessments and Data Teams:

1. **Structured time** for educators to do the work
2. **Personal participation by the leader**, making expectations clear and learning right along with the group
3. Understanding that there is **a learning curve for staff**
4. Acceptance of the fact that you must **persist until they get it**
5. A commitment that you will **observe the processes, review the CFAs,** and **provide feedback for improvement** *all along the way*

The most important advice I can offer is to *follow up, not **give** up*, and provide constant feedback for growth.

Superintendent

Stephen Ventura, Superintendent of the Edison School District in Bakersfield, California, and a former Assistant Principal, Principal, and Central Office Director, understands the necessity of personally participating in professional development sessions to learn firsthand the value of practices he intends to later institute district-wide. In a relatively short period of time, his school system has experienced significant growth in student achievement by focusing on four related professional practices, the foundational building blocks for designing and implementing a rigorous curriculum:

1. Decision Making for Results (also called Data-Driven Decision Making)

2. Priority Standards and "Unwrapping" the Standards

3. Common Formative Assessments

4. Data Teams

Stephen describes how central office leaders can establish initiatives and progress toward deep implementation:

We were thoughtful about the order of implementation and how each practice would complement and support district-wide strategies. Consequently, these four practices were implemented, one after the other, in the order that they are listed. Each new practice was dependent upon previous learning, and provided participants with the prerequisite skills necessary to reinforce and increase their awareness of leadership, teaching, and learning. The combined impact of all four of these practices was maximized through the implementation process.

Schools and districts invest millions of dollars each year to purchase programs designed to increase student achievement. It is not about programs; it's about *professional practice*. As leaders, we must recognize the difference between the two; for every dollar we invest in the competence of teachers and administrators, we will net a greater gain in student achievement than if we were to spend that same money on another program.

These practices can be applied in any school of any size, regardless of demographics and economics. With determination and focus, and a belief that this is work worth doing, it can become the culture of your school or district and will ultimately lead to improved student learning.

There are many ideas I would like to share with other administrators about our success in implementing these professional practices, but here are my top five:

1. Make sure you are **committed to full implementation by year two or three**. Decision Making for Results, Priority Standards, CFAs, and Data Teams are the four connected main initiatives that we are focused on. These are our "critical-mass" areas, where *we expect 100 percent implementation*.

2. Teachers were **compensated for professional development**. We *conducted training in the evenings* and broke each seminar into two evenings. This was paid for using federal/stimulus funds. Because we valued teacher time with payment, buy-in was a nonissue. Even though my 100-day plan could not include everything, we still were able to map out a training schedule for all four connected initiatives.

3. I cannot overemphasize the fact that we were **very purposeful in narrowing our focus** (depth over breadth). *Having only two to three focused goals is the key.*

4. Make sure you set yourself up for some short-term wins. **Short-term wins lead to long-term success.** Short-term wins for us: Ten meetings of our Data Teams in our first year, *starting with only one content area* for CFAs, and providing *regular and timely feedback* after each meeting. Our Data Team meetings are all conducted under the same roof at the same time (library, cafeteria, or auditorium) so administrators and others can *quickly visit* each meeting and *monitor progress.*

5. **Apply the *best leadership behaviors*:**
   a. Leaders must be prepared to stand up for effective practice even if changes are initially unpopular.
   b. Change leaders should share a common commitment to the notion that *ideas are more important than personalities* (this one is big).
   c. Leaders must commit to ambitious goals, maintain those goals, and provide frequent feedback (we use our Web site to do this: www.edisonsd.com).
   d. Leaders should select projects that will have the greatest impact on student achievement.

SCHOOL-LEVEL ADMINISTRATORS
Principal

Jay Trujillo is the Principal of Patriot High School in Riverside County, California. Jay has led his schools to extraordinary results. For more than five years, student achievement gains in Jay's previous high school (Rubidoux) ranked number 1 among 82 comprehensive high schools in his southern California region. In his local county alone (with 45 comprehensive high schools), Jay's school ranked number 1 in improvement over two, three, and four years, respectively. This consistent progress earned his school two Model of Excellence awards.

Jay's "top five" recommendations for school leaders are:

1. **Clearly determine what you want to see, and articulate this vision and your corresponding expectations to others** (e.g., Is this an expectation applicable to *all* staff? How many meetings must they hold each month? How many common assessments must they administer each quarter or semester?). Minimally, I believe *all* departments must have the following: Priority Standards, pacing guides, end-of-course assessments, and a

minimum of five benchmark tests (aligned to end-of-course assessments). Depending on the amount of work completed to date, some of the above may be in place already, some may not. Decide what has already been done, and determine what must yet be done.

2. **Be flexible.** Not every department will embrace change in the same way. Once departments know what is expected, allow them to tackle the needed steps in the way that best meets their needs. Some may want to immediately get into the Data Teams process. Some may want to focus on identifying their Priority Standards first. Some may want to write common assessments for upcoming units. Some may want to "unwrap" their standards. All this work is necessary, but *the order and/or how it is completed* can be determined by the teachers. This flexibility will do much to promote staff buy-in.

3. *Most important:* **Teacher leadership is key.** Having the right teachers serve as Data Team leaders will make or break success. *Do whatever you can to get the right people into these positions of leadership.* Once in place, strategically care for, feed, and support them. Celebrate their successes!

4. **Monitor.** This is perhaps the biggest challenge—especially at a high school. For example, I have 21 instructional Data Teams. Principals will have to monitor who is *not* following through on expected behaviors (e.g., meeting attendance, showing up on time, submitting data, administering common assessments). Further, principals must provide appropriate intervention and support the process.

5. **All administrators, *especially the principal,* must be involved—you must lead by example.**

Principal

Juan Cordova is a former K–8 Principal in the Marion County school system of Ocala, Florida. His advice:

1. **Participate in training sessions.** Teachers *want to see* their administrators (principal and assistant principals) in the training sessions. Since they understand that an administrator's time is his or her most precious resource, the administrator's participation sends a message about the critical importance of every component of the initiative, whether it is CFAs, Data Teams, or anything else being done.

2. **Preview expectations with clear goals.** Teachers want to know what is going to happen, both short- and long-term. This provides them with an

opportunity to digest what is being asked and to begin their planning accordingly. This also eliminates surprises along the way, and provides the administrator with the time needed to share his or her vision. It also requires the administrator to reflect upon what is being implemented, what resources are needed, and what time frames need to be developed.

3. **Allow for feedback.** Create a mechanism for teachers to give feedback and suggestions. Frequently, some of the best ideas come from those "on the ground" that have to take the ideal and make it work in a less-than-ideal setting.

4. **Think big, start small.** Sometimes we want to "eat the entire elephant" at one sitting instead of one bite at a time. If we want a new, culture-changing initiative to become "the way we do things around here," we sometimes need to *start small and build momentum* and success. As I once heard, "A good idea, badly implemented, is a bad idea."

5. **"Weed the Garden."** Too many initiatives, too many demands, not enough time, and no true understanding about what is *most* important destroys too many good ideas. If teachers are already at their maximum, find things that are not as important—or not important at all—and eliminate them. Doing this goes a long way toward fostering and sustaining goodwill among the faculty.

6. *Inspect* **what you expect.** This goes back to my first recommendation about an administrator's time being precious. If teachers see that this initiative is going to be inspected—frequently—they are more likely to come on board. The *monitoring* of any good initiative is what frequently separates a successfully implemented one from one that is later described as "Been there, done that."

Principal

Barb Pitchford is a former Principal with nearly twenty years of administrative experience at the elementary, middle, and high school levels in the Aspen, Colorado, school system. She writes:

Implementation of any initiative involves the same critical components. Although the ingredients may vary, I believe the core essentials remain the same. Here are my "top five":

1. **Leadership commitment:** This is not a "flavor-of-the-month" practice. This is about changing culture—behavior, practice, and attitude. Commit to the *critical time necessary* to create as broad a consensus as possible with key

players (teachers, board, district leadership, parents). Build the foundation together (with those who choose to play) and cultivate teacher leadership to help create the change over time. Understand the different phases of the change process to avoid the "this too shall pass" attitude that results when initiatives so often come and go.

2. **Resources:** If it's important, then resources should be there to support it: provide the needed time, money, people, and technology.

3. **Professional Development:** Workshops are not just for teachers! Be there, right there, with your teachers during professional development sessions. Be the resident expert.

4. **Accountability:** Make accountability user-friendly. When you hear teachers genuinely asking for feedback, you will know that you have arrived. To achieve this, monitor, monitor, monitor—everything and everyone, continually. Make necessary midcourse corrections and be willing to make and admit mistakes in the learning and implementation process. Celebrate progress!

And last, but absolutely imperative:

5. **Never underestimate the difficulty of change.** It takes longer than you anticipated, has unanticipated dips, causes antipathy from unexpected quarters, and gets harder rather than easier when you dig deeper. If leadership isn't behind the initiative for change, every day, in every way, with a deep unrelenting commitment, chances are likely that it will become yet another short-lived initiative. Stay the course, despite the inherent difficulties. It will all be worth it.

Principal

Loan Mascorro is the Principal of Rio Vista Elementary School in the El Monte City School District, El Monte, California. Her school's motto is *"Unlimited Possibilities."* The Rio Vista staff and the entire El Monte school district have been working diligently to implement and sustain Professional Learning Communities (PLCs) and the Data Teams process.

Her top five "must dos" for school leaders are:

1. **Provide time for teachers to collaborate and sustain Data Teams** by restructuring the daily schedule to establish planning days for teams during which they create common formative assessments and collaboratively score student work, specifically writing.

2. **Hold Data Team meetings in the same room** to ensure accountability for all, to make it possible for the administrator to be present and support all grade-level teams, and to provide the teams with the opportunity for vertical planning and collaboration.

3. **Read** *Compelling Conversations* **by Thomasina Piercy (2006).** Implementing her ideas, I meet with each of my teachers individually, four times a year, to discuss students' progress in reading comprehension, math, and writing proficiency. During these important meetings, we also discuss strategic interventions to improve student achievement.

4. **Conduct classroom walk-throughs for regular monitoring and feedback.**

5. **Communicate and celebrate.** In Douglas Reeves' book *Leading Change in Your School* (2009), he makes three key points that I have found to be particularly important:
   - "Implementing change requires focus, clarity, and monitoring" (p. 123).
   - "Communicate elements of effective instruction in clear and unmistakable terms" (p. 119). This is crucial, not only to establish buy-in, but also to promote a deep commitment to effectiveness. Doing so truly leads to celebrations for short-term wins in student performance.
   - "Individuals need immediate, continuing reinforcement to sustain meaningful changes" (p. 90). I have found that it is very effective to communicate, celebrate, and appreciate my staff on a consistent basis, to make sure they know that I recognize the hard work they do to continually hold high expectations for themselves and for their students. I want them always to be certain that I appreciate them for who they are.

Principal/Assistant Principal

Tommy Thompson is the Principal of New London High School in New London, Connecticut. He was formerly Assistant Principal of Bernie Dover Middle School in New London, where he directly oversaw the implementation of CFAs and Data Teams for several years.

His ten "must dos" (not in rank order) for administrators are:

1. **Create the infrastructure to support the system.** The administrator controls time and money. These resources should be aligned with priorities. If you are using valuable time to discuss things that could be written in a memo, you are not supporting the process.

2. **Participate as a learner in the related professional development sessions, and then become a certified trainer for that practice.** Knowing practices

in depth helps you to create the infrastructure and support teachers. The leader must know what he or she is asking people to do.

3. **Provide systematic professional development.** The message should be the same for everyone. Don't "spray and pray" by having everyone get a cursory overview only. Have everyone *learn by doing.* Don't wait to get started until everyone has had the related professional development. Start with a few people and build from there.

4. **Monitor—"don't expect what you can't inspect."**

5. **Don't try to do everything in one day.** Teachers and administrators should be reminded often that it will not be perfect the first time. It's about the *process.* Don't complicate things. Beware of information overload. Be deliberate in the "rollout" of any new professional practices.

6. **Understand that teamwork is atypical.** Prepare for the occasional hurt feelings and differing team dynamics. Never overlook developing norms for effective collaboration *first.* Show teacher leaders *how* to take on facilitation roles (they will greatly benefit from professional development to learn new skills for doing this effectively).

7. **Look for ways to make the process easier for teachers.** For example, I assembled data for teachers at first. Eventually, the teachers were able to assume that responsibility. We just wanted to show that we were supporting them and valued their time. Also, we bought software to facilitate the turnaround time of assessment results. The software provided an item analysis that was extremely useful, along with other reports. We also developed an Excel spreadsheet for teachers to use prior to purchasing the software. These are examples of how administrators are supporting the process with resources.

8. **Provide opportunities for administrators and teachers to step back and reflect on their process and products.** Give teachers sample guides and work products so they can see *how* they can improve. Have peers observe one another, share, and collaborate on what's working and what isn't. Build a professional learning community that supports each and every person. Periodically remind everyone why we are doing these things.

9. **Be up front in stating that these practices are never meant to be punitive.** Help people understand that using the CFA and Data Teams processes is not intended to set up a competition against other teachers on a team or toward other teams in the school. This will help relieve any pressure teachers may be putting on themselves to perform. Know, however, there

will be some resulting *positive* pressure to do as well as another grade level or content area that is seeing dramatic results. That's healthy, not harmful.

10. **Celebrate wins and stay positive.** Find ways to communicate the truth that "Things are getting better!" Nothing improves morale more than knowing that what we are doing is *making a difference* in the learning of our students.

The Principal's Role in Curriculum Design

Mary Jane O'Connell, former elementary school Principal in the Douglas County School District of Colorado, sees the administrator as the facilitator of "3Ps" (people, process, and product), each of which is necessary to ensure the development of a thoughtfully designed curriculum that will prepare students to meet the challenges of the 21st century. Upon my request, Mary Jane graciously provided for this chapter practical and specific actions administrators can take to successfully implement and monitor the work of curriculum design.

People

The *ideal* qualifications of people that serve on curriculum design teams include: strong interpersonal skills; outstanding recognition from students, peers, parents, and administrators; being an "activator of learning"; and being a self-motivated, continual learner. Selecting people who are knowledgeable, forward-thinking, and able to work collaboratively may seem an obvious precept. However, there are times when the selection of people to serve comes down to those who are *available.* This results in a mixed blend of those who are willing to leave their students, plan for a substitute, and work after school, on weekends, and/or during summers, along with those who are "fighting to maintain the status quo."

Process

A thoughtful approach to curriculum design is to define the parameters of the work, including specific outcomes and timelines, so that participants clearly understand their role and related responsibilities. Specific ideas necessary when communicating the process include: having clarity of vision, purpose, and outcomes; understanding the rigor required of a 21st century-oriented curriculum; knowing that the creative process is not always neat, tidy or linear; understanding the need for and careful selection of Priority Standards; providing job-embedded professional development for participants.

Administrators should lend credibility and support to the curriculum development and implementation process by initially providing faculty with the vision and then by maintaining appropriate involvement. Think of the finished curriculum as the culminating performance of an orchestra. As "conductor of the curricular orchestra," the administrator melds the talents and perspectives of all the "musicians" to create a collective and enduring masterpiece.

Establishing group processes is vitally important in organizing curriculum design. These specific processes include:

- Norms, including confidentiality expectations
- Roles (leader/facilitator, recorder, process monitor, participant)
- Decision-making guidelines
- Meeting times, dates, and locations
- A communication plan for sharing progress and gathering input

In organizing the process component of curriculum design, administrators will find it helpful to: monitor *themselves* carefully during the work and entire process; allow *others* to do the thinking, talking, and actual work; provide clarity of the vision and outcomes whenever needed or requested; provide resources, recognition, and feedback; and collaborate with the designated leaders/facilitators as needed.

Product

Architects know that *Form Follows Function*. Their knowledge of design, experience in the field, and personal inventiveness provide the building blocks that create structures of beauty and purpose. In a similar way, the architects of curriculum shape the content of what will be taught in a form that is clearly articulated and understood by colleagues, students, and parents. No longer can "sit and get" be the mode of student learning.

Specific Monitoring Actions

There are specific monitoring actions administrators can take to assist educators in effectively implementing the newly designed rigorous curricula:

- Arrange opportunities for teacher modeling, shadowing, and follow-up practice.
- Offer frequent encouragement and feedback to teachers.
- Make videos of teachers effectively delivering the "new" curriculum.

- Create *with* teachers an observation rubric for the implementation of the curriculum that specifies criteria for proficient and exemplary teacher and student behaviors.

- Use the observation rubric to:
  — conduct a specific number of classroom observations each week;
  — record the number of teachers and students displaying the targeted behaviors;
  — chart the data without displaying teacher names; and
  — use data to help define professional development or resources needed.

- Write personal notes to teachers after classroom observations to acknowledge one or more rubric criteria that they demonstrated during the visit.

- Survey students to determine their satisfaction levels with the content and quality of the new curriculum.

IN CONCLUSION

Those who create the curricular units of study are the ones who will best understand each of the related components represented on both the unit planning organizers and on the accompanying documents that provide important details. However, keep in mind that educators who were *not* part of the initial design work, but will themselves be implementing these curricular units in their own instructional programs and classes, need to thoroughly understand how and why each component is a necessary part of the integrated whole. They cannot be expected to receive the completed units and be able to implement them effectively without *sufficient* explanation from those who created the units.

To this end, administrators need to prepare a thoughtfully constructed implementation plan that includes ongoing, scheduled opportunities for professional collaboration between those who designed the units and those who did not. In addition, professional development directly related to each of the unit components is a must.

When everyone understands how the units of study were put together, why everything in them has been included, and how to effectively implement the units according to the guidelines provided in Chapter 17, my sincere hope is that *all* educators will be able to use these rigorous curricula to (1) successfully prepare their students for attainment of the grade-specific and course-specific learning outcomes and (2) assist their students *beyond* the classroom by preparing them for whatever life pathways they choose for themselves in the future.

In closing, I wish to offer my sincere thanks, respect, and appreciation to all leaders and educators for everything you have done and continue to do to benefit the students and the education communities you serve. Your dedication and commitment are sure to produce a lasting and far-reaching impact on all the students in your care.

Reader's Assignment

An effective way of sharing this chapter's valuable information with a group of administrators is to form small groups and assign a different one of these administrator commentaries to each group. Ask the small groups to read their respective commentary, discuss the key points among themselves, and then share out with the whole group the salient points of the advice given and the group members' thoughts about it.

Choose a moderator to facilitate the large-group discussions and a recorder to take notes on the discussion points raised and the participants' various responses to the advice presented. Draft an action plan for any decisions made about how to apply the advice in individual schools and in the entire school system.

1. Discuss and define the roles of those leaders (central office, curriculum supervisors, and school leaders) in your school system that are, or will be, associated with curriculum design and implementation.

2. To what degree is each of your administrators knowledgeable of the curriculum design work taking place? What further information and professional development do they need?

3. What steps do you need to take in order to create a "mindset for change"?

4. Identify from this chapter the particular *implementation* guidelines that seem most helpful for your administrators to follow.

5. Discuss and decide the procedures you will use to *monitor* implementation of the new curricula in classrooms.

6. What means will you use to provide *regular feedback* to educators?

7. How will your administrators *sustain educators' fidelity* to the new curricula once they are implemented?

APPENDIX A
Bloom's Taxonomy

Categories in the Cognitive Process Dimension

Most educators are quite familiar with Bloom's *Taxonomy of Educational Objectives* (Bloom et al., 1956). For many, understanding the levels of thinking represented in this taxonomy was a cornerstone of required educational methods courses.

In recent years, as educators have become increasingly focused on the accurate assessment of student learning, the original taxonomy has been revisited and revised. Unlike the original, the revised framework is two-dimensional. In the newer model, the two dimensions are cognitive process and knowledge. These two components operate like *X* and *Y* axes: the cognitive level (evident from a verb that represents student learning) would be placed on the horizontal axis, and the type of knowledge (evident from the nouns that represent what the student is to learn) would be placed on the vertical.

The six cognitive processes in the revised taxonomy are *remember, understand, apply, analyze, evaluate,* and *create.* These are just slightly different from the original six levels of Bloom's Taxonomy (Bloom et al., 1956). The four categories of knowledge in the revised taxonomy are *factual, conceptual, procedural,* and *metacognitive.*

This revised taxonomy works well with the "unwrapping" process and, later, in designing effective assessment items. In order to place an objective in the taxonomy, teachers must first "unwrap" a standard to discover what it requires cognitively (the verb) and knowledgewise (the nouns that delineate content and concepts). Once they have determined the correct placement, then the "bare bones" of the assessment items are set. However, the placement is important, because different types of objectives require different approaches to assessment (Anderson and Krathwohl, 2001, p. 8).

The list on the following pages contains lists of verbs that **approximate** the particular levels of student learning. It is important to "unwrap" standards and ensure each standard is placed in the taxonomy table before designing appropriate assessment items.

Cognitive process 1: *To remember*

To remember is to retrieve relevant knowledge from long-term memory (Anderson and Krathwohl, p. 67).

Verbs associated with this level: **choose, define, describe, find, identify, label, list, locate, match, name, recall, recite, recognize, record, relate, retrieve, say, select, show, sort, tell**

Cognitive process 2: *To understand*

To understand is to construct meaning from instructional messages, including oral, written, and graphic communication (Anderson and Krathwohl, p. 67).

Verbs associated with this level: **categorize, clarify, classify, compare, conclude, construct, contrast, demonstrate, distinguish, explain, illustrate, interpret, match, paraphrase, predict, reorganize, represent, summarize, translate, understand**

Cognitive process 3: *To apply*

To apply is to carry out or use a procedure in a given situation (Anderson and Krathwohl, p. 67).

Verbs associated with this level: **apply, carry out, construct, develop, display, execute, illustrate, implement, model, solve, use**

Cognitive process 4: *To analyze*

To analyze is to break material into its constituent parts and determine how the parts relate to one another and to an overall structure or purpose (Anderson and Krathwohl, p. 68).

Verbs associated with this level: **analyze, ascertain, attribute, connect, deconstruct, determine, differentiate, discriminate, dissect, distinguish, divide, examine, experiment, focus, infer, inspect, integrate, investigate, organize, outline, reduce, solve (a problem), test for**

Cognitive process 5: *To evaluate*

To evaluate is to make judgments based on criteria and standards (Anderson and Krathwohl, p. 68).

Verbs associated with this level: **appraise, assess, award, check, conclude, convince, coordinate, criticize, critique, defend, detect, discriminate, evaluate, judge, justify, monitor, prioritize, rank, recommend, support, test, value**

Cognitive process 6: *To create*

To create is to put elements together to form a coherent or functional whole; reorganize elements into a new pattern or structure; inventing a product (Anderson and Krathwohl, p. 68).

Verbs associated with this level: **adapt, build, compose, construct, create, design, develop, elaborate, extend, formulate, generate, hypothesize, invent, make, modify, originate, plan, produce, refine, transform**

Works Cited

Anderson, L. W., and Karthwohl, D. R., eds. (2001). *A Taxonomy for Learning, Teaching, and Assessing: A Revision of Bloom's Taxonomy of Educational Objectives.* New York: Longman.

Bloom, B. S., et al. (1956). *The Taxonomy of Educational Objectives: Handbook I, Cognitive Domain.* New York: David McKay.

Rigorous Curriculum Design Glossary: A Lexicon of Terms

Academic content and performance standards: General and specific descriptions of knowledge and skills that students need to acquire in a given content area.

"Aligned" pre-assessment: Contains the same concepts and skills as the end-of-unit post-assessment, but has fewer questions.

Big Ideas: The three or four foundational understandings—main ideas, conclusions, or generalizations relative to the unit's "unwrapped" concepts—that educators want their students to discover and state in their own words by the end of the unit of study. Written as *complete sentences*, not phrases, Big Ideas convey to *students* the benefit or value of learning the standards in focus that they are to remember long after instruction ends.

Common formative assessment (CFA): An "in-process" assessment based on the "unwrapped" Priority Standards for a unit of study that grade-alike and course-alike educators collaboratively create and administer to all of their students at approximately the same time. When aligned to summative assessments *of* learning (whether school-based, district- or school-division-based, or state- or province-based) they provide educators with predictive value of how students are likely to perform on those summative assessment measures *in time* for them to "change up" instruction as needed.

Common summative assessment (CSA): A culminating or final assessment that is typically graded and recorded. Even though summative, the results can be used formatively to diagnose individual student learning needs and to inform instruction accordingly, either the next day or in the next unit of study.

Compacting: Streamlining or modifying basic content to provide students with tiered assignments (see "Tiered assignments").

Curriculum: The high-quality delivery system for ensuring that all students achieve the desired end—the attainment of their designated grade- or course-specific standards.

Differentiation: "The practice of adjusting the curriculum, teaching strategies, and classroom environment to meet the needs of all students" (Tomlinson, 2001).

Differentiation strategies: Additional supports that educators use during all high-quality lessons to modify or adjust instruction for students who need a different approach in order to understand. Differentiation strategies can be used with students learning the standards-based concepts and skills in focus as well as with proficient and advanced students who need enrichment experiences that go beyond those learning targets.

Engaging learning experiences: Authentic performance tasks. *Engaging* is synonymous with interesting and compelling. *Experiences* produce personal insights that are deeper and longer lasting than explanations. A rigorous curriculum ought to provide students with meaningful learning tasks that are both engaging and experiential.

Essential Outcomes: See "Priority Standards."

Essential Questions: Engaging, open-ended questions that educators use to spark student interest in learning the content of the unit about to commence. Even though plainly worded, they carry with them an underlying rigor. Responding to them in a way that demonstrates genuine understanding requires more than superficial thought. Along with the "unwrapped" concepts and skills from the Priority Standards, educators use the Essential Questions *throughout the unit* to sharply focus instruction and assessment.

Grade-Level Expectations (GLEs) or Course-Level Expectations (CLEs): Specific descriptions of standards for particular grade levels and courses, respectively; terms vary by state and province.

Instructional Data Team: A grade-level or course-specific group of educators who are teaching the same unit of study at the same time that also includes special educators, English Language Learner educators, and other instructional specialists and student support staff. Together they complete the Data Teams step-by-step process with common formative assessment data and use the results to differentiate instruction and improve student learning.

Instructional strategies: The specific actions educators take to help students achieve specific learning targets; the variety of research-based and experience-based methods teachers use to increase student understanding.

Learning progressions: "The step-by-step building blocks students are presumed to need in order to successfully attain a more distant, designated instructional outcome" (Popham, 2008).

Learning outcomes: Often used synonymously with the term "standards."

"Mirrored" pre-assessment: Contains the exact same number and type of questions that appear on the post-assessment.

Pacing Calendar: A yearlong or course-long schedule for delivering all of the planned units of study for a designated grade level or course, *not* the instructional materials used within those units; helps educators ensure that students learn all of the grade- or course-specific Priority Standards and their related supporting standards *in the right order* through a sequenced delivery of the units; provides *suggested* horizontal "learning progressions" *within* grades and courses and *suggested* vertical "learning progressions" *between* grades and courses.

Performance assessment: A *collection* of several related standards-based performance tasks, distributed throughout a unit of study, that progressively develop and reveal student understanding of the "unwrapped" concepts, skills, and Big Ideas along the way.

Priority Standards; original term, **Power Standards:** A carefully selected subset of the total list of academic content and performance standards or learning outcomes within each content area that students must know and be able to do by the end of each school year so they are prepared to enter the *next* level of learning.

Progress-monitoring checks: Short, frequent, informal, nongraded assessments—aligned to the end-of-unit post-assessment—that help educators accurately infer student understanding during a unit of study and change instruction accordingly.

Response to Intervention: A multistep approach to providing services and interventions to students who struggle with learning that includes increasing levels of intensity.

Rigor: A level of difficulty and the ways in which students apply their knowledge through higher-order thinking skills; the reaching for a higher level of quality in both effort and outcome; the intentional inclusion of and alignment between all necessary attributes or components of a rigorous curriculum.

Rigorous curriculum: An inclusive set of intentionally aligned components—clear learning outcomes with matching assessments, engaging learning experiences, and instructional strategies—organized into sequenced units of study that serve as both the detailed road map *and* the high-quality delivery system for ensuring that all students achieve the desired end: the attainment of their designated grade- or course-specific standards within a particular content area.

Scoring guide: A written list of *specific* criteria describing different levels of student proficiency on a standards-based assessment task.

"Singletons": Educators who alone teach a particular grade level or course within an individual school.

Specially Designed Instruction (SDI): A customized instructional approach based on a special education student's particular disability or disabilities identified on the student's Individualized Education Program (IEP).

Supporting standards: Those standards that support, connect to, and enhance the Priority Standards. They are taught *within the context* of the Priority Standards but do not receive the same degree of instruction and assessment emphasis.

Tiered assignments: Learning tasks designed at different levels of complexity according to students' instructional readiness levels.

Total Physical Response: A Sheltered Instruction strategy for English Language Learners whereby students respond with body movement to show comprehension.

Unit of Study: A series of specific lessons, learning experiences, and related assessments based on designated Priority Standards and related supporting standards for a topical, skills-based, or thematic focus that may last anywhere from two to six weeks.

"Unwrapping" the standards: Analyzing and deconstructing grade-level and course-specific standards for a unit of study to determine exactly what students need to know (concepts) and be able to do (skills).

Bibliography

Ainsworth, L. (2003a). *Power standards: Identifying the standards that matter the most.* Denver, CO: Advanced Learning Press.

Ainsworth, L. (2003b). *"Unwrapping" the standards: A simple process to make standards manageable.* Denver, CO: Advanced Learning Press.

Ainsworth, L., and Viegut, D. (2006). *Common formative assessments: How to connect standards-based instruction and assessment.* Thousand Oaks, CA: Corwin.

Anderson, L. W., and Krathwohl, D. R., eds. (2001). *A taxonomy for learning, teaching, and assessing: A revision of Bloom's taxonomy of educational objectives.* New York: Longman.

Bishop, B. (2010). *Accelerating academic achievement for English language learners.* Englewood, CO: Lead + Learn Press.

Bloom, B. S., et al. (1956). *The taxonomy of educational objectives: Handbook I, cognitive domain.* New York: David McKay.

Common Core State Standards Initiative: www.corestandards.org.

Connecticut State Department of Education. (2008, February). *Using scientific research-based interventions: Connecticut's framework for RTI.* Available at: www.sde.ct.gov/sde/lib/sde/pdf/pressroom/SRBI_full.pdf.

Cortiella, C. (2006). *Parent advocacy brief: A parent's guide to response-to-intervention.* Available at: www.allkindsofminds.org/documents/Policy/WA_rti_parent_guide.pdf.

Costa, A., and Kallik, B. (2010). "It takes some getting used to: Rethinking curriculum for the 21st century." In *Curriculum 21: Essential education for a changing world.* Jacobs, H. H., p. 225. Alexandria, VA: ASCD (Association for Supervision and Curriculum Development).

Darling-Hammond, L. (1997). *The right to learn: A blueprint for creating schools that work.* New York: John Wiley and Sons.

Darling-Hammond, L. (2009, November). "Lessons from abroad: International standards and assessments." Webinar from www.edutopia.org.

Darling-Hammond, L., and Richardson, N. (2009). "Teacher learning: What matters?" *Educational Leadership, 66*(5), 47–49.

Deming, W. E. (2000). *The new economics: For industry, government, education.* 2nd ed. Cambridge, MA: MIT Press.

DuFour, R., and Marzano, R. J. (2009, February). "High leverage strategies for principal leadership." *Educational Leadership, 66*(5), 47–49.

Duke, N. K., and Pearson, P. D. (2002). "Effective practices for developing reading comprehension." In *What research has to say about reading instruction.* Farstup, A. E., and Samuels, S. J., pp. 205–242. Newark, DE: International Reading Association.

Elmore, R. F. (2000). *Building a new structure for school leadership.* New York: Albert Shanker Institute. p. 26.

Federal Register. Rules and Regulations 46761. Vol. 71, No. 156. Monday, August 14, 2006. Available at idea.ed.gov/download/finalregulations.pdf.

Fisher, D., and Frey, N. (2003). "Writing instruction for struggling adolescent readers: A gradual release model." *Journal of Adolescent and Adult Literacy, 46,* 396–407.

Fullan, M. (2005). *Leadership and sustainability.* Thousand Oaks, CA: Corwin.

George Lucas Educational Foundation: What Works in Public Education. www.Edutopia.org.

Graham, S., and Perin, D. (2007). "A meta-analysis of writing instruction for adolescent students." *Journal of Education Psychology, 99*(3), 445–476.

Gregg, L. (2010). *Power strategies for response to intervention.* Englewood, CO: Lead + Learn Press.

Hall, G. E., and Hord, S. M. (2001). *Implementing change: Patterns, principles, and potholes.* Boston: Allyn & Bacon.

Hargreaves, A., and Shirley, D. (2009). *The fourth way: The inspiring future for educational change.* Thousand Oaks, CA: Corwin.

Hattie, J. A. (1992). "Measuring the effects of schooling." *Australian Journal of Education, 36*(1), 5–13.

Hattie, J. A. (2009). *Visible learning: A synthesis of over 800 meta-analyses relating to achievement.* New York: Routledge.

Heacox, D. (2002). *Differentiating instruction in the regular classroom: How to reach and teach all learners, grades 3–12.* Minneapolis, MN: Free Spirit Publishing.

Heritage, M. (2007, October). *Learning progressions: Supporting instruction and formative assessment.* (Draft paper). Washington, DC: Council of Chief School Officers.

Isaacson, W. (2009, April 27). "How to raise the standard in America's schools." *Time, 173*(16), 36.

Jacobs, H. H. (1997). *Mapping the big picture: Integrating curriculum and assessment k-12.* Alexandria, VA: Association for Supervision and Curriculum Development.

Jacobs, H. H. (2010). *Curriculum 21: Essential education for a changing world.* Alexandria, VA: ASCD (Association for Supervision and Curriculum Development).

Kamm, C. (2009, September). *Transforming schools in the new era.* Keynote presented at the 2009 ESSARP Conference, Buenos Aires, Argentina.

Klein, A. (2008, September 24). "Groups seek to keep a spotlight on issues of testing, standards." *Education Week,* p. 24.

Kofman, F., and Senge, P. (1995). "Communities and commitment: The heart of learning organizations." In *Learning organizations: Developing cultures for tomorrow's workplace.* Chawla, S., and Renesch, J., eds. Portland, OR: Productivity Press.

Kong, A., and Pearson, P. D. (2003). "The road to participation: The construction of a literacy practice in a learning community of linguistically diverse learners." *Research in the Teaching of English, 38,* 85–124.

Lawrence-Brown, D. (2004, summer). "Differentiated instruction: Inclusive strategies for standards-based learning that benefit the whole class." *American Secondary Education, 32*(3), 34–58.

Leahy, S., Lyon, C., Thompson, M., and Wiliam, D. (2005, November). "Classroom assessment that keeps learning on track minute-by-minute, day-by-day." *Educational Leadership, 63*(3), 19–24.

Lewis, S. G., and Batts, K. (2005, Fall). "How to implement differentiated instruction? Adjust, adjust, adjust." *Journal of Staff Development, 26*(4), 28–29.

Lloyd, S. L. (2004). "Using comprehension strategies as a springboard for student talk." *Journal of Adolescent and Adult Literacy, 48,* 114–124.

Marzano, R. J. (2003). *What works in schools: Translating research into action.* Alexandria, VA: ASCD (Association for Supervision and Curriculum Development).

Marzano, R. J. (2007). *The art and science of teaching: A comprehensive framework for effective instruction.* Alexandria, VA: ASCD (Association for Supervision and Curriculum Development).

Marzano, R. J., Norford, J. S., Paynter, D. E., Pickering, D. J., and Gaddy, B. B. (2001). *A handbook for classroom instruction that works.* Alexandria, VA: McRel/ASCD (Association for Supervision and Curriculum Development).

Marzano, R. J., Pickering, D. J., and Pollock, J. E. (2001). *Classroom instruction that works: Research-based strategies for increasing student achievement.* Alexandria, VA: ASCD (Association for Supervision and Curriculum Development).

Marzano, R. J., Waters, T., and McNulty, B. A. (2005). *School leadership that works: From research to results.* Alexandria, VA: ASCD (Association for Supervision and Curriculum Development).

McTighe, J., and Brown, J. L. (2005, Summer). "Differentiated instruction and educational standards: Is détente possible?" *Theory into Practice, 44*(3), 234–244.

Nozik, S. J. (2009, May). "Why differentiating instruction should be at the top of your school improvement plan." *Diverse Learning Communities Today, 1*(4). National Association of Elementary School Principals.

Oliva, P. F. (2005). *Developing the curriculum.* 6th ed. New York: Allyn & Bacon. p. 7.

O'Shea, M. (2005). *From standards to success.* Alexandria, VA: ASCD (Association for Supervision and Curriculum Development).

Pearson, P. D., and Gallagher, M. C. (1983). "The instruction of reading comprehension." *Contemporary Educational Psychology, 8,* 317–344.

Peery, A. (2009a). *Power strategies for effective teaching.* Englewood, CO: Lead + Learn Press.

Peery, A. (2009b). *Writing matters in every classroom.* Englewood, CO: Lead + Learn Press.

Perkins-Gough, D. (2003–2004). "Creating a timely curriculum: A conversation with Heidi Hayes Jacobs." *Educational Leadership, 61*(4), 13.

Piercy, Thomasina. (2006). *Compelling conversations.* Englewood, CO: Lead + Learn Press.

Popham, W. J. (2003a, February). "The seductive allure of data." *Educational Leadership, 60*(5), 48–51.

Popham, W. J. (2003b). *Test better, teach better: The instructional role of assessment.* Alexandria, VA: ASCD (Association for Supervision and Curriculum Development).

Popham, W. J. (2004, November). "Curriculum matters." *American School Board Journal, 191*(11), p. 30.

Popham, W. J. (2007, April). "The lowdown on learning progressions." *Educational Leadership, 64*(7), 83–84.

Popham, W. J. (2008). *Transformative assessment.* Alexandria, VA: ASCD (Association for Supervision and Curriculum Development).

Reeves, D. B. (1996–2004). *Making standards work: How to implement standards-based assessments in the classroom, school, and district.* (Three editions). Englewood, CO: Advanced Learning Press.

Reeves, D. B. (2001). *101 questions & answers about standards, assessment, and accountability.* Englewood, CO: Advanced Learning Press.

Reeves, D. B. (2004a). *Accountability for learning: How teachers and school leaders can take charge.* Alexandria, VA: Association for Supervision and Curriculum Development.

Reeves, D. B. (2004b). *Accountability in action: A blueprint for learning organizations.* Englewood, CO: Advanced Learning Press.

Reeves, D. B. (2004c). *Assessing educational leaders.* Thousand Oaks, CA: Corwin Press.

Reeves, D. B. (2006). *The learning leader: How to focus school improvement for better results.* Alexandria, VA: ASCD (Association for Supervision and Curriculum Development).

Reeves, D. B. (2008). *Reframing teacher leadership to improve your school.* Alexandria, VA: ASCD (Association for Supervision and Curriculum Development).

Reeves, D. B. (2009). *Leading change in your school: How to conquer myths, build commitment, and get results.* Alexandria, VA: ASCD (Association for Supervision and Curriculum Development).

Sherer, M. (2001). "How and why standards can improve student achievement: A conversation with Robert J. Marzano." *Educational Leadership, 59*(1), 14–15.

Simmons, J. (2006). *Breaking through: Transforming urban school districts.* New York: Teacher's College Press.

Stiggins, R. J. (2005). *Student-involved assessment for learning.* 4th ed. Upper Saddle River, NJ: Prentice Hall.

Tomlinson, C. A. (2001). *How to differentiate instruction in mixed-ability classrooms.* 2nd ed. Alexandria, VA: ASCD (Association for Supervision and Curriculum Development).

Tomlinson, C. A. (1999). *The differentiated classroom: Responding to the needs of all learners.* Alexandria, VA: ASCD (Association for Supervision and Curriculum Development).

Varlas, L. (2010, March). "The basics of differentiation" (originally entitled "Responding to research"). *Education Update, 52*(3), 3.

Wagner, T. (2008, October). "Rigor redefined." *Educational Leadership, 66*(2), 20–24.

White, S. (2005). *Beyond the numbers: Making data work for teachers and school leaders.* Englewood, CO: Lead + Learn Press.

Wiggins, G., and McTighe, J. (1998). *Understanding by design.* Alexandria, VA: ASCD (Association for Supervision and Curriculum Development).

Wiliam, D. (2007–2008). "Changing classroom practice." *Educational Leadership, 65*(4), 36.

Zmuda, A., Kuklis, R., and Kline, E. (2004). *Transforming schools: Creating a culture of continuous improvement.* Alexandria, VA: ASCD (Association for Supervision and Curriculum Development). p. 169.

Index